IMPERIAL ECHOES

IMPERIAL ECHOES

Eye-Witness Accounts
of Victoria's Little Wars

by

Robert Giddings

**Blow, bugle, blow, set the wild
echoes flying**
Alfred, Lord Tennyson (1802–92)

LEO COOPER
LONDON

First published in Great Britain in 1996 by
LEO COOPER
190 Shaftesbury Avenue, London WC2H 8JL
an imprint of
Pen & Sword Books Ltd,
47 Church Street,
Barnsley, South Yorkshire S70 2AS

A CIP record for this book is available from the British Library

ISBN 0 85052 394 X

Typeset in 11/13pt Linotype Sabon by
Phoenix Typesetting, Ilkley, West Yorkshire.

Printed in Great Britain by Redwood Books, Trowbridge, Wilts

THIS BOOK IS DEDICATED TO:

ARTHUR WESLEY GIDDINGS
2nd Lieutenant, 125 Siege Battery,
Royal Garrison Artillery 1916–19

ARTHUR JOHN GIDDINGS
Bandsman, 3rd **Carabiniers,**
Prince of Wales's Dragoon Guards 1947–53

REGINALD JAMES GIDDINGS
Sapper, Royal Engineers 1947–49

Contents

Acknowledgements

The Author would like to thank the Librarian and Library staff of Bournemouth University, especially the Inter-Library Loan Department, not only for their splendid help in locating texts, even when only sparse bibliographical details were available, but also for their massive support through the location and provision of numerous volumes and quantities of source material when I was researching this book. Also the Librarian and staff at the London Library, without whom no book of this sort would really be possible.

My thanks are also due to the curators and staffs of the fine Museums of several British County Regiments. Their materials and displays were a great source of inspiration. Leo Cooper, my publisher, and Georgina Harris, his assistant, provided constant encouragement and were endlessly resourceful over the tracking down of maps and illustrations. In Bryan Watkins, I could not have had a better editor. His military experience compensated for my amateur enthusiasm and his editorial skill helped the material into shape.

RG

Introduction

... to speak a word of that just commendation which our nation do indeed deserve ... they have been men full of activity, stirrers abroad, and searchers of the remote parts of the world, so in this most famous and peerless government of her most excellent Majesty, her subjects through the special assistance and blessing of God, in searching the most opposite corners and quarters of the world ... in compassing the vast globe of the earth more than once, have excelled all nations and people of the earth. For, which of the kings of this land before her Majesty, had their banners ever seen in the Caspian Sea? which of them hath ever dealt with the Emperor of Persia ... who ever saw ... an English leger in the stately porch of the Grand Signor at Constantinople? who ever found English consuls at and agents at Tripolis, in Syria, at Aleppo, at Babylon, at Balsara, and which is more, who ever heard of Englishmen at Goa before now?

Richard Hakluyt: *Principal Navigations, Voyages, Traffics and Discoveries of the English Nation* 1589.

*

The British overseas empire really begins with these ventures by brave, reckless, buccaneering Elizabethan seafarers which Hakluyt so proudly chronicles. The thrust for empire came not so much from the desire of English monarchs for overseas conquest, but from the zeal of trading and commercial interests – initiated by such companies as the East India Company, the Levant Company or the Virginia Company. Once the foundations of settlement were made in Virginia in 1606, London was full of talk about serious colonization. By 1642 the West Indies and Bermuda had absorbed some 40,000 colonists.

Colonial trade was increased by each war the British fought overseas, with the Spanish, Dutch and French in the West Indies, North America, Latin America, the Far East, India, Africa and the Middle East. Certain aspects of the economy thrived in war – iron and other metals, leather trades, shipbuilding, woollens, chemicals. The end of each war seemed to bring Britain more overseas territory in which her merchants and empire builders could extend imperial power. The defeat of the Dutch – a nation more conscious of their maritime power than the Spanish – in a series of wars in the 17th Century gave Britain dominion over the East Indies and on the Hudson River. This allowed British influence to extend in America, pushing the French out. The Treaty of Utrecht, which concluded the War of the Spanish Succession in 1713 provided Britain with key naval bases in Hudson Bay, Newfoundland, Acadia, Gibraltar and Minorca. During the 18th Century there were only twenty-three years of peace. The Peace of Paris in 1763 left the British masters in India and North America.

But the 19th Century, and for us in these islands, more particularly the late Victorian period, was the 'Age of Empire'. The century begins with a few border, frontier and tribal conflicts in the Indian sub-continent which made Arthur Wellesley a household name. As the century unfolded, each passing year brought forth a seemingly unending series of small wars, fought mainly against resisting or rebelling native tribal armies, mostly in India, Africa and the East. By the turn of the 19th and 20th Century Britain's Empire stands at its zenith. Between 1875 and the beginning of the Great War in 1914, Britain increased its territories by over four million square miles. The word imperialism only comes into general political discourse at this time. It does not appear in the works of Karl Marx (who died in 1883). John Atkinson Hobson, the economist and publicist, wrote in *Imperialism* (1902) that the word was on everyone's lips '. . . and used to denote the most powerful movement in the current politics of the western world'.

As Empire grew, the world shrank. As E J Hobsbawm argues,

the great period of European imperialism created a single global economy:

> progressively reaching into the most remote corners of the world, an increasingly dense web of economic transactions, communications and movements of goods, money and people, linking the developed countries with each other and with the undeveloped world. . . . Without this there was no particular reason why European states should have taken more than the most fleeting interest in the affairs of, say, the Congo basin. (*The Age of Empire* 1987 p. 62)

European civilization now required this overseas world – the exotic – for its continuance, development and survival. Western civilization and its technologies needed raw materials – oil, rubber, tin, non-ferrous metals, sugar, tea, coffee, cocoa, nitrates, timber, fruit, meat, vegetables. Awareness of the exotic, the far away, of places with strange names inhabited by curious 'different' people begin to feature in European literature in the Middle Ages. Its survival is a testimony to its popularity, and far-fetched or untruthful as much of it may be, its existence certainly points to the great fascination European readers had for these faraway places. To take but one example, the *Voiage of Sir John Maundevile*, which dates from the middle of the 14th Century, purports to be an account of Sir John Mandeville's travels in Turkey, Tartary, Persia, Egypt and India. Whoever wrote these yarns travelled no further than his study, and compensated for his limited collection of volumes with his capacious imagination – for here we have the famous accounts of the fountain of youth, ant-hills of gold dust, the discovery of Noah's Ark, the dragon-princess and a race of black people who have only one large foot to hop about on, but which provides them with useful shade in the heat of the noon-day sun. By the time of Marlowe and Shakespeare we find a much more sophisticated fascination with foreign lands and their inhabitants. Shakespeare draws fine studied portraits of 'strangers' – Othello, Shylock. The curiosity about the 'other' world out there is present in the view of Egypt in *Antony and Cleopatra* and the exotic island in *The Tempest* ('When they will not give a doit to relieve a lame beggar, they will lay out ten to see a dead Indian').

India and the East were traditionally associated with riches. When Milton came to describe the glories of Satan's wealth, he could find no better images than those drawn from the mythical wealth of the East, and wrote of Satan's throne that it far outshone the wealth of Ormus and of India, where 'the gorgeous east with richest hand showers on her kings barbaric pearl and gold' (*Paradise Lost*, Book One).

By the time of Alexander Pope we are beginning to ransack the world as fast we discovered it, to provide luxuries, ornaments and consumables. The beautiful Belinda renders herself even more seductive decked with goods and finery plundered from the four corners of the earth:

> Unnumber'd treasures ope at once, and here
> The various offerings of the world appear;
> From each she nicely culls with curious toil,
> And decks the goddess with glitt'ring spoil.
> This casket India's glowing gems unlocks,
> And all Arabia breathes from yonder box.
> The tortoise here and elephant unite
> Transform'd to combs, the speckled and the white.
>
> (*The Rape of the Lock*, 1714)

Developments in print technology, transport and communication, combined with the rapid increase in popular literacy resulting from the efforts of the Sunday School movement laid the foundations of the modern newspaper industry. Jalalabad, Chillianwalla, Aboukir, Magdala, Sindh, Assaye, Mudki, Ferozeshah, Aliwal, Sabraon, Gujerat, Kandahar, Kabul, Prome, Canton, Batavia, Boomplaatz, Tel-el-Kebir, Atbara, Uluni, Majuba, Kamkula, Charasia – the names you find listed in British Regimental battle-honours sound like the invented nomenclature of Tolkien's Middle-earth, yet this was the very stuff of everyday newspaper reading matter during Queen Victoria's reign. The generation which avidly consumed information about the activities of Arthur Wellesley in the Second Maratha War, and news of British colonial wars in Burma, Ceylon, Nepal, Poona, Nagpur, Indore, Rajputan, Ashanti, China, and the North-West Frontier – also began to read about exciting actions and dangerous escapades in fiction. The French translation by Antoine Galland of the *Arabian Nights* (which was carefully upholstered so as to appeal to an already considerable fashion for oriental tales) was translated into English early in the 18th Century. The craze for 'oriental' literature flourished – Samuel Johnson published *Rasselas* 1759, Thomas Beckford's *Vathek* appeared in 1786, and Byron, Moore and Shelley supplied to need for Arabian and oriental subject matter which was a feature of romantic poetry. Clothes, furniture, music, architecture all showed a flourishing taste for the exotic.

The 19th Century was the golden age of exotic 'Eastern' décor, of the vogue for the *Arabian Nights* (one of the few books Dickens took with him on his trips across America) Egyptian furniture, genre paintings of bazaars, pornography about young English maidens shipwrecked and seduced on the coast of Algiers, 'Eastern' operas by Weber, Rossini, Mozart, Eastern tales, songs about Arab steeds, military bands rendered more exotic with African or Indian drummers or buglers (rendered even more exotic with fez, turban or tiger-skin) and the craze for 'Turkish Music' (featured in the finale of Beethoven's *Choral Symphony*). Aladdin was a popular subject for pantomime. Works such as William Henry Sleeman's *Ramaseena* (1836), Edward Parry Thornton's *Illustrations of the History and Practices of the Thugs* (1837), and Philip Meadows Taylor's *Confessions of a Thug* (1839) and *Tara: A Mahratta Tale* (1863), *Ralph Darnell* (1865) and *Seeta* (1873) and Alexander Kinglake's *Eothen* (1844) presented readers of fiction with a dazzling picture of the hot, sunny far-away world of the Orient and Middle East.

William Makepeace Thackeray (who was born in Calcutta) coloured his masterpiece *Vanity Fair* (1848) with echoes of the exotic world of the Indian sub-continent – the novel abounds with references to brandy-cutchery, brandy-pawnee, tiffin, punkahs, tiger hunts, elephants, mangoes, chutney and curry powder. Charles Dickens' successful merchant, Dombey, has important trading and commercial interests in India and the West Indies:

> Though the offices of Dombey and Son were within the City of London . . . . yet there were hints of adventures and romantic story to be observed in some adjacent objects. . . . The Royal Exchange was close at hand. . . . Just round the corner stood the rich East India House, teeming with suggestions of precious stuffs and stones, tigers, elephants, howdahs, hookahs, umbrellas, palm-trees, palanquins and gorgeous princes of a brown complexion sitting on carpets, with their slippers turned up at the toes. (*Dombey and Son* 1848)

In *Barnaby Rudge* (1841) Joe Willet serves in the American colonial wars. In *The Old Curiosity Shop* (1841) Grandfather Trent's brother returns to the rescue with money he has made in the Antipodes. Arthur Clennam, the hero of *Little Dorrit* (1855), returns to England after twenty years trading in China. Wilkie Collins' *The Moonstone* (1868) exploited all the mysterious potential of the 'East' – the Moonstone is a vast diamond which had once been set in the head of an image of an Indian Moon-god. An English army officer, John Herncastle, had killed three Brahmin guards and gained possession of it during the battle of Seringapatam. The Brahmins resolve to regain it. The uneasy and sinister atmosphere of the story is established at the very beginning by the appearance of three Indian jugglers. At all levels, the British overseas Empire made its presence felt, in novels, on the stage, in books and magazines for young people and works aimed at children.

The Empire was extended by war, and military and naval conflict in the cause of Empire becomes one of the 19th Century's main sources of excitement and romance in fiction and drama. War ceased to be domestic after the Commonwealth period (except in Ireland). The development of imperialism out of colonialism, which itself was born of the initial rather primitive and modest attempts to expand trade with overseas countries, have very close connections with developments in industrialism in the homeland. There was no final 'industrial revolution'. The system created new class antagonisms and new international relationships. The search for new raw materials, new goods, new markets, ever extending the boundaries of our trade, accumulated an Empire and brought us face to face with other (mainly European) nations who were engaged in the same search. Thus was the idea of 'abroad' created – territory overseas to be exploited, to be grabbed before anyone else grabbed it, or grabbed off somebody else if they already had it. These endeavours created the need for an army and navy to extend, to protect and police British holdings all over the world.

Major wars in the 19th Century laid the foundations of Victoria's vast Empire, celebrated in the Jubilee in 1897. There was hardly a year between her accession in 1837 and her death in 1901 when the British were not at war somewhere overseas – in India, China, Africa, the Far East, the Near East, the Antipodes. As the Revd C S Dawe wrote in *Queen Victoria and Her People*, published by the Education Supply Association for schoolchildren in 1897:

The British Empire consists not only of the United Kingdom and such large countries as Canada, Australia and India, but it comprises also a host of small settlements dotted about the world, and valuable either for purposes of war or commerce. In consequence of our Empire being world-wide, there is scarcely a month when peace reigns in every part of it. We have generally some little war on hand.

The British were ever conscious of the fact that somehow this was simply part of God's plan for the world. In a textbook routinely issued to military cadets at the turn of the 19th and 20th Centuries we find this quite baldly stated:

It is not without some reason, beyond our ken, that the greatest Empire in the world, the greatest Empire of the White Race, happens to hold these lands on the other side of the globe, as well as the temperate regions in North America and South Africa. The wonderful growth of the British Empire, from pole to pole, has been attributed to various sources: by our friends, to British enterprise and statesmanship; by our enemies, to our alleged qualities of greed and cunning. . . . And they cannot reasonably be held to account for such geographical phenomena as the Gulf Stream bearing warm breezes to the British Islands, or the monsoons coming at the right time to water the parching plains of British India. The same inscrutable causes which placed England's geographical position in the centre of the land hemisphere arranged that the great mass of the habitable lands on the earth should be in the temperate zone, where men can best live. (J Fitzgerald Lee: *Imperial Geography*, published in India in 1903, and dedicated to Lord Kitchener, Commander-in-Chief in India).

In public entertainment, musical hall, popular theatre, postcards, comics and other ephemera, the Victorian consciousness was steeped in the idea of war as something irresistibly fascinating, which happened a long away. The public were early treated to military displays, field day demonstrations with bands, mock battles, mass troop movements and fireworks (sketched by Thomas Rowlandson and James Gillray, satirised by Charles Dickens in *Pickwick Papers*). In 1880 the Royal Tournament was inaugurated. The element of 'show' was vital and soldiers still wore their red coats right up to end of the century. The Sudan campaign of 1895 was the first time khaki was worn.

The young male readership was directly addressed in *Boys' Own Paper* (started in 1879) and encouraged to be 'masculine' – often in the reproving tones of a schoolmaster ('*Eyelashes*: Leave your eyelashes alone. Cut them indeed! One would think you were a silly girl!') The periodical pushed the idea that the outside world was an exciting adventure playground (*The Fetish Hole: A Story of East Africa* and *Up the Essequibo: The Story of a Boy's Adventures in British Guiana*) and projected the armed forces as an almost inevitable career for its readers. *Boy's Own Paper* carried articles about the practicalities of military life (*The Barrack Bugler and his Calls* and *A Young Soldier's Life Under Canvas*) and played up the glamour and excitement of the services (*Campaigning as it is Today: A Young Officer's Experience in the Soudan*). It was a poetic and glorious thing to die for one's country (*The Powder Monkey's Last Message Home*).

At the height of Britain's imperial sea-power it was the done thing to dress schoolboys in sailor-suits, complete with straw hats. The penny-dreadful market adapted itself to the needs of the day. There were thrilling yarns of campaigning abroad, slaying millions of natives and escaping from treacherous foreigners in the four corners of the globe. Characters in comics actually took part in real campaigns. The popular strip-cartoon duo Weary Willie and Tired Tim served in South Africa, and were rewarded for their unusual vigour, zeal and dedication to duty: 'Timmy, my noble friend', said Lord Roberts, 'I appoint you Governor of Pretoria at thirty bob a week.'

Very young children were introduced to the glamour and myth of Empire at their mother's knee. One of the most popular and frequently reprinted works produced for the development of the young mind in the last century – *The Child's Guide to Knowledge; Being a Useful Collection of Useful and Familiar Questions and Answers on everyday Subjects, Adapted For Young Persons, And Arranged in the Most Simple and Easy Language. By a Lady* – contains a superbly brief history of the Empire:

Q   *Where was the Mogul's empire?*
A   *In Hindostan, in Asia: it now belongs to England.*
Q   *Pray when did the English first establish themselves in Hindostan or India?*

A   In the year 1610, when a company of English merchants settled at Surat, about 150 miles north of Bombay.

Q   But when may it be said that the foundations of our Empire over this immense country were first laid?

A   By the great victory of Lord Clive, won June 2nd 1757, over Nabob Suraj ah-Dowlah at Plassey, about 100 miles north of Calcutta.

Q   Who consolidated the British power?

A   Warren Hastings, who was appointed the first Governor-General of India in 1772.

Q   What great General distinguished himself in India at an early age?

A   The first Duke of Wellington, then Sir Arthur Wellesley, who won the battle of Assaye, September 23rd. 1803.

Q   Have many additions been made to our Empire since that time?

A   Yes: the most memorable are the conquest of Scinde, by the late General Sir Charles Napier in 1843, and of the Punjaub [Punjab] by Lord Gough in 1846.

Q   Pray where are Scinde and the Punjaub situated?

A   On the North-West Frontier of India

Q   Is not the extent of India very great?

A   Yes: it is about fifteen times the size of Great Britain, and contains a population estimated at 200 millions.

Q   Are we not responsible as a nation for the well-being of this immense multitude?

A   Yes: God has made England the most powerful of all nations, and we ought, therefore, to govern with mercy and justice.

Q   Why?

A   Because, if we do so, He will continue to bless and prosper us.

Q   What does India produce?

A   Rice, cotton, silk, flax, hemp, sugar, opium, tobacco, and many other things.

The Empire is now officially dismembered. It occasionally surfaces in public memory as a fleeting memory, captured, like a random dream, in films about India or newspaper obituaries of old colonial administrators, soldiers or sailors. From time to time a television drama series may draw on Empire as a backcloth for some action. But, like a long lost relative, it is likely to crop up from time to time. It is not currently fashionable to quote G K Chesterton with approval. Nevertheless, while in the course of researching this book, ransacking one of the numerous second-hand bookshops whose resources are so valuable when seeking memoirs of deceased and forgotten Major-Generals, I bought a battered old volume of his articles from the *Illustrated London News*. Among other wholly characteristic garrullities, there were some interesting comments about the United States of America and the problems of government organization, communication and geographical size. Few are willing to admit this in good company today, but Chesterton does sometimes get hold of the right end of some very important sticks. There, staring at me on the page, was a brilliant comment on the nature of empire:

> There is no such thing as a great power. What is spread out before us is a great weakness. The system in extending its communications always decreases its efficiency; and there never was an empire upon this earth that did not go further and fare worse.

This comment seemed apt at the time. So many of the conflicts dealt with in this book occurred at far-flung corners of Empire, where the fabric of control and communication was stretched so thin as almost to be fraying. The more I read about these escapades, the more I was convinced that here were so many stories that needed telling, and telling – insofar as was possible – in the words of those who experienced these events.

As far as personal experience goes, I was born too late and in the wrong part of the world to have much actual knowledge of Empire. The Empire Exhibition took place a decade before I was born. I was two years old in 1937 when the Congress Party won the Indian elections and the Imperial Conference was held in Lonon. I was twelve when India achieved its independence. But I grew up surrounded by memories, debris and distant echoes of Empire. As a boy I spent some years in hospital, and one Christmas several of my friends clubbed together to buy me a suitable book for Christmas 1946 – *The Empire Youth Annual* (which strongly plugged the 'children of all nations' line). I loved it.

Empire Day, 24 May (Queen Victoria's birthday) was still celebrated when I was a boy. In Bath, where my formative years were spent, I was frequently made aware of strong imperial associations, seeing the retired military, colonial and administrative families taking tea in the Pump Room. Pressing my face against junk shop windows in Walcot Street or Manvers Street, I was sometimes able to see a dress sword, accoutrements, a cavalry trumpet, medals, portraits of Sir Garnet Wolseley, Lord Kitchener, General Gordon; paintings and engravings of engagements with exotic names such as Ferozeshah, Omdurman, Multan, Ghazni. I once actually saw a real 19th Century infantryman's shako, which I dearly wanted. It was wholly beyond the family purse. But I could still dream. There were numerous military tattoos in those days, and I was thrilled to see and hear all the imperial and colonial troops and their pipes, bands and drum corps. Rasping, echoing bugles, skirling pipes and the deep, rich sonorities of British military bands filled me with echoes of empire. Marches redolent of those old campaigns and conflicts – *Punjaub, Secunderabad, 79th's Farewell to Gibraltar, The Thin Red Line, Tel-El-Kebir, The Haughs of Cromdell, The Campbells Are Coming, Goodbye, Dolly Gray* and, of course, Safroni's masterpiece, *Imperial Echoes* (which was used on BBC wireless to herald the news broadcasts). Then there were Korda's films – *The Four Feathers, The Drum* – and Hollywood's epics with C Aubrey Smith, Victor McLaglan, Ronald Colman, Shirley Temple, Errol Flynn (with Indian Princes played by Sabu) *Gunga Din, Lives of a Bengal Lancer, Rhodes of Africa, Elephant Boy, Wee Willie Winkie, Clive of India* – I saw them all at the local flea-pit. At school I traded cigarette cards – *Makers of Empire, Regimental Uniforms, Drum Banners and Standards, Military Headwear, Uniforms of the British Empire Overseas.* In spare moments at home I pored over ancient Victorian volumes – *Boy's Own Paper* and *British Battles on Land and Sea* – acquired from elderly relatives. *Chums Annual* I had from my sister's boyfriend, who served in Sierra Leone.

Gradually, during my adolescence, various parts of the British Empire broke free from the mother yoke and became separate nation states. In 1958, the year I graduated at university, Empire Day was officially renamed Commonwealth Day. I can remember reading the Editorial in the *Daily Express* at the time of this 'momentous change' some comment to the effect that officially the name of the day had been altered to 'Commonwealth' Day, 'but the British people will remember'. As, of course, we do. The delicate fingering of the nerve ends of collective memory must in part account for the immense success of Attenborough's *Gandhi*, and Granada Television's drama series, *The Jewel in the Crown*. The tremendous impact of living memory was demonstrated in Stephen Peet's brilliant documentary television series for BBC, *Tales of India* (1978). Reminders still crop up from time to time, sometimes from unexpected quarters.

There is obviously a sound historical basis for the fact that the British national domestic beverage is Indian tea. No nation's taste in food is so international and cosmopolitan, – Indian, Chinese, Middle Eastern, Far Eastern – and the experience of Empire has been a very powerful shaping influence here. The great British craze for curry is very important evidence. An extraordinary amount of unsuspected but revealing information is to be found between the covers of Pat Chapman's *Good Curry Restaurant Guide* (1991). There were only six Indian Restaurants in Britain in 1950. The die-hard Blimps had to trek all the way to London to enjoy a good sweat at *Veeraswarmy's*. Ten years later there were three hundred. Then came several successive revolutions, including fashions for Tandoori cooking, the introduction of unusual and enterprising ideas for curry dishes (certainly encouraged if not actually initiated by Madhur Jaffrey) and then came Balti. Today there are more curry restaurants in Britain than anywhere else in the world – including India. There are approximately seven thousand of them, from Thurso to Penzance – John o' Groats to Land's End. There are curry houses in the Shetlands and the Channel Islands. There are more Indian restaurants in London (over one thousand five hundred of them) than in Delhi. The names of the restaurants are frequently redolent of Empire – *Khyber Pass, British Raj, Kathmandu, Bengal Lancer, Days of the Raj, Jalalabad, Lancers, Far Pavilions, Gurkha, Jewel in the Crown, Viceroy of India.*

But what of the soldiers and sailors and their officers who actually acquired and policed this vast Empire? What was it actually like to go up the Irrawaddy, hack through the jungle, sweat across the Sudan? I had often wondered. It was while I was researching a previous book on writings about war that I first began to come across really interesting first-hand accounts of historic military action. I began to acquire a real interest in the memoirs of the old military commanders, and to scan their accounts of actions long past in the far-flung parts of empire. It was often that casual, on the spot, feeling which I found appealing.

From time to time I came across old army periodicals which carried the stories by other ranks of engagements in these small wars. Again and again I was struck by the fresh and vivid quality of the writing.

It dawned on me that here was a considerable resource from which might be assembled an alternative 'non-official' history of some of the landmarks in British imperial history, which might bring the past back to life, culled from the writings of people who were actually there at the time. This, in essence, is what I have tried to do in this book. This is a collection of 'imperial echoes', grouped together on the basis of their location. There is no attempt to create a complete story-of-empire illustrated with eye-witness-accounts. The excerpts have been chosen because I thought they were interesting and worth reading. The vast majority of the text is quoted material, with background accounts only insofar as they are needed to reflect the points behind the fascinating 'echoes'. Because the 'echoes' are the whole point of the book, and give it whatever life and purpose it may have, I have left them entirely as written – warts and all. This may mean that there are a number of inconsistencies, especially in the spelling of place names. It could be argued that this, in fact, increases the curious authenticity of much of the writing. I have attempted to clear up some possible confusion by putting the modern spelling in square brackets after the old spelling on the occasion of first use. The stories speak for themselves. And they speak volumes.

Robert Giddings
Poole, Dorset
June 1995.

INDIA AND THE RAJ
1799–1858

1. Wellington in India (1799–1803)

The major European colonial powers had been rivals in India for many years, rich with pickings for European investors after the collapse of the Mogul empire, (whose dynasty was destroyed by the Marathas [Mahrattas]) but by the close of the 18th Century the Portuguese and Dutch had been out of the running for some time. British domination over France had been achieved as the result of Robert Clive's forward policies and secured as a result of the Seven Years War, 1756–1763.

Although under the Treaty of Paris (10 February, 1763) France and Britain had to restore their mutual conquests, French power was really at an end as she was not allowed to rebuild her fortifications in India and the British had control over Bengal, which they had conquered from the Indians. The British East India Company almost had the authority of a delegated state – with its own officials, officers, administrators and armed forces. British military supremacy was further endorsed by the presence in Madras from the mid-18th Century of an outstanding British regular regiment, the 39th Regiment of Foot, later named the Dorset Regiment (whose regimental motto *Primus in Indis* tells its own story). France's direct rival to the British East India Company – *Compagnie des Indes* – was dissolved in 1769. The series of Mysore wars fought between 1766–1799, culminating in the battle of Seringapatam 6 April, 1799, left the British masters of southern India.

The Governor-General of India, Richard Wellesley, enacting the policies of William Pitt the Younger, had ensured that all traces of French influence in India were wiped out. In consequence, there were no remaining foundations on which Bonaparte could rebuild French power in the subcontinent by exploiting the Marathas. This final campaign saw brilliant service by the Governor General's younger brother, Arthur Wellesley, later known to the world as the Duke of Wellington.

Seringapatam was defended by the Sultan of Mysore, Tipu Sahib, who was killed in the final battle. The garrison numbered 22,000 of the Sultan's best troops, with 240 guns. The besieging British and native forces numbered 35,000 and 100 guns. The final onslaught began at noon on 3 May, 1799, and by half past two it was all over. As Sir Herbert Maxwell describes in his biography of Wellington:

> On 30th April a heavy fire was poured from the British batteries at close range, and on 3rd May the breach was pronounced practicable. The assault was committed to General Baird, who marched 4,300 men into the trenches before dawn on 4th May, and kept them concealed till past noon – the hour when Asiatic troops are generally most drowsy. At one o'clock Baird led the assault under a heavy fire from the fort, Wellesley being left in command of the reserve in the advanced trenches. The resistance was fierce, but the assailants swept all before them: at half-past two they were in complete possession of the fort, the palace, and the town.
>
> Brave Tipú Sultan, lame as he was from an old wound, and despondent as he had been ever since his defeat at Malavelly, fought like a tiger to his last breath. When the British mounted the breach he placed himself, musket in hand, behind a traverse, and kept firing on the assailants till the backward rush of his own men carried him away. His body was found among five hundred corpses piled together in the gateway of the interior work.
>
> The British lost in the assault 8 officers and 75 men killed, besides upwards of 300 wounded and missing; the total loss among the 20,000 men actually engaged in the siege, which lasted exactly a month, being 22 officers

and 310 men killed, and 45 officers and 1,164 men wounded and missing.

General Baird having applied to be relieved in order to make his report in person to the Commander-in-chief, Colonel Wellesley, as next senior officer, took over the command on the morning of the 5th, and became responsible for the security of the town and the property therein. A stern task it was, for war was a worse affair for non-combatants and private citizens in those days than it has been rendered since by the common assent of civilised nations.[1]

Seringapatam was then subject to what was customary in war at this period – plunder, violence and destruction. We may gather something of the troops' behaviour from this excerpt from a letter written by Arthur Wellesley to his brother on 8 May, 1799:

It was impossible to expect that after the labour which the troops had undergone in working up to the place, and the various successes they had had in six different affairs with Tippoo's troops, in all of which they had come to the bayonet with them, they should not have looked to the plunder of this place. Nothing, therefore, can have exceeded what was done on the night of the 4th. Scarcely a house in the town was left unplundered, and I understand that in camp jewels of the greatest value, bars of gold, etc., etc., have been offered for sale in the bazaars of the army by our soldiers, sepoys, and foreigners. I came in to take command on the 5th, and by the greatest exertion, by hanging, flogging, etc., etc., in the course of that day I restored order among the troops, and I hope I have gained the confidence of the people. They are returning to their houses, and beginning again to follow their occupations, but the property of every one is gone.[2]

*   *   *

The extension of British power in India under the crown and the East India Company was threatened again by Bonaparte's incursions into Egypt and India. Native Indian forces exposed to the French were well equipped and trained. Tipoo Sahib, in

5

particular, had been a great ally of the French; this was attested by evidence captured at Seringapatam. Two Maratha leaders, Doulut Rao Sindhai and Jaswant Roa Holkar, commanded vast efficient armies. At the turn of the 18th and 19th Centuries, the Sikhs were united by the warrior Ranjit Singh who controlled most of the Punjab. In the civil war between rival Maratha chieftains, Baji Rao and Holkar, the British supported Baji Rao. He was defeated at the Battle of Poona in 1802. When the British demand for his reinstatement was refused, British military offensives were launched in the Deccan and Hindustan, and Wellington, who commanded 9,000 regulars and 5,000 native troops, restored Baji Rao as Sindhai's forces withdrew to the south.

Wellington pushed further into Maratha territory and took Ahmednagar (11 August, 1803). It was agreed to divide the British forces, one part to be commanded by Colonel Stevenson, the other by Wellington. The two forces were to attack the rebels from either side on the morning of 24 September. Wellington took 4,500 regulars (19th Light Dragoons, 4th, 5th, 7th Madras Native Cavalry, a detachment of Madras Infantry, a detail of Bombay Artillery, the 74th and 78th Highlanders and four battalions of 12th Regiment Madras Sepoys) with him and advanced to the confluence of the Jua and Kelna rivers. Here he unexpectedly faced Maratha forces of 30,000 cavalry, 10,000 French-trained foot soldiers and 200 guns, the combined forces of Sindhai and his ally, the Rajah of Berar. There was no time to contact Stevenson. He resolved to attack the Mahrata forces across the ford.

This was the Battle of Assaye, news of which turned Sir Arthur Wellesley into a household name:

On the 21st September, the whole of the Mahratta army, joined by their infantry, of which there were sixteen battalions of regulars, was encamped about the village of Bokerdun, and between that place and Jaffeirabad. On the same day, General Wellesley and Colonel Stevenson met at Budnapoor, when it was agreed that the two divisions, then in the neighbourhood of each other, should move separately, and attack the enemy on the morning of the 24th. They accordingly marched on the 22nd; Colonel Stevenson

6

by the western, and on ascending a rising ground, the host of the confederates was seen extending in a vast line along the opposite bank of the Kailna river, near its junction with the Juah. Their army amounted to upwards of 50,000 men, of whom more than 30,000 were horse, and 10,500 were regular infantry supported by upwards of one hundred guns. The handful of British troops, which now moved straight down upon this formidable array, did not exceed four thousand five hundred men, but the general sentiment was that of their commander, 'they cannot escape us.' As General Wellesley drew nearer the enemy's line, he found their right composed entirely of cavalry, and that their cannon and infantry, which it was his object to take and destroy, were on their left, near the village of Assaye. He, therefore, moved round and passed the Kailna river at a ford beyond the enemy's left flank, forming his infantry into two lines, and his cavalry as a reserve in a third, with his right towards the Juah, and his left on the Kailna. The horse belonging to the Peishwa and Raja of Mysore, accompanying General Wellesley, formed at a distance across the Kailna but had little or no share in the conflict. The position thus occupied by the British, between the two rivers and near their junction, not only brought them upon their object, but was of importance in diminishing the front of the enemy, who changed their position as the British turned the flank of their old ground, and were now drawn up in two lines, one of them fronting the British troops, the other running at a right angle to their first line, with the left of both resting on the fortified village of Assaye. In this situation as the British lines were forming, the Mahrattas opened a heavy cannonade, the execution of which is described as terrible. The picquets of the infantry and the 74th regiment which were on the right suffered particularly; the picquets were for a time halted, and the officer in command of them when urged to advance, sent word that the guns were disabled, and the bullocks killed. General Wellesley received the message with the utmost composure, and coolly replied, 'Well, tell him to get on without them.' The whole line without artillery was exposed to a dreadful fire of round and grape; the ranks of the 74th were completely thinned, and a large

7

body of the Mahratta horse charged them: the order was given for the advance of the British cavalry—the 19th Light Dragoons, who only drew 360 swords, received the intimation with one loud huzza! Accompanied by the 4th Native Cavalry, who emulated their conduct throughout this arduous day, the 19th passed through the broken but invincible 74th, whose very wounded joined in cheering them as they went on, cut in and routed the horse, and dashed on at the infantry and guns. Never did cavalry perform better service or contribute more to the success of a battle. The British infantry likewise pressed forward, the enemy's first line gave way, fell back on their second, and the whole were forced into the Juah at the point of the bayonet; the fugitives, on gaining the opposite bank were followed, charged and broken by the cavalry; but some of their corps formed again and went off in good order. One large body of this description was pursued and routed by the British cavalry, on which occasion Colonel Maxwell, who commanded them, was killed. As the British line advanced they passed many individuals of the enemy who either appeared to have submitted, or lay apparently dead. These persons rising up turned their guns on the rear of the British line, and after the more important points of the victory were secured, it was some time before the firing thus occasioned could be silenced. The enemy's horse hovered round for some time, but when the last body of infantry was broken, the battle was completely decided, and ninety-eight pieces of cannon remained in the hands of the victors. The loss was severe; upwards of one-third of the British troops lay dead or wounded, but they had, considering the circumstances, achieved a triumph more splendid than any recorded in Deccan history.

Of the enemy, twelve hundred were killed, and the whole neighbourhood was covered with their wounded.[3]

Like so many of Britain's most successful generals in the nineteenth Century, Wellington cut his teeth as a field commander in those bloody Indian battles and the experience they gave him was to pay enormous dividends in the Peninsular. Those same battles were also forging new traditions for the

British infantry and cavalry, whose colours, standards and guidons still tell the tale through the battle honours with which they are emblazoned.

Notes

1. Sir Herbert Maxwell, *The Life of Wellington* (1899)
2. Lieutenant Colonel John Gurwood (ed.), *The Dispatches of Field Marshal the Duke of Wellington during his Various Campaigns in India, Denmark, Portugal, Spain, the Low Countries and France* (1834–38)
3. James Grant Duff, *A History of the Mahrattas* (1826)

2. A Bloody Campaign
(The Gurkha War 1814–16)

'The Indian Government, observing that a gradual invasion was being persistently made into the all-important valley of the Ganges, now endeavoured to regulate the frontier, and early in 1812, Lord Minto offered to do so . . . but he received for reply that the Nepalese were within their rights and had not yet occupied all that was due to them. Commissioners from both sides, however, were at last assembled for a judicial investigation of the various claims . . . and upon examination it became apparent that the Gurkhas had no vestige of a right to any of the fiefs they had seized. . . . It was evident . . . that force would have to be employed if the question was to be settled. For a long time the Gurkhas had been unmolested, and in spite of frequent remonstrances they were approaching little by little within a perilous proximity to the centre of the Bengal provinces; it was therefore necessary to arrest this invasion, which, far from being confined to two or three points, had been allowed to menace the whole length of the frontier.'[1]

By 1814 British domination in northern India was seriously challenged by 'depredations, encroachments and murders committed by the Gurkhalese on our frontiers, continuing to increase in spite of all remonstrances and attempts at pacific settlement'. It was resolved that there was no alternative between a degrading submission to these raiding parties, or a vigorous expedition into Nepal, driving these warriors back within their own boundaries. It was official British thinking that no challenge to British authority was to be endured, as whenever the natives begin to lose their reverence for our arms, our 'superiority in other respects' sinks in proportion, and forbearance to such insolence is no virtue. The mountain tribesmen of Nepal had a high reputation, and their unpunished insolence would incite other natives to challenge British authority. The expedition launched into Nepal in 1814 was supported by a high sense of delivering justice and punishment in equal measure. General Sir David Ochterlony met very stiff resistance. In fact, the column under his command was the only conspicuously successful one to enter Nepal. The natives, bravely commanded by Amar Singh, were only finally quelled after a bloody campaign ending at Katmandu in 1816.

Ochterlony's tactics were to crush the various Gurkha mountain citadels systematically and one by one – Nahan, Jytuk, Jumpta, Kalunga, Mornee, Nallaghur, Yarraghur, Ramghur, Malouen, Irkea – in the rugged hill country of southern Nepal, thus ultimately destroying the native forces' safe havens.

One major memorable event of the war was the death of Sir Robert Rollo Gillespie at Kalunga in 1814. Already famed for campaigns in Java and Sumatra, Gillespie was killed in a forlorn hope at the siege of Kalunga.

Kalunga was besieged by Gillespie's forces in October, 1814, and bravely defended by Bulbudder Singh. British assaults on the fort proved extremely costly, an additional handicap to their initial efforts being the lack of heavy guns. After over a thousand casualties had been suffered, the guns arrived and the fort was shelled for three days. Only seventy of Balbudder Singh's troops survived this onslaught, from an original force of 600, but they were able to flee to safety before the British occupied the fort.

Gillespie died leading his forces, making himself conspicuous to encourage the bravery of his troops:

> To whatever causes the failure was owing, whether in the ordinary nature of human accidents, by which well-concerted plans are not properly understood on the part of those who are entrusted with the execution of them, or in

the want of that promptitude which could alone ensure success, no reflection can be cast upon the memory of the commander, either on account of the plan of the assault, or his conduct in endeavouring to recover the fortune of the day. It was certainly reduced to a forlorn hope, and as such, the general considered it to be his duty to expose himself in the most conspicuous manner, that, if possible, his example might inspire and rouse the emulation of his troops into another vigorous and effectual attack upon the place. The heroic sentiment which occasioned this sacrifice has carried the renown of the British arms to a height of splendour, that, in point of radical virtue, and permanent utility, has far exceeded the Grecian and Roman glory. That daring spirit of bold enterprize, which in Europe has stamped with immortality so many illustrious names, will be found peculiarly needful in the vast and complicated regions of the east, where, from the character of the people, and the tenure of our possessions, we shall be continually obliged to maintain a high military attitude. But the effect of that power must depend on the commanding talents and unshackled energy of the generals who are employed in the service; for where there are jarring interests, it is obvious the seeds of dissatisfaction will produce error and confusion, defeat and disgrace

It is distressing to reflect that an invaluable life was here cut off by a voluntary act of devotion for the public good, which might have been preserved for many years of active service and honourable retirement, had all who were with him been equally animated in the cause of their country. But in this case it was a mournful satisfaction for him to say with the Spartan commander, in a situation of extreme difficulty, 'Whatever misconduct shall happen in this battle, I shall either conquer or die.'

The body of Major-General Gillespie being laid in spirits, was conveyed to Meerat for interment, and a monument has been there erected to his memory by the officers who served under his command.[2]

*   *   *

Bloody and bitterly fought though this first encounter between the British and the legendary fighting men of Nepal may have been, it marks the start of an association between the two countries that survives to this day in the form of the highly regarded and deeply respected Brigade of Gurkhas, the only mercenary force to form an established element of the British Army. The Gurkhas' prowess in battle in two world wars, fighting alongside their British comrades-in-arms, struck fear into the hearts of some of the world's most redoubtable soldiers. Since 1945 Gurkha troops have been engaged, time and again, in lesser wars and insurgencies and have never failed.

Notes

1. Major JFG Ross-of-Bladensburg, *The Marquess of Hastings KG* (1893)
2. *A Memoir of Major General Sir Robert Rollo Gillespie, Knight Commander of the Most Honourable Order of the Bath (1816)*

3. The Destruction of Maratha Power (The Third Maratha (and Pindari) War 1817–18)

'. . . an irregular assembly of several thousand horsemen, united, by preconcerted agreement, in some unfrequented part of the country. They set off with little provision; no baggage, except the blanket on their saddles; and no animals but led horses, with bags prepared for the reception of their plunder. If they halted during part of the night . . . they slept with their bridles in their hands: if in the day, whilst the horses were fed . . . their swords were laid by their sides, and their spears generally stuck in the ground at their horses' heads.'[1]

*

Towards the end of 1817, large numbers of plundering bands of freebooters, Pindaris, began raiding forays in central and southern India which seriously threatened the maintenance of social order. Their numbers were swelled by former Maratha soldiers. The Maratha chiefs, on the face of it, had agreed to support British rule, but secretly connived at these depredations.

Two British armies, totalling 20,000 troops, one commanded by General Lord Francis Rawdon-Hastings, the other by Sir Thomas Hyslop, were organized to restore order. The problem was to suppress the Pindaris without stirring up the Marathas, who could put 200,000 men into the field, with 500 guns, and were bound to relish any possibility of embarrassing their erstwhile conquerors. Trouble flared in some British garrisons in Poona. This is an account of the methods of operation of these bandits by James Baillie Fraser, who had travelled extensively in India and Persia:

The principal leaders at this time were the following:—The celebrated Cheetoo, whose *durra*, or horde, was estimated at from 10,000 to 15,000; Kurreem Khan, at this time, only 4,000; Dost Mahomed and Wasil Mahomed, 6,000; inferior and independent leaders, 8,000.

These chiefs all haunted the valley of the Nerbudda, and the mountains to the north and south of it. There they had their camps and strongholds, where, by sufferance of the fixed powers, they bestowed their families and property when absent on expeditions, and there they themselves dwelt and pastured their horses during the rains and hot weather. By the time of the *dussera* – an annual festival occurring at the end of October or beginning of November – each chief planted his standard in his camp, and to these flocked all loose spirits and lawless adventurers who sought to partake of their fortunes. There were formed their plans of rapine and plunder, and there they trained their horses for hard work and long marches. By the end of the *dussera*, when the rivers generally become fordable, they shod their horses, chose leaders, and set forth upon their projected *lubhur*, or foray. The party usually ranged from one to several thousands. Of these, the proportion of good and well-mounted cavalry was usually that of 400 out of every 1,000, and these were always armed with long spears and swords; besides which, every fifteenth or twentieth man had a matchlock. The rest were of all sorts, looties or common scamps, attendants, slaves, or followers of the camp, mounted as each man could manage, on tattoos or ponies, and armed with every sort of weapon they might possess. Thus, without baggage or encumbrances, their progress was so rapid as almost to mock pursuit; and the barbarous atrocities they committed, their ingenuity of tortures to extort property, and their system of wanton destruction were beyond the power of description.

Under such a progress of devastation, it is obvious that every country they visited must have become a waste, which grew wider and wider as the mere exhaustion of its resources caused the freebooters to spread further, until cultivation and cultivators alike disappeared from the land. No language can paint the melancholy scale of desolation to which the Rajepoot [Rajput] dominions were reduced. . . .[2]

* * *

On 21 December, 1817, Sir Thomas Hyslop's forces defeated the Holkar of Indore and his army (30,000 cavalry and 5,000 infantry) at Mahidpur. The Maratha losses totalled 3,000, the British 778 killed and wounded.

The following year Rawdon-Hastings' army pursued and destroyed the Maratha and Pindari forces, his campaign culminating in their surrender on 2 June, 1818. Rawdon-Hastings' journal gives valuable insight into imperial/colonial thinking of this period. He seemed to believe that a veneer of Anglo-Christian culture would render the new citizens of these conquests co-operative and harmless, but he does give much thought to the complexity of the issues and problems facing the extension of British power in India:

> June 10th. – The radical policy of the Mahrattas was oddly avowed lately by an agent of Scindiah's. The rights or possessions of the Mahratta chiefs are strangely intermixed with those of the different rajahs between the Jumna and the Nerbudda. In one instance there was a district enveloped in the territories of the Rajah of Boondee, the annual revenue of which was divisible in equal portions between the latter chief, Holkar, and Scindiah. As the two Mahratta Princes kept agents there to watch over their shares, there was an obvious chance of quarrels; and we wished to secure the Boondee chief, who had been taken under our protection, against any vexatious pretention on the part of his neighbours. It was therefore proposed that Scindiah should cede his title to any income from the district in question, and should receive from us certain villages

producing a rent considerably beyond what we wished him to give up. A strong disinclination to close with this proposal was manifested. When it was urged that Scindiah would not only be a great pecuniary gainer by the exchange, but that he would acquire a tract which actually connected itself with his old possessions, and would be exclusively his, the Mahratta negotiator denied that the circumstance of sole occupancy could be an advantage to his master equal to what the maharajah enjoyed by his co-partnership in the Boondee district. On surprise being expressed at this assertion, he explained it by saying, 'We Mahrattas have a maxim that it is well to have a finger in every man's dish.' His meaning was, that there was solid value in pretexts for interference which would afford opportunities of pillage or extortion.

June 17th. – Bajee Rao has submitted and placed himself in the hands of Sir John Malcolm. He had been so surrounded that resistance or retreat was equally impossible. That he will live tranquilly on the generous allowance (equal to one hundred thousand pounds yearly) which we have assigned to him, is not believed by me. His intriguing spirit never will be at rest. . . . In the meantime, this event terminates the war, and completes the destruction of the Mahratta power. The resources of Scindiah will now dwindle into absolute insignificance; and he must, without recurrence to a subsidiary treaty, look to the British Government for the maintenance of his authority over his own subjects. The dispersed plunderers having now no head under whom they could reunite, will look out for other modes of subsistence; and it is to be hoped that a tranquility will prevail in central India which we may improve to noble purposes. The introduction of instruction into those countries, where the want of information and of principle is universal, is an object becoming the British Government. It is very practicable. Detachments of youths who have been rendered competent at the Lancasterian schools in Bengal under the missionaries, should be despatched under proper leaders to disseminate that method of teaching. Its progress would soon enable numbers to read and comprehend books of moral inculcation in the Hindostanee language. Lady

Hastings caused a compilation of apologues, and of maxims relative to social duties, to be printed for the use of her school at Barrackpore. It was not only studied, to all appearance profitably, by the boys, but many individuals of high caste in the neighbourhood used to apply for the perusal of copies. It has all the attraction of a novelty, while the simplicity of what it recommends is likely to make impression on minds to which any reflection on the topics was never before suggested.[3]

✻   ✻   ✻

In a clash that was so typical of the years of British rule in India, a firm hand and the imposition of the rule of law had been followed by a genuine attempt at the establishment of an enlightened and benevolent administration – though, as Hastings had well recognized, the complexity of the task and the scope for further misunderstanding and conflict was limitless, as the story of the Raj would prove.

Notes

1. James Grant Duff, *A History of the Mahrattas* (1826)
2. James Baillie Fraser, *Military Memoir of Lieutenant Colonel James Skinner, CB, Many Years a Distinguished Officer Commanding a Corps of Irregular Cavalry in the Service of the Honourable East India Company* (1851)
3. The Marchioness of Bute (daughter of the Marquess of Hastings), ed, *The Private Journal of the Marquess of Hastings KG, Governor-General and Commander-in-Chief in India* (1858)

4. A Splendid Tenacity
(The First Sikh War 1845–46)

The national independence of the Sikh character may dictate the attempt to escape from under foreign yoke; for however benevolent be our motives and conciliating our demeanour, a British army cannot garrison Lahore, and the fiat of a British functionary cannot supersede that of the Darbar throughout the land, without our presence being considered a burden and a yoke.[1]

*

The Sikhs are a sect of dissenters from Brahmanical Hinduism, and originated in the Punjab. The First Sikh War, sometimes called the Sutlej Campaign, flared up as part of the revolt of the Sikh Army – which became uncontrollable after the death of Ranjit Singh in 1839. Ranjit Singh had allied himself to the British and organized the Sikh Army in the European style, with the aid of French officers. This finally put paid to Afghan influence in the Punjab. Ranjit Singh attempted to form a Sikh state and extended territorially, adding Multan, Kashmir and Peshawar to Sikh possessions. However, he had always hesitated to cross the Sutlej and take the Mulwa, who were under British protection. His death was followed by intrigue, serious unrest and lack of leadership. Belief in British invincibility received a severe jolt after the catastrophes in the First Afghan War, and the annexation of Sindh provoked fears of a British attempt on the Punjab. On 11 December, 1845, a Sikh army of 20,000 crossed the Sutlej into British Indian territory. The British had anticipated the Sikhs' intentions and had massed troops at Ferozepore, Ludhiana and Umballa.

British troops marched 150 miles to Moodkee [Mudki] to protect Ferozepore from Sikh attack. They were resting in the early afternoon of 18 December when news was brought that the Sikh army – 10,000 infantry, 2,000 cavalry and twenty-two guns – were advancing to do battle. In the opening artillery exchange the British guns, though heavily outnumbered, soon silenced the Sikh field pieces. British cavalry charges drove the Sikhs from position after position, supported by accurate infantry fire. Darkness prevented the victory from being followed up.

In the early morning of 21 December the British advanced from Moodkee to attack the Sikhs at Ferozeshah. Sir Hugh Gough, the British commander, intended to attack while the light was good, but he was overruled by Sir Henry Hardinge, the Governor-General, who took precedence from his superior civil authority. Hardinge wished to postpone any attack until the army was joined by Sir John Littler's force from Ferozepore. The two armies did not combine until the mid-afternoon. On this occasion the British artillery failed against the enemy's, and in the infantry engagement the British found they were fighting an extremely formidable foe. The fighting continued sporadically throughout the night and by morning the British found that they had captured 73 cannon and that they were now masters of the field.

A fresh Sikh army then arrived, commanded by Tej Singh, but after one half-hearted attack, inexplicably, it withdrew. The Sikh forces then retreated behind the Sutlej and attacked once more in January, 1846. A brilliant British victory was achieved under the command of the remarkable Sir Harry Smith at Aliwal on 28 January, a battle remembered particularly for the spectacular charge by the 16th Lancers which broke the Sikh square. The enemy fled the field, leaving 67 guns. The final engagement of the campaign was fought at Sobraon on 10 February when Sir Hugh Gough inflicted a terrible defeat on the Sikh armies which sustained casualties in excess of 10,000 and the loss of 70 guns. The British then advanced to Lahore, where the Treaty of Lahore was signed on 11 March.

British losses in the First Sikh War were more than was usual at this time for campaigns fought in India. There are several reasons for this, which Gough fully understood. One was the splendid tenacity of the Sikhs. Secondly, the Sikh Army, as we know, had been organized and trained in the European tradition. Another fact was the lack of energy displayed by the Sepoy forces fighting on the British side. About 11,000 British and sepoy troops fought at Moodkee, 17,000 at Ferozeshah and 16,000 at Sobraon. At Moodkee 215 were killed, at Ferozeshah 694 and at Sobraon 320. The total wounded amounted to 4,441.

Sir Hugh Gough wrote to his son on 18 April, 1846:

There were three good causes for the heavy loss in the two first battles. First, the army generally had not recovered themselves from the fearful disasters in Afghanistan, the latter operations in which country were so unjustly lauded for political purposes. . . . The second was the natural consequence, the Native Army almost dreaded the Sikh which had never been beaten, and which they looked on as invincible. The third was that the Native Army participated in the general feeling throughout India of a desire that we should not overthrow the only remaining powerful Native Hindu Government. This is a fact that can be proved. Not that the Native Army had a wish to lose their 'salt' (as they term their maintenance), but they decidedly did not wish to see the Lahore Government annihilated. These three causes made it necessary for the European portion of the army, especially the European officers of the Native Corps, to be foremost in the fight, and to expose themselves in a manner most creditable to them, but in many instances fatal. These are facts, but facts that cannot be brought before the world, and I must bear the brunt. It is rather hard my actions in China were not accounted of any moment, because they were effected without much, indeed with very little loss. In India, I am a reckless savage, devoid of stratagem and military knowledge, because my loss is severe; whilst the reasons, to any person knowing the army I fought with, and that I contended with in both countries, must be obvious, and could not be misinterpreted. In China, my force was almost exclusively European, whilst the force I contended with, although as brave and much more athletic than the Indian, was totally without military knowledge, and allowed me, in every instance, to turn their flank and to bring the great weight of my force upon a less powerful portion of them, thus making their artillery of no use, from their immovable construction. Not so the Mahrattas and Sikhs. They were both peculiarly military nations with a powerful artillery as well served as our own, infinitely superior in numbers and in the weight of metal in their guns. Led by officers accustomed to war, and in the latter instance [the Sikhs] having a confidence in themselves and in their tactics, from the knowledge that they had never been beaten, whilst they had before their eyes the fearful disasters of the first Cabool [Kabul] Army, and the retreat (for it can be taken in no other light) of the second, which they gave themselves the credit of having covered:—but I find that I am entering into a justification of my conduct, and I feel as a soldier that such is not necessary. Let the world carp, let them call me savage, incompetent, and what they please; I am ready to bear all their taunts, rather than throw a shade over the bright laurels the Indian army have won. Posterity will do me justice.[2]

* * *

The story of Empire is littered with examples of commanders upon whose heads public obloquy has been heaped and, as we shall see, it would not be the last time that so distinguished a soldier as Gough should suffer in this way. Nor would he be the last to suffer from political interference in the conduct of his battles.

Notes

1. Sir Henry Montgomery Lawrence (1806–57) British Resident in Lahore, Punjab
2. Robert Rait, *The Life and Campaigns of Hugh, First Viscount Gough, Field Marshal* (1903)

5. The Punjab Annexed
(The Second Sikh War 1848–49)

*The battle was now at its highest, and the air had become filled
with shot, shell and smoke. Trumpets were sounding, drums
beating, bugles sounding, colonels and other officers hollering,
when all of a sudden came the order for the 3rd Light Dragons
to charge. I could see the 9th Lancers and the black cavalry doing
the same. . . . It now seemed that the battle was drawing to a
close, as we could see the enemy in full retreat. Lord Gough came
down to the front. . . . His leg was bleeding at the knee. A piece
of shell had struck him I afterwards heard. The old man said:
'Thank you, 3rd Light, a glorious victory, men!' As soon as he
had been down the cavalry front, we got the order to advance in
pursuing order. The whole of the regiments . . . covered eight or
ten miles of front. . . . We pursued the poor flying devils to the
banks of the Indus river.*[1]

*

The Punjab remained a British protectorate for two years after
the First Sikh War with Sir Henry Lawrence as Resident. The
proud Sikhs, however, were not convinced of British military
superiority. The native rulers constantly intrigued to regain their
power. Hence, a power struggle was inevitable and hostilities
broke out after two British officers were murdered during an

outbreak of insubordination at Multan in April, 1848. Matters might have been contained, but Lieutenant Herbert Edwardes, Lawrence's assistant, who advanced on Multan with a force of Pathan frontier troops, could do no more than keep matters in check at Multan while waiting for an addition force of Bombay troops under General Sir William Sampson Whish.

Gough perceived that it was better to wait and campaign in the cold season and avoid the Sikh government in Lahore joining in, which would consequently involve considerable British strength to suppress. Multan was invested during August by Whish in conjunction with the Sikh general, Shere Singh who was loyal to him during the Siege of Multan. However, Shere Singh went over to the rebels and what had begun as a local rising became a national war, native support for which was fanned by the fall of Multan.

Gough crossed the Sutlej river on 9 November and fought the Battle of Chillianwallah on 13 January, 1849. The Sikh artillery took the British by surprise early in the morning, demonstrating that they had advanced out of their entrenchments. Gough decided on immediate retaliation, though he had been hoping to join forces with Whish from Multan. The Sikhs had the advantage of position and strength in guns. Gough's infantry began to advance at 3 o'clock in the afternoon. British losses were considerable – 2,338 – and the 24th Regiment lost all their officers in a few minutes. However, by evening the British possessed the Sikh line and Gough was cheered by his troops. Nevertheless, his losses were considered unacceptable at home and by the East India Company and Charles Napier was sent to replace him in command.

News and commanding officers travelled slowly during Victoria's reign, and by the time Napier arrived on the scene, Gough had fought his brilliant crowning victory at Gujerat. This account of Chillianwallah is from Gough's own Report:

Having learned from my spies, and from other sources of information, that Shere Singh still held with his right the villages of Lukhneewallah and Futteh Shah-ke-Chuck, having the great body of his force at the village of Lolianwallah, with his left at Russool, on the Jhelum, strongly occupying the southern extremity of a low range of difficult hills intersected by ravines, which extended nearly to that village, I made my arrangements accordingly that evening, and communicated them to the commanders of the several divisions; but, to ensure correct information as to the nature of the country, which I believed to be excessively difficult and ill adapted to the advantage of a regular army, I determined upon moving on this village, Chilianwallah, to reconnoitre.

On the morning of the 13th the force advanced. I made a considerable detour to my right, partly in order to distract the enemy's attention, but principally in order to get as clear as I could of the jungle, on which it would appear the enemy mainly relied.

We approached the village about twelve o'clock, and I found on a mound close to it a strong picket of the enemy's cavalry and infantry, which we at once dispersed, obtaining from the mound a very extended view of the country before us, and the enemy drawn out in battle array, he having, either during the night or that morning, moved out of his several positions and occupied the ground in our front, which, although not a dense, was a difficult jungle, his right in advance of Futteh Shah-ke-Chuck, and on his left the furrowed hills before described.

The day being so far advanced, I decided upon taking up a position in the rear of the village, in order to reconnoitre my front, finding that I could not turn the enemy's flanks, which rested upon the dense jungle extending nearly to Hailah . . .

The engineer department had been ordered to examine the country before us, and the quarter-master general was in the act of taking up ground for the encampment when the enemy advanced some horse artillery and opened fire on the skirmishers in front of the village. I immediately ordered them to be silenced by a few rounds from our heavy guns, which advanced to an open space in front of the village. The fire was instantly returned by nearly the whole of the enemy's field artillery, thus exposing the positions of his guns, which the jungle had hitherto concealed.

It was now evident that the enemy intended to fight, and would probably advance his guns so as to reach the encampment during the night.

I therefore drew up in order of battle, Sir Walter Gilbert's division on the right, flanked by Brigadier Pope's brigade of cavalry, which I strengthened by the 14th Light Dragoons, well aware that the enemy was strong in cavalry upon his left. To this were attached three troops of horse artillery, under Lieutenant Colonel Grant. The heavy guns were in the centre.

Brigadier Campbell's division formed the left, flanked by Brigadier White's brigade of cavalry, and three troops of horse artillery, under Lieutenant Colonel Brind. The field batteries were with the infantry divisions . . .[2]

Whish marched to join Gough on 18 February, as the Sikh armies encamped at Gujerat. The British now had superiority in artillery for the first time in these Sikh wars, and a picked force of 24,000 men. On 21 February at 7.30 am the British opened hostilities at Gujerat with an artillery barrage of two and a half hours duration, and Gough ordered a general advance at 11.30. Within an hour and a half Gujerat was in British hands, while the cavalry pursued the remnants of the Sikh forces:

At 7.30 A.M. the battle began, and after an obstinate defence the Sikh artillery was forced to fall back before the terrific fire poured into it. It would have been well if the cannonade had been continued for another half-hour upon the villages of Burra and Chota Kalra. For within them lay concealed large bodies of the enemy, which were able to inflict heavy losses as Gilbert's troops advanced to take them. To the great satisfaction of the gallant old Commander-in-Chief, Burra Kalra was carried at the point of the bayonet by the 3rd Brigade under Penny, consisting of the 2nd Europeans and the 31st and 70th Native Infantry, while a portion of Hervey's brigade, led by Colonel Franks of Her Majesty's 10th Foot, was equally successful in its attack upon Chota Kalra. The Sikh artillery and the lines of infantry behind them fell back, and it seemed as if the battle was decided. But just at this moment the too rapid advance of a portion of the British infantry left a gap between the centre and the left of their line, into which the Sikhs threw themselves with a furious onslaught. The ammunition of some of the British guns gave out at the critical moment; but Colin Campbell saw the danger, and the fire of part of his artillery thundered upon the Sikhs, whose rout now became complete. Turning to the east, Campbell pursued the flying foe, while the Bombay column hotly followed them to the west of the town. Then the British cavalry, who, during the engagement of the infantry, had repeatedly charged the Sikh cavalry under Akram Khan, son of the Amir Dost Mahomed, joined in the pursuit, and nightfall alone put a stop to General Thackwell's operations. The losses on our side were small, about 100 killed and 700 wounded. On the following morning Gilbert was at the heels of the disorganised and broken Sikh army in the direction of the Jhelum, while Campbell scoured the country with a division of infantry, and Bradford with Nicholson pushed on for twenty-four miles in to the hills. Fifty-three out of the enemy's fifty-nine pieces of artillery were left in our hands, and all the guns lost by us at Ramnagar and Chilianwalla were recaptured. The whole of the Sikh camp and baggage were taken, and the fugitives, throwing away their arms and uniforms, hid themselves in their villages; while the Afghan horse stampeded from the field and never drew rein till they were safe across the Jhelum. A few of the Sikhs rallied on the other side of that river under cover of a detachment of 5000 men and six guns which had been sent across some time before under Sher Sing's brothers, but this rally in no way affected the completeness of the victory. Those who managed to get across destroyed their boats, so that Gilbert was delayed by having to seek for fords, and when he crossed on the 27th to a large island in midstream, they were gone. On and on they went, past Rohtas, occupying a splendid position in the Bakriula Pass, and abandoning it on the first approach of their pursuers, while their allies the Duranis withdrew from Attock and hurried off to Peshawar. Of these latter, Lord Dalhousie, writing to Sir James Hogg, said, 'I hear from Kabul that the Dost is in great discredit, and the people in the utmost alarm, expecting our arrival for punishment. The Khaibaris would not come up to the scratch. I offered them two lakhs to close the pass effectually. Of course I was not fool enough to pay them beforehand. They said they would, but they did nothing, and said the Duranis ran so fast that they had not time to stop them.'[3]

Thus ended the Second Sikh War. The Punjab was now annexed to British India.

Notes

1. Sergeant John Pearman, 3rd Light Dragoons, at the Battle of Gujerat, 21 February, 1849
2. *Letters and Dispatches of Field Marshal Sir Hugh Gough* (1865)
3. Sir William Lee Warner, *The Life of the Marquis of Dalhousie KT* (1904)

6. The Indian Mutiny (1857–58)

On the 31st of March the 19th Native Infantry was disbanded at Barrackpore. . . . The 19th Regiment was in open mutiny, the 34th was in league with it, 2nd Grenadiers were sympathetic. Not less than 5,000 men were in a state of obstinate fanaticism, which any incident might change to fury. . . . In these circumstances a strong force of English troops and well-affected natives were despatched to the scene of disorder. The two QUEEN'S regiments with the cavalry and artillery occupied one side, the native regiments the other, and the 19th Native Infantry, the mutinous corps, were in the midst. A proclamation was read, and they were told they must lay down their arms. They were disposed to resist, but the preparations and firmness of Major-General HEARSEY, the officer in command, and himself a native of India, thoroughly cowed them. They yielded, piled their arms and were marched off. . . . It is thought that the 34th must be disbanded, and a native regiment at Dinapore is only held in check by the presence of English troops.[1]

*

'There was not much sleep that night in our camp. . . . Each of us looked carefully at the loading of our pistols, the filling of our flasks and getting as good protection as possible for our heads

*which would be exposed so much in going up the ladders. I
wound two turbans round my old forage cap with my last letter
from the hills in the top.'[2]*

*

It all began on 22 January, 1857. It was strictly speaking, a
mutiny, not a rebellion or revolution, for the disturbances originated in the armed forces. There had been mutinies in the native
army before the Indian Mutiny of 1857, but these had been easily
suppressed. There were minor grievances before the outbreak.
Regular native soldiers were anxious that a new development,
recruiting native soldiers for general service only, might effect the
pension rights of long-standing native soldiers. Also, there had
been rumours among both the Hindu and Mohammedan soldiers that it was the British intention to undermine their
religions. Sepoys who served in Scinde had been given bonus pay,
and this was resented among those whose service was not so
rewarded. But it was the issue of the greased cartridge for the
Enfield rifle which brought matters to an immediate and frightening crisis.

The British Government desired to establish which of four different manufactured cartridges was the best suited to the Indian
climate. The military authorities were fully aware of the delicacy
which would be needed. Unless it was known that the grease
employed in the cartridges was not of a nature to offend the religious observances of caste, it would be best to issue them to
European soldiers only. The cartridges were tested and a particular kind were requisitioned from the arsenal at Woolwich. They
were made up and dispatched but the greasing process was
undertaken in India. The work was done by low caste Hindus.
On the 22 January, 1857, at Dumdum, between Calcutta and
Barrackpore, one of these low caste workmen asked a grenadier,
who was a high caste Brahmin, for a drink of water from his
flask. The request was refused as the Brahmin believed his flask
would thus have been defiled. The grenadier then received the
retort that he need not be so particular, as the Hindu workman
asserted, he would be defiled soon enough as the cartridges in
use were greased with cow fat.

This incident was contained as the Hindu soldiers' alarm was quietened when the authorities assured them that in future cartridges would be greased with wax. Matters broke out a week later when a British officer was threatened with a loaded musket by a native soldier, Mungul Pandy, who shot his horse from under him. Pandy was tried and executed, but discontent spread. A native regiment was broken up and disbanded on account of the fear of mutiny. Native soldiers in Oude, hearing of the disbanding of the 19th Regiment and other regiments, had to be disbanded, for fear of mutiny.

The first big explosion came at Meerut, when over eighty native soldiers refused to use the new cartridges during carbine practice and were sentenced to ten years' imprisonment with hard labour at their court martial. On 9 May, 1857, when the sentence was read out at parade, and they were stripped of their uniforms and put in irons, feelings ran very high. Rioting broke out the following evening while the servicemen were at church, the jail was stormed and all the prisoners let out, a British officer was shot and hacked to pieces and then a general massacre of Christian men, women and children erupted. The mutineers then fled to Delhi and, incredibly, were not adequately pursued.

At Delhi the Meerut mutineers were joined by other native troops and a general slaughter ensued of all the Europeans they could find. Brigadier General John Nicholson, whose valour was legendary (a brotherhood of Fakirs in Hazara regarded him as a demi-god and began the worship of *Nikkul-Seyn*) who was in command in the Punjab wrote in a letter to Herbert Edwardes, Commissioner at Peshawar:

> Let us propose a Bill for the flaying alive, impalement or burning of the murderers of the women and children at Delhi. The idea of simply hanging the perpetrators of such atrocities is maddening.

News of the mutiny spread and the entire Bengal Army from Delhi to Calcutta joined in the revolt:

> While sepoy regiments were revolting throughout the whole breadth of Northern India, and a handful of British troops was painfully toiling to control them; while Henry Lawrence was struggling, and struggling even to death, to

maintain his position in Oude [Oudh]; while John Lawrence was sagaciously managing the half-wild Punjaub at a troublous time; while Wheeler at Cawnpore, and Colvin at Agra, were beset in the very thick of the mutineers; while Neill and Havelock were advancing up the Jumna; while Canning was doing his best at Calcutta, Harris and Elphinstone at Madras and Bombay, and the imperial government at home, to meet the trying difficulties with a determined front – while all this was doing, Delhi was the scene of a continuous series of operations. Every eye was turned towards that place. The British felt that there was no security for their power in India till Delhi was retaken; the insurgents knew that they had a rallying-point for all their disaffected countrymen, so long as the Mogul city was theirs; and hence bands of armed men were attracted thither by antagonistic motives. Although the real siege did not commence till many weary weeks had passed, the plan and preparations for it must be dated from the very day when the startling news spread over India that Delhi had been seized by rebellious sepoys, under the auspices of the decrepit, dethroned, debauched representative of the Moguls.

It was, as we have already seen . . . on the morning of Monday the 11th of May, that the 11th and 20th regiments Bengal native infantry, and the 3rd Bengal cavalry, arrived at Delhi after a night-march from Meerut, where they had mutinied on the preceding evening. At Delhi, we have also seen, those mutineers were joined by the 38th, 54th, and 74th native infantry. It was on that same 11th of May that evening saw the six mutinous regiments masters of the imperial city; and the English officers and residents, their wives and children, wanderers through jungles and over streams and rivers. What occurred within Delhi on the subsequent days is imperfectly known; the few Europeans who could not or did not escape were in hiding; and scanty notices only have ever come to light from those or other sources. A Lahore newspaper, three of four months afterwards, gave a narrative prepared by a native, who was within Delhi from the 21st of May to the 23rd of June. Arriving ten days after the mutiny, he found the six regiments occupying the Selimgurh and Mohtabagh, but free to roam over the city; where the sepoys and sowars, aided by the rabble of the place, plundered the better houses and shops, stole horses from those who possessed them, 'looted' the passengers who crossed the Jumna by the bridge of boats, and fought with each other for the property which the fleeing British families had left behind them.[3]

It was the British intention to regain control of Delhi as soon as possible, but a few days after beginning his rescue expedition underway General George Anson died of cholera on 27 May, 1857. Sir John Lawrence, chief commissioner in the Punjab, then led a force of 3,000 to Delhi and his elder brother, Sir Henry Lawrence, reinforced the defences at Lucknow. British reinforcements at Calcutta were gathered by Sir Charles John Canning, Governor-General of India, even though he was slow to apprehend the full seriousness of the events then unfolding before him.

* * *

The most notorious atrocity of the Mutiny was the horrific Cawnpore Massacre of June, 1857. Dandu Panth, (Nana Sahib), the Rajah of Bitpur, with a native force, besieged the British garrison at Cawnpore for three weeks. Major-General Sir Hugh Massy Wheeler, a veteran of the Afghan and Sikh wars, capitulated on terms after a brave defence. As the disarmed British troops were embarking on river transports Nana gave the order for a general massacre of the men. Women and children were imprisoned. Wheeler himself was among the slain. This is how British readers read about the event:

THE INDIAN MUTINY

During the last fortnight, the career of rebellion has remained unchecked throughout India, except at Futteh-pore, where the mutineers, under Nana Saheb, have been thrice defeated by the British troops. On the morning of the 17th instant, General Havelock, who left Allahabad with about 2,000 Europeans, consisting of the 64th Regiment, 78th Highlanders, Madras Fusiliers, and a company of

Royal Artillery, attacked and totally defeated the insurgents, capturing eleven guns, and scattering their forces in
utter confusion in the direction of Cawnpore. . . . This
splendid victory was gained without a single casualty on the
side of the British, not a man being touched by the fire of
the enemy.

FRIGHTFUL TRAGEDY AT CAWNPORE

These glorious successes are dimmed by a frightful tragedy
which has occurred at Cawnpore, where Sir Hugh Wheeler
and a small band of Europeans had long held out against
fearful odds. It appears from the conflicting reports published regarding this melancholy catastrophe, that after Sir
Hugh Wheeler was killed, the force at Cawnpore accepted
the offer of safety made by Nana Saheb and the mutineers.
The treacherous miscreant, however, whose hands were
already stained with the blood of the luckless fugitives from
Futtyghur, opened fire on the boats in which the party were
allowed to enter, and destroyed them all. Other accounts
state that the wives and children of the officers and soldiers,
consisting of 240 persons, were taken into Cawnpore, and
sold by public auction, when, after being treated with the
highest indignities, they were barbarously slaughtered by
the inhabitants. There is, notwithstanding, a faint hope that
some few have escaped the general massacre as it is said that
Nana Saheb has more than a hundred European prisoners
in his hands, whom he intends to hold as hostages. These
are probably the remains of General Wheeler's force at
Cawnpore.[4]

The military historian Sir John William Kaye, who served in
the artillery in Bengal and became Secretary of the India Office,
wrote in his three volume *History of the Sepoy War* (1864–76):

There was not a soldier in the garrison who did not recoil
from the thought of surrender – who would not have died
with sword or musket in hand rather than lay down his
arms at the feet of the treacherous Mahratta.

Major-General Sir Henry Havelock, an officer of vast experience in campaigns in India, Afghanistan and Persia, led the expedition (2,500 strong) to relieve Lucknow. His comment at the time, is recorded in his *Memoirs* (1860):

> My lot is cast for Lucknow. The enterprise of crossing the Ganges, opposed by double my number, is not without hazard. But it has, to me, at sixty-three, all the charm of a romance. I am as happy as a duck in thunder.

Havelock's force covered 126 miles in nine days during July – the hottest season of the year – wholly routing Nana Sahib's forces at Fatephur, Aong and Cawnpore, where the victorious British discovered the true horrors of Cawnpore:

> We reached Cawnpore, the scene of the Nana Sahib's massacre of the poor defenceless European men, women and children. Just outside the place we halted near a fine house which was, however, empty, and while waiting for the order to march on, we strolled into it. Even there there had been murder if one could judge by the crimson stain where blood had spurted on the wall and by the smear of a bloody hand. Our Camp was pitched at each side of the road, and that evening we all paid the now-famous well etc. a visit as well as the house close to it in which before their massacre the women and children were confined. The house was a small one, being as well as I can now remember one long room with a verandah in front and rear and the back verandah looked into a courtyard or zenana compound, on the other three sides of which were walls with a door leading out of that on the left to the path to the well. In the courtyard itself grew a babul tree and near the well between it and the house were three or four large trees and some low scrubby thicket of thorny shrubs. The inside of the house was of course bare of furniture and there was no matting or carpet on the floor, but instead blood, thick clotted blood looking like Russian leather, with which the walls also for three or four feet from the ground were spattered, and in some places smeared as if a great spout of it had gushed out on them, while here and there were marks where the murderers had dried their

bloody hands by rubbing them against the walls in which were also deep sword cuts, as if some poor victim had dodged aside from the blow. There were also several pencil inscriptions, noting the date of arrival there, and memoranda of deaths of friends or relatives, or short prayers for help. Bonnets, slippers, hats, stays and various other articles of female clothing, with tresses and plaits of hair were scattered about with fragments of books, most, if not all of them Bibles and prayer books. Some of the bonnets and hats were hanging from the beams in the back verandah, which as well as the back yard was covered thick with clotted blood. All the way to the well was marked by a regular track along which the bodies had been dragged and the thorny bushes had entangled in them scraps of clothing and long hairs. One of the large trees to the left of this track going to the well had evidently had children's brains dashed out against its trunk, for it was covered thick with blood and children's hair matted into the coarse bark, and an eye, glazed and withered could be plainly made out pasted into the trunk. A few paces on and you stood by the well itself, now the receptacle of all these poor mangled bodies. It looked old and going fast to decay for the bricks and mortar had given way and crumbled in many places round the low edge, I think it must have been dry or very nearly so. After peering into it for some time until the eyes had become accustomed to the gloom, you could see members of human bodies, legs and arms sticking up browned and withered like those of a mummy. But there was no putrid smell or anything of that kind that I could perceive. Those dead arms of our murdered country people seemed to be making a mute appeal to us from the darkness below; far more eloquent than words they called to Heaven for vengeance on the ruthless perpetrators of untold atrocities, and many a vow was registered over that well never to spare should they be met with hand to hand in the approaching struggle for the Relief of Lucknow, but four short marches now lay between us and that city where we knew the garrison with a crowd of women and children, were daily subject to the attacks of the Cawnpore, and thousands of similar ruffians all eager to repeat the horrors of the place where we now stood; but we had to curb our impatience to go to their relief and had days still to wait the coming of Sir Colin Campbell, the new Commander-in-Chief, who with a large force was now pushing up country.[5]

Havelock waited for reinforcements before beginning the advance to relieve Lucknow. Delhi was stormed by a British force of 4,000 under Brigadier General John Nicholson, who was himself killed. Of his assault force, 1,574 were killed and wounded.

* * *

Sir Henry Lawrence, the Chief Commissioner of Oudh, had moved the European families in his area into the Residency at Lucknow, as the situation in Oudh began to deteriorate, and to put measures in hand to stock Lucknow with food and ammunition. Taking the rank of Brigadier General, he also assumed command of all the troops in Oudh and formed a defensive garrison of British and loyal native regiments. Improvements to the defensive works were also put in hand.

Although the storm burst on 30 May, Lawrence was able to continue his defensive work for a month until Lucknow became invested on 1 July. Three days later he was dead, having been struck by a shell on 2 July. His second-in-command, Colonel John Eardley Wilmot Inglis, who had served gallantly in Canada and the Punjab, assumed the acting rank of Brigadier General and took command.

From 1 July to the end of September, when a relief force under Havelock and Outram arrived to reinforce the garrison, the fight continued incessantly. Outram had been appointed to succeed Havelock but had generously allowed the latter to continue to direct the operations that he had begun, although he was unable to resist the temptation to interfere from time to time, which did not make for an easy command situation. On establishing their force in the Residency, after hard fighting, Outram assumed complete command.

The siege continued until a further force of 4,500 men under the Commander-in-Chief, General Sir Colin Campbell, arrived, to the skirl of the pipes playing 'The Campbells are coming', on 17 November. Within his force was Campbell's beloved 93rd of

Foot – part of the Highland Brigade at Balaclava and famed as 'the thin red line'. Fighting like heroes, the Scots forced their way into the city, inflicting formidable casualties on the enemy, heavily supported by the 53rd and the 4th Punjab Infantry. An invaluable element of Campbell's army was a naval train of heavy guns commanded by Captain William Peel of HMS *Shannon* which did much to swing the outcome of the battle in Campbell's favour.

Despite the blow inflicted upon the mutineers, they were still very much alive and Campbell decided that the garrison must withdraw, an operation carried out with immense skill by Outram and Havelock. The strain of the siege upon the families had been immense and some idea of life inside the Residency during those terrible weeks may be gathered from this diary extract:

Thursday, 20 August. A good deal of shelling has been going on this morning, but it is mostly our own. . . . It rained in the evening a good deal. A poor little child next door to us died of cholera; it was only taken ill about one o'clock and it was dead before seven. The poor mother was in a dreadful state just before it died, and afterwards perfectly calm. While we were undressing she came and asked if we had an empty box we could give her to bury the poor little thing in. We had not one long enough . . .

Thursday, 27 August. Colonel Inglis had a most merciful escape last night. He was standing on the bastion at Mr Gubbins's house, close to Mr Webb when he was killed. They saw the round shot coming, and went down to avoid it, but it hit Mr Webb, and a native who was with him, killing them both instantaneously. It makes one shudder to think how death is hovering about and around us all; busy indeed has he been amongst this little garrison. Mrs Thornhill had a little girl last night. Sir Henry Lawrence's things are being sold today [he had recently been killed]; heard of a ham being sold for £7 and a tin of soup sufficient only for one day's dinner for £1.5s.!!! Money has ceased to be of any value, and people are giving unheard-of prices for stores of any kind – one dozen brandy £20; one small box of vermicelli, £5; four small cakes of chocolate, £2.10s.!!! . . .

Monday, 5 October. Today we have begun to restrict our-selves to two chuppatties each a day; and soon, I fear, we shall have to eat horseflesh; but as yet we have beef and rice. I have been hungry today, and could have eaten more, had I had it. Seven men and three officers came in today from the Fureed Bux, badly wounded. Mrs Roberts came to see us this morning, and told us the chloroform at the hospital is all gone. Mrs Omiley's children both died in one hour a day or two ago . . .

Sunday, 18 October. We have been out of soap for some days and are now obliged to wash with what is called 'bason' (ground grain made into a paste with water). It is a nice clean thing, and the best substitute for soap.[6]

This account by Sir Colin Campbell of the relief of Lucknow is contained in his official dispatch to the Governor-General of 18 November, 1857:

THE RELIEF OF LUCKNOW

From His Excellency the Commander-in-Chief to the Right Honourable the Governor-General.
HEAD-QUARTERS, SHAH NUJJEEF,
LUCKNOW, *Nov.* 18, 1857.

My Lord, – I have the honour to apprise your Lordship that I left Cawnpore on the 9th November, and joined the troops under the command of Brigadier-General Hope Grant, C.B., the same day, at Camp Buntara, about six miles from Alumbagh.[7]

There being a few detachments on the road, I deemed it expedient to wait till the 12th before commencing my advance.

On the day I marched early for Alumbagh.

The advanced guard was attacked by two guns and a body of about 2,000 infantry. After a smart skirmish the guns were taken; Lieut. Gough, commanding Hodson's Irregular Horse, having distinguished himself very much in a brilliant charge by which this object was effected.

The camp was pitched on that evening at Alumbagh. This place I found to be annoyed to a certain extent by guns placed in different positions in the neighbourhood.

I caused the post to be cleared of lumber and cattle, and placed all my tents in it.

I made my arrangements for marching without baggage when I should reach the park of Dilkoosha, and the men were directed to have three days' food in their haversacks. I changed the garrison at Alumbagh, taking fresh men from it, and leaving her Majesty's 75th Regiment there, which had been so much harassed by its late exertions.

On the 14th, I expected a further reinforcement of 600 of 700 men, who joined my rear guard after my march had commenced in the morning of that day.

As I approached the park of Dilkoosha, the leading troops were met by a long line of musketry fire.

The advance guard was quickly reinforced by a field battery and more infantry, composed of companies of her Majesty's 5th, 64th, and 78th Foot, under the command of Lieut.-Col. Hamilton, her Majesty's 78th Highlanders, supported by the 8th Foot. After a running fight of about two hours, in which our loss was very inconsiderable, the enemy was driven down the hill to the Martinière, across the garden and park of the Martinière, and far beyond the canal. His loss was trifling, owing to the suddenness of the retreat.

The Dilkoosha and Martinière were both occupied Brigadier Hope's brigade being then brought up and arranged in position in the wood of the Martinière at the end and opposite the canal, being flanked to the left by Captain Bourchier's field battery and two of Captain Peel's heavy guns.

Shortly after these arrangements had been made the enemy drew out a good many people and attacked our position in front. He was quickly driven off, some of our troops crossing the canal in pursuit. On this occasion the 53rd, 93rd, and a body of the 4th Punjaub Sikhs, distinguished themselves.

With the exception of my tents, all my heavy baggage, including provisions for fourteen days for my own force and that in Lucknow, accompanied me on my march across country to Dilkoosha, covered by a strong rearguard under Lieutenant-Colonel Ewart, of her Majesty's 93rd Highlanders. This officer distinguished himself very much in this difficult command, his artillery, under Captain Blunt, Bengal Horse Artillery, assisted by the Royal Artillery, under Colonel Crawford, R.A., having been in action for the greater part of the day. The rearguard did not close up to the column until late next day, the enemy having hung on it until dark on the 14th. Every description of baggage having been left at Dilkoosha, which was occupied by her Majesty's 8th Regiment, I advanced direct on Secunderbagh early on the 16th. This place is a high-walled inclosure of strong masonry of 120 yards square, and was carefully loopholed all round. It was held very strongly by the enemy. Opposite to it was a village at a distance of a hundred yards, which was also loopholed and filled with men.

On the head of the column advancing up the lane to the left of the Secunderbagh, fire was opened on us. The infantry of the advance guard was quickly thrown in skirmishing order, to line a bank to the right. The guns were pushed rapidly onwards, viz., Captain Blunt's troop, Bengal Horse Artillery, and Captain Traver's, Royal Artillery, heavy field battery. The troop passed at a gallop through a cross-fire from the village and Secunderbagh, and opened fire within easy musketry range in a most daring manner. As soon as they could be pushed up a stiff bank, two 18-pounder guns, under Captain Travers, were also brought to bear on the building. Whilst this was being effected, the leading brigade of infantry, under Brigadier the Hon. Adrian Hope, coming rapidly into action, caused the loopholed village to be abandoned; the whole fire of the brigade being then directed on the Secunderbagh. After a time a large body of the enemy, who were holding ground on the left of our advance, were driven in by parties of the 53rd and 93rd, two of Captain Blunt's guns aiding the movement. The Highlanders pursued their advantage and seized the barracks, and immediately converted them into a military post, the 53rd stretching in a long line of skirmishers in the open plain, and driving the enemy before them.

The attack on Secunderbagh had now been proceeding

for about an hour and half, when it was determined to take the place by storm through a small opening which had been made. This was done in the most brilliant manner by the remainder of the Highlanders and the 53rd and the 4th Punjaub Infantry, supported by a battalion of detachments under Major Barnston. There never was a bolder feat of arms, and the loss inflicted on the enemy, after the entrance of the Secunderbagh was effected, was immense – more than 2,000 of the enemy were afterwards carried out. The officers who led these regiments were Lieutenant-Colonel Leith Hay, her Majesty's 93rd Highlanders; Lieutenant-Colonel Gordon, her Majesty's 93rd Highlanders; Captain Walton, her Majesty's 53rd Foot; Lieutenant Paul, 4th Punjaub Infantry (since dead); and Major Barnston, her Majesty's 90th Foot.

Captain Peel's Royal Naval Siege Train then went to the front and advanced towards the Shah Nujjeef, together with the field battery and some mortars, the village to the left having been cleared by Brigadier Hope and Lieutenant-Colonel Gordon.

The Shah Nujjeef is a domed mosque with a garden, of which the most had been made by the enemy. The wall of the inclosure of the mosque was loopholed with great care. The entrance to it had been covered by a regular work in masonry, and the top of the building was crowned with a parapet. From this, and from the defences in the garden, an unceasing fire of musketry was kept up from the commencement of the attack. This position was defended with great resolution against a heavy cannonade of three hours. It was then stormed in the boldest manner by the 93rd Highlanders, under Brigadier Hope, supported by a battalion of detachments under Major Barnston, who was, I regret to say, severely wounded; Captain Peel leading up his heavy guns with extraordinary gallantry within a few yards of the building, to batter the massive stone walls. The withering fire of the Highlanders effectually covered the Naval Brigade from great loss, but it was an action almost unexampled in war. Captain Peel behaved very much as if he had been laying the *Shannon* alongside an enemy's frigate. This brought the day's operations to a close.

On the next day communications were opened, to the left rear of the barracks, to the canal, after overcoming considerable difficulty. Capt. Peel kept up a steady cannonade on the building called the mess-house. This building, of considerable size, was defended by a ditch about twelve feet broad and scarped with masonry, and beyond that a loopholed mud wall. I determined to use the guns as much as possible in taking it. About three p.m., when it was considered that men might be sent to storm it without much risk, it was taken by a company of the 90th Foot, under Captain Wolseley,[8] and a picket of Her Majesty's 53rd, under Captain Hopkins, supported by Major Barnston's battalion of detachments under Captain Guise, Her Majesty's 90th Foot, and some of the Punjaub Infantry under Lieutenant Powlett. The mess-house was carried immediately with a rush. The troops then pressed forward with great vigour, and lined the wall separating the mess-house from the Motee Mahal, which consists of a wide inclosure and many buildings. The enemy here made a last stand, which was overcome after an hour, openings having been broken in the wall, through which the troops poured, with a body of Sappers, and accomplished our communications with the Residency. I had the inexpressible satisfaction, shortly afterwards, of greeting Sir James Outram and Sir Henry Havelock, who came out to meet me before the action was at an end. The relief of the besieged garrison had been accomplished. The troops, including all ranks of officers and men, had worked strenuously and persevered boldly in following up the advantages gained in the various attacks. Every man in the force had exerted himself to the utmost, and now met with his reward.

It should not be forgotten that these exertions did not date merely from the day that I joined the camp; the various bodies of which the relieving force was composed having made the longest forced marches from various directions to enable the Government of India to save the garrison of Lucknow. Some from Agra, some from Allahabad – all had alike undergone the same fatigues in pressing forward for the attainment of this great object. Of their conduct in the field of battle the facts narrated in this despatch are sufficient evidence, which I will not weaken by any eulogy of mine.

In a subsequent report, dated 'Alumbagh, Nov. 25', Sir Colin Campbell records the incidents connected with the evacuation of the Lucknow Residency. After giving an account of three days' skirmishes with the enemy, he continues:

Having led the enemy to believe that immediate assault was contemplated, orders were issued for the retreat of the garrison through the lines of our pickets at midnight on the 22nd.

The ladies and families, the wounded, the treasure, the guns it was thought worth while to keep, the ordnance stores, the grain still possessed by the commissariat of the garrison, and the state prisoners, had all been previously removed.

Sir James Outram had received orders to burst the guns, which it was thought undesirable to take away; and he was finally directed silently to evacuate the Residency of Lucknow at the hour indicated.

The dispositions to cover their retreat and to resist the enemy, should he pursue, were ably carried out by Brigadier the Hon. Adrian Hope; but I am happy to say the enemy was completely deceived, and he did not attempt to follow. On the contrary, he began firing on our old positions many hours after we had left them. The movement of retreat was admirably executed, and was a perfect lesson in such combinations.

Each exterior line came gradually retiring through its supports, till at length nothing remained but the last line of infantry and guns, with which I was myself to crush the enemy if he had dared to follow up the pickets.

The only line of retreat through a long and tortuous lane, and all these precautions were absolutely necessary to insure the safety of the force.

During all these operations, from the 16th inst., Brigadier Greathed's brigade closed in the rear, and now again formed the rear-guard as we retired to Dilkoosha.

Dilkoosha was reached at 4 a.m. on the 23rd inst. by the whole force.

On the 22nd the enemy attacked at Dilkoosha, but was speedily driven off, under Brigadier Little's orders.

I moved with General Grant's division to Alumbagh on the afternoon of the 24th, leaving Sir James Outram's division in position at Dilkoosha, to prevent molestation of the immense convoy of the women and wounded, which it was necessary to transport with us. Sir James Outram closed up this day without annoyance from the enemy.'

I have the honour to be, my Lord, your Lordship's most obedient humble servant. C. CAMPBELL., General, Commander-in-Chief.[9]

On withdrawing, Campbell left a covering force outside Lucknow and, in March, 1858, he returned with a substantial force to recapture the city. The mutineers had not yielded easily and the operation involved ten days' bitter fighting.

*   *   *

The mutiny deteriorated into a guerrilla war. Between April and June, 1858, General Sir Hugh Rose engaged the rebel leader Tantia Topi in a series of battles which brought the Mutiny to its end – Jhansi, Kunch, Kalpi and finally at Gwalior on 19 June, 1858, where the rebel forces were led by the Rani of Jhansi in person. She was among the slain.

The Mutiny was now at an end. British reprisals were terrible. Rebel leaders, native officers, those detected in treasonable correspondence with Tantia Topee, Nana Sahib, the Rani of Jhansi or any other of the rebel leaders, were hanged or blown away from guns. Charles Dickens was among those in Britain who had hoped that a similar thoroughness would be exerted in looking after the maimed and wounded soldiers on their return to the mother country. He wrote in the journal *All the Year Round* about the conditions pertaining on the troopships used to transport returning troops which arrived at Liverpool:

Any animated description of a modern battle, any private soldier's letter published in the newspapers, any page of the records of the Victoria Cross, will show that in the ranks of the army, there exists under all disadvantages as fine a sense of duty as is to be found in any station on earth. Who doubts that if we all did our duty as faithfully as the soldier does his, this world would be a better place? There may be greater difficulties in our way than in the soldier's. Not disputed. But, let us at least do our duty towards *him*.

I had got back again to that rich and beautiful port and I was walking up a hill there, on a wild March morning. My conversation with my official friend Pangloss, by whom I was accidentally accompanied, took this direction as we took the up-hill direction, because the object of my uncommercial journey was to see some discharged soldiers who had recently come home from India. There were men of HAVELOCK's among them; there were men who had been in many of the great battles of the great Indian campaign, among them; and I was curious to note what our discharged soldiers looked like, when they were done with.

In this agreeable frame of mind I entered the workhouse of Liverpool. — for, the cultivation of laurels in a sandy soil, had brought the soldiers in question to *that* abode of Glory.

Before going into their wards to visit them, I inquired how they had made their triumphant entry there? They had been brought through the rain in carts, it seemed, from the landing-place to the gate, and had then been carried upstairs on the backs of paupers. Their groans and pains during the performance of this glorious pageant, had been so distressing, as to bring tears into the eyes of spectators but too well accustomed to scenes of suffering. The men were so dreadfully cold, that those who could get near the fires were hard to be restrained from thrusting their feet in among the blazing coals. They were so horribly reduced, that they were awful to look upon. Racked with dysentery and blackened with scurvy, one hundred and forty wretched soldiers had been revived with brandy and laid in bed.

My official friend Pangloss is lineally descended from a learned doctor of that name, who was once tutor to Candide, an ingenious young gentleman of some celebrity. In his personal character, he is as humane and worthy a gentleman as any I know; in his official capacity, he unfortunately preaches the doctrines of his renowned ancestor, by demonstrating on all occasions that we live in the best of all possible official worlds.

'In the name of Humanity,' said I, 'how did the men fall into this deplorable state? Was the ship well found in stores?'

'I am not here to asseverate that I know the fact, of my own knowledge,' answered Pangloss, 'but I have grounds for asserting that the stores were the best of all possible stores.'

A medical officer laid before us, a handful of rotten biscuit, and a handful of split peas. The biscuit was a honey-combed heap of maggots, and the excrement of maggots. The peas were even harder than this filth. A similar hand-ful had been experimentally boiled six hours, and had shown no signs of softening. These were the stores on which the soldiers had been fed.

'The beef—' I began, when Pangloss cut me short.

'Was the best of all possible beef,' said he.

But, behold, there was laid before us certain evidence given at the Coroner's Inquest, holden on some of the men (who had obstinately died of their treatment), and from that evidence it appeared that the beef was the worst of possi-ble beef!

'Then I lay my hand upon my heart, and take my stand,' said Pangloss, 'by the pork, which was the best of all pos-sible pork.'

'But look at this food before our eyes, if one may so mis-use the word,' said I. 'Would any Inspector who did his duty, pass such abomination?'

'It ought not to have been passed,' Pangloss admitted.

'Then the authorities out there—' I began, when Pangloss cut me short again.

'There would certainly seem to have been something wrong somewhere,' said he; 'but I am prepared to prove that the authorities out there, are the best of all possible authorities.'

I never heard of any impeached public authority in my life, who was not the best public authority in existence.

'We are told of these unfortunate men being laid low by scurvy,' said I. 'Since lime-juice has been regularly stored

47

and served out in our navy, surely that disease, which used to devastate it, has almost disappeared? Was there lime-juice aboard this transport?'

My official friend was beginning 'the best of all possible—' when an inconvenient medical forefinger pointed out another passage in the evidence from which it appeared that the lime-juice had been bad too. Not to mention that the vinegar had been bad too, the vegetables bad too, the cooking accommodation insufficient (if there had been anything worth mentioning to cook), the water supply exceedingly inadequate, and the beer sour.

'Then the men,' said Pangloss, a little irritated, 'were the worst of all possible men.'

'In what respect?' I asked.

'Oh! Habitual drunkards,' said Pangloss.

But, again the same incorrigible medical forefinger pointed out another passage in the evidence, showing that the dead men had been examined after death, and that they, at least, could not possibly have been habitual drunkards, because the organs within them which must have shown traces of that habit, were perfectly sound.

'And besides,' said the three doctors present, one and all, 'habitual drunkards brought as low as these men have been, could not recover under care and food, as the great majority of these men are recovering. They would not have strength of constitution to do it.'

'Reckless and improvident dogs, then,' said Pangloss. 'Always are – nine times out of ten.'

I turned to the master of the workhouse, and asked him whether the men had any money?

'Money?' said he. 'I have in my iron safe, nearly four hundred pounds of theirs; the agents have nearly a hundred pounds more; and many of them have left money in Indian banks besides.'

'Hah!' said I to myself, as we went up-stairs, 'this is not the best of all possible stories, I doubt!'

We went into a large ward, containing some twenty or five-and-twenty beds. We went into several such wards, one after another. I find it very difficult to indicate what a shocking sight I saw in them, without frightening the reader from

48

the perusal of these lines, and defeating my object of making it known.

O the sunken eyes that turned to me as I walked between the rows of beds, or – worse still – that glazedly looked at the white ceiling, and saw nothing and cared for nothing! Here, lay the skeleton of a man, so lightly covered with a thin unwholesome skin, that not a bone in the anatomy was clothed, and I could clasp the arm above the elbow, in my finger and thumb. Here, lay a man with the black scurvy eating his legs away, his gums gone, and his teeth all gaunt and bare. This bed was empty, because gangrene had set in, and the patient had died but yesterday. That bed was a hopeless one, because its occupant was sinking fast, and could only be roused to turn the poor pinched mask of face upon the pillow, with a feeble moan. The awful thinness of the fallen cheeks, the awful brightness of the deep set eyes, the lips of lead, the hands of ivory, the recumbent human images lying in the shadow of death with a kind of solemn twilight on them, like the sixty who had died aboard the ship and were lying at the bottom of the sea, O Pangloss, GOD forgive you!

In one bed, lay a man whose life had been saved (as it was hoped) by deep incisions in the feet and legs. While I was speaking to him, a nurse came up to change the poultices which this operation had rendered necessary, and I had an instinctive feeling that it was not well to turn away, merely to spare myself. He was sorely wasted and keenly susceptible, but the efforts he made to subdue any expression of impatience or suffering, were quite heroic. It was easy to see, in the shrinking of the figure, and the drawing of the bed-clothes over the head, how acute the endurance was, and it made me shrink too, as if *I* were in pain; but, when the new bandages were on, and the poor feet were composed again, he made an apology for himself (though he had not uttered a word), and said plaintively, 'I am so tender and weak, you see, sir!' Neither from him nor from any one sufferer of the whole ghastly number, did I hear a complaint. Of thankfulness for present solicitude and care, I heard much; of complaint, not a word.

I think I could have recognised in the dismalest skeleton

there, the ghost of a soldier. Something of the old air was still latent in the palest shadow of life I talked to. One emaciated creature, in the strictest literality worn to the bone, lay stretched on his back, looking so like death that I asked one of the doctors if he were not dying, or dead? A few kind words from the doctor, in his ear, and he opened his eyes, and smiled – looked, in a moment, as if he would have made a salute, if he could. 'We shall pull him through, please God,' said the Doctor. 'Plase God, surr, and thankye,' said the patient. 'You are much better to-day; are you not?' said the Doctor. 'Plase God, surr; 'tis the slape I want, surr; 'tis my breathin' makes the nights so long.' 'He is a careful fellow this, you must know,' said the Doctor, cheerfully; 'it was raining hard when they put him in the open cart to bring him here, and he had the presence of mind to ask to have a sovereign taken out of his pocket that he had there, and a cab engaged. Probably it saved his life.' The patient rattled out the skeleton of a laugh, and said, proud of the story, 'Deed, surr, an open cairt was a comical means o' bringin' a dyin' man here, and a clever way to kill him.'[10]

*   *   *

It has ever been thus, as Kipling would protest so eloquently in his poem 'Tommy'. Whilst matters may have improved to a marked degree, the story of the post-war years of this century reflect a remarkable unwillingness on the part of officialdom to respond with true generosity to the needs of its disabled ex-servicemen and their bereaved dependants. That this is not simply a British disease is reflected in the plight of America's Vietnam veterans, who still feel bitterly that they are despised and rejected.

Notes

1. *The Times* 19 May, 1857
2. Captain Richard Barter, 75th Foot (The Gordon Highlanders), writing of the night before the assault on Delhi, 15 September, 1857. Richard Barter, *The Siege of Delhi – Mutiny Memories of an old Officer* (1869)

3. William Chambers and Robert Chambers, *The History of the Revolt in India* (1859)
4. *The Sunday Times* 30 August, 1857
5. Barter *op.cit.*
6. Adelaide Case, *Day by Day at Lucknow* (1858)
7. Alumbagh was a defended locality outside Lucknow, as was Secunderbagh.
8. Wolseley. Later to become a Field Marshal and Commander-in-Chief of the Army.
9. Lawrence Shadwell, *Life of Colin Campbell*, Lord Clyde (1881)
10. Charles Dickens, The *Great Tasmania*'s Cargo in *All the Year Round*, vol. 3 No. 54, 5 May, 1860

PAGODAS, PALACES AND *PAHS*

7. Crushing an Expansionist Policy (The First Burma War 1824–26)[1]

In April, 1824, it was my lot, and a proud and happy lot I thought it, to hold the rank of ensign in the Madras European Regiment . . . and never shall I forget the shouts of joy with which we welcomed the intelligence of a war with the Burmese. . . . The day that brought the news was . . . one of rejoicing, especially to the youngsters among us . . . the well known professional toast of 'Prize-money and promotion' and the more barbarous one of 'A bloody war and a sickly season' were given and drunk.[1]

*

In the early 19th Century Burma conducted an expansionist policy, engaging in frequent conflict with Siam and from time to time threatening British influence in India. In 1815 Arakan rebels attempted to drive the Burmese back from Chitttagong, and the Burmese invaded Assam in 1819, the inhabitants looking to the British East India forces to protect them. Three years later Burmese incursions into Manipur and Cachar were ineffectively resisted by British troops, supporting the native rulers.

The Burmese military commander, Maha Bandula, the governor of Assam, resolved to deal the British a decisive blow, and invaded India from Assam and Arakan in March, 1824. This led to the First Burma War. The British forces were commanded by

Sir Archibald Campbell, who had served in India since 1788 and distinguished himself at Seringapatam. He had also given sound service during the Peninsula campaign with Sir John Moore in 1808.

The British forces embarked on the campaign with considerable zest and the initial stages were straightforward. Rangoon was taken with little opposition, but the British soon began to suffer depredation from being so far removed from their supply lines. Clothing deteriorated, food supplies were extremely poor, sanitation was bad. Ravaged by disease, the British then found themselves encircled by a courageous enemy who was not prepared to yield without a good fight. A young English officer serving with the Madras Fusiliers recorded the impact of jungle warfare on catering and costume:

My regiment brought with it from India a full mess establishment of butchers, bakers, cooks, &c.; but their occupation was soon almost a dead letter, for where there is no market, there can be no mess, and though every effort was made to keep up our social meetings at the mess-table, even to foraging in the jungle for such of the vegetable tribe as might supply the place of greens, it was found to be such uphill work that 'ere a month had elapsed the mess was broken up *nem. con,* till matters took a more favourable turn. Well can I recall the scrambling scene that took place as soon as the dishes – which, however, were 'few and far between' – appeared on the tables! Ceremony was out of the question, hunger now ruled the roast, and the longest and strongest arm carried the day! The viands had scarcely touched the board when there was a simultaneous rush towards the centre, a charge with forks into the very dishes, and the affair was over! This unequal distribution of the loaves and fishes, however, could not last; the operations of the mess were consequently suspended, and we broke up into small parties of twos and threes, to keep the pot boiling as we best could. Ingenuity was now ever upon the stretch to add to the scanty meal, and experiments were tried, by the most enterprising amongst us in gastronomy, upon such of the animal tribe within our reach as promised nutrition without being detrimental. W—, of ours, exerted his skill upon a squirrel, which animals are plentiful in most parts of the East; this he roasted and ate, and declared to be very palatable: whether he continued to feast upon them I cannot remember. Paddy-birds (so called from their frequenting the rice or paddy-fields,) a kind of stork, were now in full requisition for curries, disguised in which shape they were greedily devoured, though in India we had ever considered them as unfit for food as a crow or kite. There was a kind of pulse, call *dhall*, served out to us occasionally by the commissariat, which was a coarse substitute for peas; and of this, with the addition of some ration beef or pork, we made an inferior soup, which, if it did not nourish us much, had the effect of filling us out most effectually. . . . This system of diet, combined with the constant exposure, by day and night, to heavy tropical rains, to which military operations rendered us liable, could not but work together for evil; and melancholy were the effects soon produced thereby on the health of the troops, both European and native. . . . When troops are on active service in the East, great license is permitted in the way of costume; in fact, the Regulations could not very well be enforced where there are no army tailors to supply deficiencies. On such a barbarous and distant service as that in question, it may well be imagined we were soon a most motley group, and would have contrasted rather strangely with the Foot Guards at St. James's. My own corps ran riot very much in this particular, our colonel not being over strict as to dress. Many wore trowsers made of a coarse blue calico, used for lining tents (this was *my* favourite material); others wore white, and some tartan; in fact, every one suited his own *taste*, and all the colours of the rainbow were soon seen in the ranks, *uniform* being now, as applied to dress, quite a misnomer. There were times when Falstaff himself might have been ashamed of us. Amongst the officers there was great diversity of taste as to head-dress, some wearing the high oil-skin shako, others foraging caps of various shapes. Moustaches also were encouraged here and there by an aspiring few. As for gloves, I suppose there were hardly half a dozen pair amongst us, and of course we were soon altogether independent of such luxuries.

Irregularities in dress, however, though very unseemly on a parade in garrison, are of little or no importance on active service, when men should not be harassed about trifles; the main object then should be to keep the bayonets bright and the powder dry.[2]

* * *

By February, 1825, the British forces had broken through the defence cordon created by the Burmese commander, Mahu Bandula, and were ready to advance up the Irrawaddy. Sir Archibald Campbell had a column of 2,500 with a flotilla of 60 vessels, with sailors and additional troops numbering over 1,500. Bandula was killed in the Battle of Danubyu on 2 April, 1825. His courage in defending his country was respected by the invading British, as is recorded in the official record of the war compiled by Horace Hyman Wilson, who had served as an assistant surgeon for the East India Company in Bengal:

After halting two days at Henzada, to prepare carriage for the stores, the army resumed its march along the right bank, and came before Donabew on the 25th: a communication was opened with the flotilla on the 27th, and both divisions zealously co-operated in the reduction of the place. Batteries, armed with heavy artillery, were constructed without delay. Spirited attempts to interrupt their progress were frequently made by sorties from the work; and on one occasion Bundoola ordered out his elephants, seventeen in number, each carrying a complement of armed men, and supported by a body of infantry. They were gallantly charged by the body-guard, the horse artillery, and rocket troop, and the elephant drivers being killed, the animals made off into the jungle, whilst the troops retreated precipitately within their defences, into which rockets and shells were thrown with a precision that rendered the post no refuge from danger.

The mortar and enfilading batteries opened on the 1st of April, and their breaching batteries commenced their fire at day-break on the 2nd, shortly after which the enemy were discovered, in full retreat, through the thicket. The entrenchments were immediately taken possession of, and considerable stores, both of grain and ammunition, as well as a great number of guns of various descriptions, were captured. The sudden retreat of the enemy, it was ascertained, was occasioned by the death of their general, Maha Bundoola, who was killed on the preceding day by the bursting of a shell. With him fell the courage of the garrison, and the surviving chiefs vainly attempted to animate the men to resistance. The death of Bundoola was a severe blow to the Burman cause. He was the chief instigator of the war, and its most strenuous advocate, and in courage and readiness of resource, displayed great abilities to maintain the contest. He was a low and illiterate man, who had risen to power by his bravery and audacity. When the war broke out he professed himself ready, and no doubt thought himself able, to lead a Burman army to the capital of British India, and wrest from its Government the lower districts of Bengal. Although not present in the action at Ramoo, he commanded in Arakan, and derived additional reputation from the result of that campaign. When called to the defence of the territory of his sovereign, he anticipated fresh triumphs, and engaged to conduct the invaders captives to Ava. The operations at Rangoon taught him a different lesson, and, although they seem not to have shaken his pertinacity and valour, they inspired him with a new spirit, and engrafted courtesy on his other military merits. Of this the reply, he is reported to have returned to the summons sent him by General Cotton, is a remarkable instance. He is said to have answered, 'we are each fighting for his country, and you will find me as steady in defending mine, as you in maintaining the honour of yours. If you wish to see Donabew, come as friends, and I will show it you. If you come as enemies, LAND!'[3]

*   *   *

The British then occupied Prome and Burmese forces under Maha Nemyo threatened them on all sides with field fortifications. At the end of November the British forces broke through and routed the Burmese totally, advancing as far as Yandabo, the then capital. This final stage of the campaign is described by Major J.J. Snodgrass, Military Secretary to Sir Archibald Campbell, and Political Agent in Ava:

The first division led in files along the narrow path, and Brigadier General Cotton, with the Madras division, which followed in the rear, was directed to explore every opening that presented itself during the march, and to use his utmost endeavours to force a passage through the forest to the right, so as to reach any part of the Burmese position – his coming upon and attacking which, would be the signal for a general assault in front.

After two hours' march, the first division debouching into a plain upon the river side, opened a communication with the flotilla, and at the same time drew up in front of the stockaded heights of Napadee. Nothing can exceed the natural obstacles opposed to an advance upon these heights, independent of the artificial means, which the enemy had not failed to employ, to render his situation in every respect secure: the range of hills he occupied, rise in succession along the banks of the Irrawaddy, the second commanding the first, and the third the second; their base is washed by the river on one side, and they are covered, by the forest, from the approach of any force upon the other. The only road to the heights lay along the flat open beach, until checked by the abrupt and rugged termination of the first hill, up the sides of which the troops would have to scramble, exposed to the fire of every gun and musket on its summit; and in addition to these difficulties, the enemy had a numerous body of men stockaded along the wooded bank, which flanks and overlooks the beach for the distance of nearly a mile, in front of the position, and whom it was absolutely necessary to dislodge, before the main body could be attacked. This service was speedily accomplished, by six companies of the Eighty-seventh Regiment penetrating through the jungle in the rear of the flanking works, and carrying one of the stockades which protected the advanced line to the rear; and the enemy, finding himself exposed in this quarter, speedily withdrew his advance division, leaving the beach open to the bottom of the first hill, round the base of which he still occupied two strong redoubts. The flotilla now moved forward, and commenced a spirited cannonade on both sides of the river, while the troops were still halted, in the anxious expectation of hearing a fire open from some part of the Madras division to the right. Fruitless and unavailing, however, was every endeavour to penetrate the forest which separated that corps from the Burmese position; and it became at last necessary to assault it in the front, by the only approach it appeared to have.

During the attack, the flotilla pushing rapidly past the works, succeeded in capturing all the boats and stores which had been brought down for the use of the Burmese army. The defeat of the enemy on the left bank of the Irrawaddy was now complete: between forty and fifty pieces of artillery were captured, and the matériel of his army taken or destroyed: his loss, in killed and wounded, had been very severe; and by desertion alone, he had lost at least a third of his men.

The corps of Sudda Woon alone, protected by the intervention of a broad and rapid river, had escaped unpunished, and so carefully were his men concealed from observation, that some time elapsed before it could be ascertained whether his whole force remained in their stockades, or they were only occupied by a rear-guard; it was at length, however, established beyond a doubt, that the right corps still occupied its original ground, and arrangements were immediately made for driving them from it.

On the morning of the 5th, details were embarked for that purpose, on board the flotilla; and a brigade of rockets, and a mortar-battery, having, during the night, been established on a small island in the middle of the river, within good range of the stockades, at day-break, in the morning, they opened their fire, which was immediately answered from several pieces of artillery from the opposite shore. The troops being landed at some distance above the stockades, commenced the attack in flank and rear, while the batteries and men-of-war's boats cannonaded them in front; and the enemy, already disheartened, and panic-struck with the severe punishment they had seen their centre corps sustain, upon the second, evacuated, after a feeble resistance, their line upon the river, retreating to a second line of stockades which they had prepared in the jungle in their rear. Here they were not allowed long time to rest: the troops, following up their first success, and unaware of the existence of any second line, came suddenly upon the crowded works, whose confused and disorderly defendants, unable to retreat through the narrow gates of their inclosure, and too much alarmed to offer effectual opposition, became an easy conquest to the assailants: hundreds fell, in the desperate effort to escape, and the nature of the country alone prevented the whole corps from being taken; which, dispersed and broken, now fled in all directions through the woods.

The Burmese surrendered Assam, Arakan and the coast of Tenasserim and their domination of this area of South-East Asia was then at an end.

Notes

1. Captain F.B. Doveton, First Madras European Fusiliers, *Reminiscences of the Burmese War in 1824–6* (1852)
2. *Ibid*
3. Horace Hyman Wilson, *Narrative of the Burmese War in 1824–26, as Originally Compiled From Official Documents* (1852)
4. J.J. Snodgrass, *Narrative of the Burmese War, Detailing the Operations of Major-General Sir Archibald Campbell's Army, From Its Landing at Rangoon in May 1824, to the Conclusion of a Treaty of Peace at Yandaboo in February 1826* (1827)

8. Hong Kong the Prize
(The First Opium War 1839–42)

It seems quite useless to kill the Chinese. It is like killing flies in July.[1]

*

Warren Hastings, while Governor-General of India, had the opium trade farmed for a term of years and showed the profits in the public accounts of the East India Company. It was his honest opinion that opium was 'a pernicious article of luxury which ought not to be permitted but for the purpose of foreign commerce only!' A few years after this pronouncement the Directors of the East India Company wrote: 'If it were possible to prevent the use of the drug altogether, except strictly for the purpose of medicine, we would gladly do it in compassion to mankind'. But the fact was that opium was extremely profitable and the British East India Company required a monopoly over the trade with China, one of the best customers. European nations – Portuguese, Dutch as well as British – found business difficult to conduct with the Chinese. But the lure of Chinese silver, silk, tea, porcelain, wallpaper, furniture and other luxuries was irresistible. However, the Celestial Empire regarded all Europeans as barbarians, with whom trade on equal terms was impossible. In Chinese eyes, Europeans came not to trade but as vassals bearing tribute. Only one port, Canton, was open for trade from abroad, and only then through a group of officially designated Chinese merchants, known as 'the Hong'.

By 1834 the industrial revolution in England brought pressure from British trading interests, over and above those of the Eat India Company, to bring the Company's monopoly of the Chinese trade to an end. As the pressure for trade in China consequently increased, the friction with the Chinese developed. The question of imported opium brought matters to a head.

The Chinese government had officially banned the import of opium for some time, but corrupt Chinese officials connived at the trade. The Celestial Empire took the serious step of dispatching a special commissioner, Lin Tse-hsui, to put down this illicit trade. His ruthless measures resulted in armed conflict in November, 1839 – a British frigate spectacularly sunk a fleet of junks after Lin Tse-hsui had demanded the destruction of millions of pounds worth of opium stored in Canton warehouses. The following year a British force of 4,000 under Sir Hugh Gough (East India Company native troops as well as regular soldiers), escorted by a naval squadron, occupied the island of Chusan at the entrance of Hangchow Bay, blockading Hong Kong and Canton. British amphibious operations concentrated largely on centres south of the Yangtze. The Chinese were constantly defeated and attacks alternated with British attempts at negotiation. In February, 1841, they captured the Bogue Forts and began to move up the Pearl River. By the end of May Canton was in British hands. The expeditionary force began to move up the coast of China to Amoy and Ningpo. The invading troops suffered extreme hardship from illness and poor supplies. At times 50 per cent of the troops were ill, but East India Company stock was doing well and the Government, War Office and Admiralty paid little attention to criticism of the way the Chinese War was being handled.

* * *

In 1842 the British captured Shanghai. On 21 July the fall of Chingkiangfoo menaced Nanking and the Chinese then sued for peace. The final engagements were fought during extremely hot weather:

... the Chinese, who had trusted entirely to the defences of Woosung, offered practically no opposition, but winds and currents were the cause of considerable delay. On the evening of the 16th the General and the Admiral made a reconnaissance of the neighbourhood of Kinshan and Chinkiangfoo; still no opposition was offered, and the inhabitants crowded to the shore to gaze at the steamer. It was not till the night of the 20th that the whole fleet had assembled, and by that time, Sir Hugh Gough and Sir William Parker had agreed upon the method of the assault.

The city of Chinkiangfoo lay in immediate proximity to the Imperial Canal, which flowed beneath its western and southern faces, joining the Yangtse-kiang near the western angle of the city wall, and thus serving as a moat. On the north and east the city rose to a range of heights, and at some distance away there was a steep hill connected by a narrow ridge with a lower height, both of which commanded the northern angle of the city. On each there was a joss-house. The island of Kinshan lay little more than a thousand yards from the entrance of the canal and the western suburb of the city. It proved to be a mere rock, not more than a few hundred yards in circumference, and quite useless for military purposes because commanded from the shore; but it was employed by Sir Hugh as a means of observation.

The assault was fixed for the morning of July 21, and as the capture of Woosung had been a purely naval operation, the place of honour was, on this occasion, given to the military forces. A considerable number of Chinese troops had been descried on the northern hills commanding Chinkiangfoo, and three encampments were observed on the slope of the hills south-west of the city. Sir Hugh decided to cut these off, while, at the same time, an assault was being directed against the western wall. For this purpose he divided his troops into three brigades, under Major-General Lord Saltoun, Major-General Schoedde, and Major-General Bartley respectively; in addition to the Artillery, under Lieutenant-Colonel Montgomerie. The second brigade, under General Schoedde, was entrusted with the attack on the north; the first, under Lord Saltoun, with that on the south-western encampments; and the third, under General Bartley, with the assault on the city walls.

The first and second brigades landed at daylight on the morning of July 21; the latter immediately commenced its movement on the heights, while the former remained to cover the disembarkation of the guns and of the third brigade. Sir Hugh then ordered Lord Saltoun to move on the encampments with the 98th Regiment, nine companies of the Bengal Volunteers, and the flank companies of the 41st Madras Native Infantry, accompanied by three guns and a detachment of Sappers. The remaining companies of the Bengal Volunteers were sent along a path which led them between the encampments and the city and enabled them to make an attack upon the enemy's right flank. They were unperceived by the Chinese and had the honour of alone commencing the onslaught: but they were soon supported by Lord Saltoun, who experienced no difficulty in expelling the enemy. Meanwhile the third brigade had been assembled in front of the wall, along with the Cameronians, who had been detached from Lord Saltoun. The guns were in position, and Sir Hugh decided on forcing the west gate. Powder-bags were placed in front of the gate, which was then blown in by Captain Pears. A long archway appeared in front, through which the troops entered. They found themselves in a large outwork, and separated by an inner gate from the town. But, at this moment, the inner gate was seized by General Schoedde, and all further difficulty, in this connexion, was removed.

General Schoedde had been successful in driving the enemy from the northern hills and in destroying their works. He had been further instructed to make a feint upon the north and east walls, but was given discretionary powers to convert his diversion into a real attack, should he deem it advisable. For this purpose, detachments of artillery and sappers had been added to his brigade. He had decided to act upon these powers, had escaladed the walls at the north angle, cleared the ramparts on the western side, and carried, after considerable resistance, the inner gate, where he met the party which was accompanied by Sir Hugh in person.

The heat was now intolerable, and was telling on the British force, several of whom died from its effects. Sir Hugh was, therefore, anxious to place the men under cover, to await the approach of nightfall before continuing the assault. The Tartar city was yet untouched, and its capture could be safely postponed: but two operations had to be carried through immediately. A body of Tartar troops had been driven, without the possibility of escape, into the western outwork; they refused to surrender, and most of them were shot down or destroyed in the burning houses. It remained to clear the walls and occupy all the gates, and General Bartley's troops, in effecting this object, met with considerable resistance from about 1,000 Tartars, who had obtained cover under some enclosures. Flank attacks from the 48th and 55th Regiments soon dispersed them, and the exhausted men obtained a respite till six o'clock in the evening, when parties were pushed into the Tartar city. They found that the enemy had, as at Woosung, destroyed themselves. The General's house had been burned by his own orders, and he himself had perished in the fire. Sir Hugh's dispatch tells of the horror of the sight – 'Dead bodies of Tartars in every house we entered, principally women and children thrown into wells or otherwise murdered by their own people. A great number of those who escaped our fire committed suicide after destroying their families; the loss of life has been appalling, and it may be said that the Manchu race in this city is extinct.' It was little wonder that Sir Hugh again wrote home, 'I am sick at heart of war and its fearful consequences.' The frightful heat rendered it impossible to take any systematic measures to prevent the Chinese robbers from plundering the town, and the only redeeming feature of the scene was the hope that it would bring about the conclusion of the war.

The British casualties were 144 in all; among whom three officers and thirty-one rank and file were killed. About a seventh of the casualties occurred from the effects of the intense heat of the sun.[2]

On 29 August, 1842, the Treaty of Nanking was signed. It provided for the ceding of Hong Kong to Great Britain and for the opening of foreign residence and commerce with Canton, Amoy, Foochow, Ningpo and Shanghai on reasonable terms.

Notes

1. Sidney Smith, Letter to George Phillips, (1842)
2. Robert Rait, *The Life and Campaigns of Hugh First Viscount Gough, Field Marshal* (1903)

9. A Fair if Savage Fight
(The First Maori War 1843–48)

We stormed up in close order, elbows touching when we crooked them; four ranks, only the regulation twenty-three inches between each rank. There we waited in a little hollow before the pa, sheltered by the fall in the ground and some tree cover. We got the order 'Prepare to charge'; then 'Charge'. Up the rise we went at a steady double, the first two ranks at the charge with the bayonet. . . . When we were within about fifty paces of the stockade front we cheered and went at it with a rush. . . . The whole front of the pa flashed fire and in a moment we were in a one-sided fight – gun flashes from the foot of the stockade and from loopholes higher up . . . yells and cheers and men falling all around. . . . Not a single Maori could we see. They were all safely hidden in their trenches and pits, poking the muzzles of their guns under the foot of the outer palisade. What could we do? We tore at the fence, firing through it, thrusting our bayonets in, or trying to pull it down, but it was a hopeless business.[1]

*

The Polynesian canoe-men who had settled in what is now known as New Zealand by the 14th Century lived in peace for centuries, untroubled by European colonists until the 18th Century. Abel Jansen Tasman found the Maoris living reasonably peaceably with one another when he coasted along the western part of the archipelago in 1642. James Cook annexed the territory for Britain in 1769, but the Government at home disavowed the act. Missionaries made some inroads, and then other European traders followed. Then the British Government, learning that a French colonising company, *Le Compagnie Nanto-Bordelaise* had been formed, with the encouragement of Louis Philippe, to colonise the territory, dispatched Captain William Hobson RN with the authority to annex New Zealand to Australia and to declare himself Lieutenant-Governor in January, 1840. He was able to negotiate a fairly neat bargain with about five hundred Maori chieftains, enshrined in the signing of the Treaty of Waitangi. The Maoris agreed to surrender their sovereign rights to Queen Victoria, in exchange for the guarantee of their possession of forests and lands, and the Crown would have the sole purchase rights on any land which the Maoris might want to sell. French endeavours thus having been forestalled, the British then began the proper settlement of the country. Broken promises and violent disputes over dubious land purchases led to tribal wars, collectively known as the First Maori War 1843–48.

The war was in many ways a shock to the British. The resistance, skill, tenacity, inventiveness and energy displayed by the Maori forces was wholly unexpected to European troops deceived by traditional thinking about the vulnerability of native forces in colonial wars. Sir John Fortescue describes the Maoris as 'the grandest native enemy'[2] British armies had so far encountered. Gurkha and Sikh armies, which the British had encountered before the First Maori War, had to a considerable extent modelled themselves on the European soldiers they themselves had encountered, but Maori warriors were wholly original in their strategy, tactics and code. They were armed with indigenous weapons such as spears, axes and clubs, to which muskets and rifles were added as and when these could be obtained from traders. An outstandingly original contribution to the nature of colonial wars was the Maori fortification, the *pah*. This was a hastily constructed fort of wood and earth, replete with inter-connecting trenches and well hidden rifle emplacements. The building was protected by and lined with branches and flax. The edifice was roofed with timber covered with a good layer of fern. The combination of visual camouflage and physical protection was extremely effective. As ranks of orderly British infantry advanced in close order, twenty-three inches between each rank, they offered a prime target at about a hundred yards from the hidden Maori marksmen in the *pah*, poking their firearms through the loopholes in the palisade. We have an excellent eye-witness of the impression these fortifications made on British forces at the time preserved in the journals of Major Cyprian Bridge, who was initially in command during the opening of hostilities:

> The pa was built on a slight eminence, was square of shape, but zigzagged at the corners in order to bring a crossfire to bear on its assailants. It had three rows of tree-trunk palisades, fifteen feet in height, sunk to several feet in the ground, each tree-trunk five to six feet inches in diameter, set close together. A mass of stone rubble, collected from volcanic debris strewn about, further strengthened the foundations of the pekerangi (or outer fence). The palisading was carefully caulked with green flax to prevent enemy bullets penetrating the apertures; loopholes were everywhere prepared to facilitate the defence, and to render its storming still more difficult, a deep trench was dug between each of the wooden walls.[3]

However, the Maori ideal was a fair if savage fight at an agreed time and place. No quarter was given or expected. Hand-to-hand combat was preferred. They fought naked so that movement was unrestricted. Some wore short aprons or woven war cloaks. Shields were not carried. Tattooing gave the men an unusual appearance:

> . . . the men were all stripped for action, but I also noticed that the appearance of nakedness is completely taken away by the tattooing, the colour of the skin, and the arms and equipment. The men in fact look much better than when dressed in their Maori clothing. Every man is without exception covered with tattooing from knees to waist; the face is also covered with dark spiral lines.[4]

71

The British soon learned that they were fighting a formidable enemy:

When I got up close to the fence and saw the strength of it and the way it resisted the united efforts of our brave fellows . . . my heart sank within me lest we should be defeated . . . a bugle in the rear sounded the retreat . . . and then all that were left prepared to obey its summons carrying off the wounded with us. We had suffered very severely and many were killed or wounded whilst retiring as the enemy increased their fire upon us as they saw us in retreat. It was a heart rending sight to see the number of gallant fellows left dead upon the field and to hear the groans and cries of the wounded for us not to leave them behind.[5]

The war dragged on and eventually the Maori tribes sued for peace in 1848, and successful negotiations were handled by Sir George Grey, Governor of South Australia. The New Zealand Company, with their policy of developing the country, believed that New Zealand should have representative institutions, and the government had in fact passed legislation to bring this into effect in 1846. Grey opposed the intention of dividing the country in Maori and European districts, as he perceived the Maoris would not accept a government in which they played no part. The Act was suspended and replaced by new legislation in 1852, but the land question was bound to surface again, and trouble brewed with the Maori belief that their traditions, culture and way of life was to be swamped by settler civilisation.

Notes

1. Corporal William Free, 58th Regiment of Foot (2nd Battalion, The Northamptonshire Regiment) (1845)
2. Sir John Fortescue, *The History of the British Army* (1927)
3. Major Cyprian Bridge, *Journal of Events on an Expedition to New Zealand* (1845)
4. Frederick Manning, *Old New Zealand* (1876)
5. Bridge, *op cit*

1. **Maratha Wars:** After the Maratha surrender at Amritsar, December, 1805, an uneasy peace followed in the Punjab. A representative of the Commanding British force salutes his Highness Futteh Sing Rao, a Maratha Chief, 20 January, 1812. The 3rd Maratha War broke out in 1817.

2. **First Afghan War, 1839-1842:** Somerset Light Infantry and Shah Shujah's Irregular Horse at Jellalabad (*Painting by David Cunliffe [detail]*).

V. R.

NOTICE.

HIS HONOR THE SUPERINTENDENT OF THE SOUTHERN DIVISION IN MAKING PUBLIC THE FOLLOWING STATEMENT, TRUSTS THAT IT WILL GO FAR TO ALLAY THE ALARM AND ANXIETY WHICH THE INHABITANTS OF WELLINGTON AND ITS NEIGHBOURHOOD HAVE UNDOUBTEDLY SUFFERED UNDER THE RECENT VERY TRYING CIRCUMSTANCES, AS HE HAS NOW CONFIDENT REASON TO BELIEVE FROM THE VERY LATEST INTELLIGENCE, THAT NO ATTACK UPON THE TOWN OF WELLINGTON IS MEDITATED.

The TROOPS under Major Last,—the Marines and other Force from H.M.S. Calliope, under Capt. Stanley,—the Militia and Volunteers of the Town,—together with our Native Allies now in the Field in considerable strength,—will, his HONOR confidently trusts, be a sufficient guarantee to the Inhabitants that any serious apprehension need no longer be entertained. Should, however, a new and unforseen danger appear, the INHABITANTS will be warned by the ALARM, which will be the FIRING of TWO GUNS, upon which Signal the MILITIA, VOLUNTEERS, and others bearing Arms are requested to Repair to the FORTS at THORNDON & TE ARO, where, as also at the BARRACK Lambton-Quay, all persons requiring protection should proceed.

IN THE DISPOSITION OF THE ABOVE FORCE, STRONG RELIANCE MAY BE PLACED THAT EVERY POSSIBLE CARE HAS BEEN TAKEN TO ENSURE THE PROTECTION REQUIRED.

BY COMMAND,

S. E. GRIMSTONE,
SECRETARY.

WELLINGTON, MAY 21, 1846.

3. Public Notice, Wellington, New Zealand, May, 1846.

4. **Battle of Aliwal, 28 January, 1846:** The 16th Lancers (The Queen's Lancers) charging the Sikhs at the Battle of Aliwal. (*Lithograph by Laby and Ogg, after painting by CB Spalding*).

5. **Second Sikh War:** Sketch of scene in the Great Bazaar after the Siege of the city of Multan on 2 January, 1849.

6. **Kaffir War:** Loss of the *Birkenhead*, 1852.

7. **Crimean War:** Battle of Inkerman, 5 November, 1854. 50,000 Russians attacked allied position held by some 15,000 troops under Lord Raglan and General Pelissier. Fought in dense fog, the Russians endured heavy losses and withdrew.

8. **Crimean War:** Fitzroy James Henry Somerset, Lord Raglan, 1788-1855.

9. **Indian Mutiny:** Sir Henry Havelock 1795-1857.

10. **Indian Mutiny:** Repelling a sortie before Delhi.

11. **Indian Mutiny:** 93rd Highlanders storm Secunderabagh, Lucknow, November, 1857.

12. **Abyssinian Campaign, 1867:** One of the nine formidable mortars King Theodore used against Napier's troops.

14. Sir Garnet Wolseley 1833-1913. "I have but one great object in this world and that is to maintain the greatness of our Empire."

13. Lord Napier of Magdala 1810-1890.

15. **Zulu War, 1879:** Natal Native Infantry Contingent.

16. **Second Afghan War:** Battle of Maiwand, 27 July, 1880. A small British force under General Burrows was routed by the Afghan Army under Ayub Khan with a loss of 32 officers and 939 men killed and 17 officers and 151 men wounded. Survivors escaped to Kandahar. (*Painting "The Last Eleven", Berkshire Regimental Museum, Reading*).

17. Egyptian Campaign, 1882: 1st Life Guards and Grenadier Guards. Note sun goggles and face masks for desert service.

18. Madhist Uprising: 85th York and Lancaster Regiment in action, March, 1884.

10. A Subaltern's War
(The Second Burma War 1852–53)

At the end of 1851 the King of Ava had insulted a British flag at Rangoon, and opened fire at HMS Fox *which had been sent to the Irrawaddy to obtain an apology. So began the Second Burmese War, to follow the course common to every campaign in that province of the Indian Empire up to its final pacification. Organised resistance was soon overcome. Martaban, Rangoon and Bassein taken in April 1852, but terms offered were contemptuously rejected, and local chiefs sallied forth defiantly from their stockades to raid our friends and loot our lines of communication. The minor expeditions required to reduce these raiders to order enabled junior officers to show their mettle, and the wars in Burma were nicknamed 'Subalterns' Wars'.*[1]

The Second Burmese War was the result of internal tensions created by tyrannic and cruel rulers with a streak of madness in their blood and the avaricious and immoral treatment of nations attempting to trade. British ships had suffered considerably and a squadron was sent to Rangoon to demand redress. Several thousand Burmese troops were assembled and British ships fired on. Lord Dalhousie sent an ultimatum which expired on 1 April, 1852. Thus began the Second Burmese War. Resistance was easily overcome and Dalhousie proclaimed the annexation of Pegu Province in December, 1852:

73

The Court of Ava having refused to make amends for the injuries and insults which British subjects had suffered at the hands of its servants, the Governor-General of India in Council resolved to exact reparation by force of arms.

The forts and cities upon the coast were forthwith attacked and captured. The Burman forces have been dispersed wherever they have been met; and the province of Pegu is now in the occupation of British troops.

The just and moderate demands of the Government of India have been rejected by the King. The ample opportunity that has been afforded him for reparing the injury that was done has been disregarded; and the timely submission, which alone could have been effectual to prevent the dismemberment of his kingdom, is still witheld.

Wherefore in compensation for the past, and for better security in the future, the Governor-General in Council has resolved, and hereby proclaims, that the province of Pegu is now, and shall be henceforth, a portion of the British territories in the East.

Such Burman troops as may still remain within the province shall be driven out. Civil government shall immediately be established, and officers shall be appointed to administer the affairs of the several districts.

The Governor-General in Council hereby calls upon the inhabitants of Pegu to submit themselves to the authority, and to confide securely in the protection of the British government, whose power they have seen to be irresistible, and whose rule is marked by justice and beneficence.

The Governor-General in Council having exacted the reparation he deemed sufficient, desires no further conquest in Burma, and is willing to consent that hostilities should cease.

But if the King of Ava shall fail to renew his former relations of friendship with the British Government, and if he shall recklessly seek to dispute its quiet possession of the province it has now declared to be its own, the Governor-General in Council will again put forth the power he holds, and will visit, with full retribution, aggressions, which, if they be persisted in, must of necessity lead to the total subversion of the Burman State, and to the ruin and exile of the King and his race.[2]

Burmese stability was further undermined by an internal revolution in which the king was deposed by his brother, Mindon Min. The British negotiated a commercial treaty, which was not actually agreed in the event but hostilities were terminated.

*　*　*

This was the campaign in which the young Garnet Wolseley – who was to become the Empire's major troubleshooter and the original of Gilbert and Sullivan's 'very model of a modern Major General' – tasted action. His being severely wounded but surviving reaffirmed his belief that the Almighty had created him for great purposes:

> I had been nearly a year in the Army and had done nothing. This oppressed me, for I was vain enough to think that if only I could have the chance I should make something of it. The world was still before me, but my prospects were far from encouraging. I was eaten up by an inward fire of ambition – selfish and personal perhaps – an intense longing for active service in the field. . . . I have often been asked by foolish people if I never felt nervous when in danger. I don't think that many men when in action have time to be nervous. . . . But I often thought to myself before the bullets began to whistle near one, whether or not I should be killed that day. I can honestly say the one dread I had – and it ate into my soul – was that if killed I should die without having made the name for myself which I had always hoped a kind and merciful God might permit me to win. All through my life – sinner though I have been – I trusted implicitly in God's providence, I believed He watched specially over me and intended me for some important work.[3]

Unlike Wellington, Wolseley would have little experience of command in major engagements but as a field commander in a host of minor wars, he would have few equals. The phrase 'All Sir Garnet', meaning 'everything properly organised and shipshape', was widely used in the Army and reflects the affection and respect he commanded among his soldiers.

Notes

1. Major General Sir Frederick Maurice and Sir George Arthur, *The Life of Lord Wolseley* (1924)
2. Sir William Lee-Warner, *The Life of the Marquis of Dalhousie* (1904)
3. Field Marshal Viscount Wolseley, *The Story of a Soldier's Life* (1903)

11. Burning the Summer Palace (The Second Opium War 1856–60)

We had re-established our supremacy from the Himalayas to the Carnatic, and could at last spare sufficient troops to bring his Tartar Majesty of Peking to reason.[1]

*

You would scarcely conceive the beauty and magnificence of the palaces we burned. . . . It made one's heart sore.[2]

*

China was in a state of turmoil during the 1850s as a result of the Taiping Rebellion against the Manchu dynasty. This showed itself in a series of internal disorders resulting from the reactions against the tyrannic rules of the Hsien-Feng emperor. A new dynasty – Taiping t'ien-kuo – was established in Nanking. China lapsed into widespread insurrection.

The years between the end of the First Opium War in 1842 and the outbreak of the Second in 1856 were in truth a time of troubled truce with foreign powers as well. As far as the European signatories were concerned, not enough had been granted – there was no provision for travel into the interior of China or for residence except in the five open ports, there was no diplomatic intercourse through resident representatives in Peking. From the Chinese standpoint the treaty arrangements were an outrageous incursion on their dignity, extracted by force by western barbarians. The opium trade was still a source of irritation. On 8 October, 1856, an incident occurred which was sufficient to spark another war – a British registered vessel, the *Arrow*, with a Chinese crew, was boarded by Chinese officials. But the British had their hands full containing suppressing the Indian Mutiny and fighting the war in Persia. They had to content themselves for the time being with a few minor forays in the neighbourhood of Canton. The French and British, still full of the co-operative spirit which had enabled them to endure the stresses of the Crimean War, agreed to act together. The French found the killing of a missionary, Chapdelaine, in Kwangsi on 29 February 1856 sufficient cause to join in the conflict.

In June, 1859, envoys came to take up residence in Peking and to exchange the ratification of the trade agreements contained in treaties signed by the Chinese with the Russians, Americans, French and British. They found the road by Tientsin blockaded and were directed along the route used by bearers of tribute. The Russians went by another route but the Americans travelled the way indicated by the Chinese officials. The British and French decided a show of force was required. The British attacked the Taku forts guarding the entry of the Peiho River, below Tientsin. The subsequent action was reported in the *North China Herald*:

> On the 25th June, the negotiations with the Chinese having come to nothing but a put off to gain time, the Admiral (Sir James Hope) with his flag flying in the *Plover*, followed by the gun-boats *Lee, Cormorant, Opossum, Banterer, Starling, Forester, Kestrel, Janus* and *Haughty*, proceeded to take up a position off the Peiho forts, ready to attack in case the Chinese should offer any resistance to clearing away the barriers. At 2 pm, the stations being pretty well obtained, with the exception of *Starling* and *Banterer*, who were on shore – the former on the south and the latter on the north bank – the *Plover* and *Opossum* weighed; the latter proceeded to clear away a passage through the iron stakes which composed the first obstruction. Two of these having been drawn, the *Plover* followed by *Opossum*,

passed them, and also the second boom, which had been destroyed by the Flag-Captain on the previous night. On arriving at the second she attempted, together with the *Opossum*, to break through it, but without effect; almost immediately a single gun was fired at her, and directly all the masks were rolled up, a tremendous fire was opened up on the squadron, and the action became general. The *Lee*, by signal from the *Plover*, passed through the stakes to the support of the Admiral. The *Plover* and *Opossum* were, however, soon obliged to slip, the fire being too heavy for them, and, followed by the *Lee*, dropped clear of the stakes at 3.15. The gun-boat *Plover* suffered very much in killed and wounded. An officer was sent to the reserve to order up reinforcements, but the tide was too strong for the boats to attempt to pull up. The American flag-officers very kindly offered to tow the boats up to a position to enable them to reach the gun-boats. At 4.30 the enemy's fire slackened considerably, orders were sent down to the reserve for the marines and naval brigades to prepare to land, and the *Forester* and *Opossum*, together with the *Toewan*, proceeded and towed them to the *Nimrod*, the place of rendezvous. At an early period of the action the Admiral had been wounded on board the *Plover* by a splinter in the thigh, and that vessel was almost entirely disabled. He shifted his flag to the *Opossum*; when there he took his station on the caboose, and thence issued his orders until a round-shot cut the mainstay on which he was leaning, and caused him to fall on the deck, a height of some eight feet, breaking a rib and severely shaking him. After a short time he left the *Opossum* . . . and proceeded to the *Cormorant*, where he remained. At 5.45, the boats having assembled alongside, *Nimrod* pushed for the shore as near to the stakes as possible, and opposite to the left bastion, about 600 yards distance from it. The landing here was composed of mud about knee-deep, and the greatest difficulty was experienced in getting up the scaling-ladders and bridges. The marines and naval brigades, a small portion of which had only just landed, pushed to the front under a heavy fire from six guns in flank and in front. The fire from the walls of the jingalls, rifles, and arrows was very heavy.

No check had hitherto taken place, but here a ditch five feet deep and ten broad occurred, and the men, having no choice, plunged across and thereby wetted their ammunition. A party of some fifty officers and men again pushed on and crossed another wet ditch, which took them within twenty yards of the wall. . . . It was now about nine o'clock, and darkness had set in. The position of the landing-party was most precarious: fifty officers and men alone remained in the first ditch, and about a hundred and fifty in the second. Many had been killed and wounded; and with the exception of a small body one hundred and fifty yards further back, no reinforcements appeared to be offering, and the men already at the front were perfectly exhausted, and without dry ammunition or rifles fit to use. The officers in vain encouraged their men to charge to the wall, but it was ineffectual; the men were few and done up; and even if they had, they never could have carried them against the thousands that lined the walls. Under these circumstances the commanding officers dispatched an officer to the rear to ask for instructions.

The gunboats did the best they could. The *Lee*, *Kestrel* and *Haughty* were sunk and the *Cormorant*, *Plover* and *Starling* ran aground. Other vessels were so damaged as no alternative was left except to abandon them. The assault was an admitted failure. News of the defeat of the European forces by the Chinese was received with incredulity by British readers. A Special Correspondent wrote from Hong Kong:

The astounding intelligence of our total defeat at the Peiho came upon us like a clap of thunder. 464 men were killed and wounded; three gunboats were sunk, and several very much damaged; the Admiral was wounded, and many officers were killed. A steamer has been dispatched to Calcutta for reinforcements, and it is expected that in two months 10,000 will be out here. The treaty is at an end, and war, real war, is the order of the day. Every precaution has been taken at Canton, from which place I came down yesterday, though still now no attempt has been made against us. Our force has fallen back on Shanghai, and at present we are not acquainted with the enemy's movements.[3]

It was widely believed that the Chinese were greatly assisted in their military efforts against the allies by the Russians. A report in the *Ceylon Observer* gave some convincing details:

> The belief is universal throughout the squadron that Europeans manned the batteries as well as Chinese. Men in grey coats, with closely-cropped hair, and with Russian features, were distinctly visible in the batteries, and the whole of the fortifications were evidently of European designing. Some of those who advanced near to the wall go so far as to declare that they heard men calling for 'more powder' in Russian; and this morning it is reported that dead bodies floated out of the river, dressed in Chinese clothes, but having incontestably Russian faces.

* * *

Early in May, 1860, Anglo-French forces gathered in Hong Kong and a joint action was planned for the Gulf of Chihli – 11,000 British forces under Lieutenant Sir James Hope Grant, and 7,000 French under General Cousin Montauban would take part. The Taku forts were taken and the expedition moved up towards Tientsin and Peking.

The Chinese pleaded for an armistice and a delegation was sent into the Chinese lines led by Sir Harry Smith Parkes. The party was seized on 18 September and imprisoned. Parkes was made to kow-tow (kneel) before the Chinese commander and rub his face in the dust; he was placed in chains and starved. In all thirty-nine delegates were seized by the Chinese. Several were murdered there and then; the remainder were imprisoned and tortured. The Allies continued their advance and preparations for the assault on Peking were made. During the assault, the Summer Palace was looted and another bid for peace was made by the Chinese. Among the terms agreed was the return of Sir Harry Smith Parkes' party. Only nineteen men had survived. The British demanded reparations of £100,000 for the families of those murdered, as well as considerable territorial concessions and the surrender of the Kowloon promontory, opposite Hong Kong. The French obtained permission for their missionaries to lease or buy land and to build houses in the interior. The Russians gained modifications of their frontier and a stretch of the coast which was to become the site of Vladivostok.

As retribution for the torture and murder of European prisoners and general treachery, the British decided to burn down the Summer Palace. This account appeared in the *Daily News*:

It having been ascertained that their ill-treatment began in the Emperor's Summer Palace, it was determined to burn it to the ground, to mark in some tangible way the detestation entertained of the Chinese treachery and cruelty. Accordingly . . . a proclamation explaining to the people the motives which dictated this deed of vengeance was issued and disseminated in Peking . . . General Michel's division marched out to the Palace. The scene there in the morning, on the bank of the large lake, from the old palace, was very lovely. The lake is about five miles in circumference. Its northern shore is fringed with wood, and here and there above the trees could be seen the tops of graceful pagodas and fanciful josshouses. High above all those rose a stately pavilion; its base of stone, the upper part built of wood supported on pillars, towering in the air, as conspicuous objects for miles around. On the other side of the lake is a beautiful stone bridge of many arches, leading to an island, on which, embosomed in trees and overhanging the lake, was a gaily-painted summer-house. . . . The troops were scattered in parties over the whole place to fulfil their mission, and at two o'clock in the afternoon the scene was greatly changed. On every side and in every direction, from the hills above and the valley below, from every sheltered rock and clump of trees, dark columns of smoke rose into the air. A strong wind was blowing, and soon the fierce flames rose through the smoke, and palace, and temple, and pavilion and summer-house were in a blaze. . . . All night long the smoke and flames were rising to heaven, and obscuring the sky and stars; and today the work of vengeance is still going on. . . . It is to be hoped that the dark canopy of smoke which since yesterday forenoon has been resting over Peking will convey to the Chinese magnates, in no insignificant language, the danger and the folly of refusing any longer to comply with our demands. . . .

It seemed at the time that a distant trouble spot had been restored to order. The previous treaties of 1842–44 and 1858–60 were now seen to define the terms and conditions by means of which relations between the West and the Chinese were to be conducted, and although the details were slightly altered over the years, these terms remain in legal operation until 1943. In fact matters were far from stable. The Chinese had allowed their sovereignty to be weakened more than they realized. This proud people had at one time believed that while Europeans had one eye, they had two, and the rest of the world was blind. But now foreigners were removed from Chinese jurisdiction, they no longer controlled the tariff and by allowing Christian missionary organizations to buy land and build houses, they had officially established Christian communities as an empire within an empire. The Chinese state was weakened from within, and would continue to face pressure from without. The flames of the Summer Palace would die out, but the situation would be subject to the risk of further conflagration.

Notes

1. Field Marshal Sir Garnet Wolseley, First Viscount Wolseley, *The Story of a Soldier's Life* (1903)
2. From a letter written by Captain Charles Gordon ('Chinese Gordon', later murdered in the Sudan) on the punitive burning of the Yuen-Ming palaces, after the signing of the Peace Treaty with China, 24 October, 1860.
3. *The Illustrated London News*, 17 September, 1859

12. A Formidable Foe
(The Second Maori War 1860–70)

*The men were tearing their way through the high fern and scrub,
and impeded with their greatcoats, which with their trousers
were soon in rags, and plunging in the swampy ground to the
knees, scattered and divided by the fern which was up to their
chins whilst they held up their heavy pouches.*[1]

The indigenous natives of New Zealand, even after their defeat
in the first Maori War, had tried to retain their hold over the central area of North Island by organizing a league against
land-selling and the election of a king. Conflict with the colonists broke out in 1860 and ten years of intermittent guerrilla
warfare, now known as the Second Maori War, followed. Unfortunately, tribal jealousy led to poor co-operation against their
common enemy, but their immense bravery impressed the well-
equipped and efficiently trained soldiery sent against them. Time
and again the Maoris proved a formidable foe – in engagements
round Mount Egmont, at Orakkau, at Tauranga and in the deep
forests of Wanganui they resolutely held their own against British
regiments and colonial riflemen. As in the previous war, the colonists found the frontal storming of the Maori *pa* a very costly
manner of conducting warfare. The Maoris were fortified by
their deep anti-Christian fanatical belief, the Hau-Hau cult.
Before fighting, the warriors worked themselves up into ferocity

with fierce singing and yelling which their white opponents found unnerving. This is an eye witness account of the moments just before an assault, as the colonial forces watched a Maori *pa* receive reinforcements:

The natives in the *pa* had seen the arrival of succour as well as we had, and repeated cheers and volleys announced their appreciation of the sight. From the forest responsive cheers soon established a sympathetic intercourse between the two separate bodies, and I must confess that as far as I was concerned, at least, the enthusiasm was all on their side. Some Maori trumpeter in their *pa* commenced one of those high-pitched shouts, half-song, half-scream, that travel distinctly over long distances, particularly from range to range. He was giving the reinforcements some instructions. I have never been able to find out what they were, though we had plenty of interpreters with us. I went to the picket with reinforcements, and extended a line of skirmishers along the brow of the hill in the tea-tree scrub. There was open ground between us and the line of forest in which the reinforcements were, and they had to cross that opening if they wanted to come to us.

About this time, the natives in the *pa* commenced a war dance. Of course, we could see nothing of it, but we could hear it – the measured chant – the time keeping yell – the snort and roar – the hiss and scream – the growl and bellowing – all coming from three hundred throats in measured cadence, working up their fury into a state of maniacal, demoniacal frenzy, till the stamping of their feet actually shook the ground.

There was soon an echo in the forest of this pandemoniacal concert. Another chorus of three or four hundred throats made the woods tremble with their wrath of lung and thundering stamp of feet. Twice it subsided, and skirmishers appeared, firing lustily into us. I must confess there was something impressive in these two savage hordes linking their spirits over this distance into a bond of wrathful aid, lashing one another's fury into a higher heat by each succeeding yell echoing responsive in each breast. Yet when the result of all this volcanic wrath broke against us, when the simple crack of our carbines sent line after line of their skirmishers back into the bush, then the third war dance to get up steam became almost a laughable affair.[2]

Some of the best Maori warriors, such as the chiefs Rophata and Kemp fought on the white side, and brought many of their tribesmen over with them. Poor white generalship, however, caused the war to drag on, although the conflict was more vigorously pursued after 1865 when General Sir Trevor Chute took over from Major-General Sir Thomas Simpson Pratt and Major-General Sir Duncan Alexander Campbell.

The Maoris fought on until utterly exhausted and were finally wooed to the conference table by Sir Donald McLean, who had had many years experience negotiating with them, and had taken the precaution of thoroughly learning to communicate with them in their own language. He was mainly instrumental in obtaining the admittance of Maoris to the national Assembly of 1867 and brought about final peace in with the natives in 1870.

Notes

1. Colonel James Edward Alexander, *Incidents of the Maori War* (1863)
2. Major G.F. von Tempsky, *Memoranda of the New Zealand Campaign in 1863 and 1864* (1864)

THE EASTERN QUESTION

13. An Expensive and Dangerous Garrison (The First Afghan War 1839–42)

Dangerous it is, but if it succeeds, it is worth all risks; the rebels have not even fulfilled even one article of the Treaty, and I have no confidence in them; and if by it we can only save our honour, all will be well; at any rate, I would rather suffer a hundred deaths than live the last six weeks over again.[1]

Sir William Hay Macnaghten (1793–1841), diplomatist, Envoy and Minister to the Afghan court at Kabul. He made this comment on 23 December, 1841, immediately prior to his meeting with Akbar Khan, son of the deposed ruler of Afghanistan. Akbar Khan murdered him.

*

The instability of Afghanistan was a serious problem to British interests. Threatened from the west by Persia and from the Punjab on the east, internally torn by revolts and power struggles it was a constant temptation to Russian interference. The Russians supported the claims of Dost Muhammad to control Afghanistan. The British East India Company hoped that the Tripartite Treaty, signed on 29 July, 1838, would preserve the region from incursion either from Persia or Russia, and that stability would be guaranteed by their support of the new ruler of Afghanistan,

Shah Shuja. Dost Muhammad refused to allow the claims of Shah Shuja to the throne and the British made the refusal of their demands a *casus belli*.

The Army of the Indus commanded by Sir John Keane, 21,000 strong, gathered in Upper Sind [Scinde], and in April, 1839, had taken Kandahar. Shah Shuja was crowned in the leading mosque. Ghazni was stormed on 21 July and Dost Mahammad fled northwards. Leaving a garrison at Kabul, Sir John Keane returned to India. British interests in Afghanistan were represented by Sir William Hay Macnaghten and Sir Alexander Burnes and 8,000 of the Company's troops.

Dost Mohammad's son, Akbar Khan, raised a rebellion in 1841 against the British. Akbar personally murdered Macnaghten at a meeting arranged to discuss matters in December 1841. The garrison at Kabul was commanded by Major-General William George Keith Elphinstone, a veteran of the Napoleonic wars. Elphinstone's garrison was surrounded and early in January 1842 the British capitulated. The Afghans agreed to grant the evacuating British safe conduct out of the country. Elphinstone died before the final catastrophe always associated with his name.

The forces leaving the country included 690 British troops, 3,800 Indian troops and 12,000 followers – wives, children, servants. In the depths of the winter they were harassed, plundered and butchered by the Afghans throughout their terrible journey. They made a final stand with about twenty muskets at Gandamak in the Khyber Pass road on 13 January 1842. Most were massacred, a few were taken prisoner. The only survivor to reach Jalalabad alive was Dr William Brydon, an army surgeon. Among those who were captured and imprisoned at Kabul was Lady Florentia Sale, wife of Colonel Robert Henry Sale. (She was later rescued during Sir George Pollock's invasion of Afghanistan in September, 1842). This account of the Gandamak massacre is from her journals:

The ladies were mostly travelling in camel-panniers and were mixed up with the baggage and column in the pass; here they were heavily fired on and many camels were killed. On one camel were, in one pannier, Mrs Boyd and her youngest boy Hugh, and in the other Mrs Mainwairing and her infant, scarcely three months old, and Mrs Anderson's eldest child. This camel was shot. Mrs Boyd got a horse to ride, and her child was put on another behind a man, who, being shortly after unfortunately killed, the child was carried off by the Afghans. Mrs Mainwairing, less fortunate, took her own baby in her arms. Mary Anderson was carried off in the confusion. Meeting with a pony laden with treasure, Mrs Mainwairing endeavoured to mount and sit on the boxes, but they were upset, and in the hurry pony and treasure were left behind, and the unfortunate lady pursued her way on foot, until after a time an Afghan asked her if she was wounded, and told her to mount behind him. This apparently kind offer she declined, being fearful of treachery, alleging as an excuse that she could not sit behind him on account of the difficulty of holding her child when so mounted. This man shortly after snatched her shawl off her shoulders, and left her to her fate.

Mrs Mainwairing's sufferings were very great; she not only had to walk a considerable distance with her child in her arms through the deep snow, but had also to pick her way over the bodies of the dead, and dying, and wounded, both men and cattle, and constantly to cross the streams of water, wet up to the knees, pushed and shovelled about by men and animals, the enemy keeping up a sharp fire, and several persons being killed close to her. She, however, got safe to camp with her child . . .

Poor Sturt was laid on the side of a bank, with his wife and myself beside him. It began snowing heavily; Johnson and Bygrave got some coarse blanket thrown over us.

Dr Bryce came and examined Sturt's wound and he dressed it, but I saw by the expression of his countenance that there was no hope. He afterwards kindly cut the ball out of my wrist, and dressed both my wounds. Half of a Sipahee's pall had been pitched, in which the ladies and their husbands took refuge. We had no one to scrape the snow off the ground in it. Captain Johnson and Mr Mein first assisted poor Sturt over to it, and then carried Mrs Sturt and myself through the deep snow. Mrs Sturt's bedding (saved by the nurse riding on it, whom we kept up close with ourselves) was now a comfort to my poor wounded son. He suffered dreadful agony all night, and intolerable thirst, and most grateful did we feel to Mr Mein for going out constantly to the stream to procure water; we had only a small vessel to fetch it in, which contained but a few mouthfuls. To sleep in such anxiety of mind and intense cold was impossible. There were nearly thirty of us packed together, without room to turn.

The Sepoys and camp-followers, half-frozen, tried to force their way, not only into the tent, but actually into our beds, if such resting places can be so called . . . a pelisse of sheepskin half spread on the snow, and the other half wrapped over one. Many poor wretches died round the tent in the night. The light company of the 54th Native Infantry, which left Kabul thirty-six hours previously eighty strong, was reduced to eighteen. This is only one instance which may fairly be taken as a general average of the destruction of our force.[2]

The British garrison at Ghazni was compelled to surrender to Akbar's army but Kandahar and Jalalabad held out. An expedition was prepared in Nindia to relieve these garrisons and to rescue the British prisoners. It was led by General Sir George Pollock. The campaign was brilliantly planned and executed under Pollock's command, and he personally instructed the officers and troops to travel as lightly as possible to reduce baggage and the need for transport, bearers and draught animals – mules and camels. The Khyber Pass was regarded as particularly threatening to Pollock's army of British and native troops, but the expeditionary force traversed it successfully in the spring of 1842:

At half-past three on the morning of the 5th April, the troops were under arms, the camp struck, and, according to arrangements previously made, the treasure, ammunition, and baggage placed on the road leading from Jumrood towards the entrance of the Khyber Pass. Quickly, and without beat of drum or sound of bugle, the British force moved off in the dim twilight, towards the Shadi Bhagiaree mouth of the pass, and the crowning columns prepared to ascend the heights on either side. The hearts of the bravest – and there were gallant soldiers there who had fought in many climes, under the Iron Duke in the Peninsula, and at Washington and New Orleans – even the hearts of these, who had many a time looked death in the face, must have beat quicker with proud hope and high expectation, as they glanced upwards at the terrific crags towering above them, or cast a look at the no less tremendous gorge yawning at their feet, like the mouth of an open sepulchre. It was now their immediate duty to surmount these precipices, and boldly assail the defile that 'oped its ponderous jaws' before them; and yet so marvellously had the *morale* of the Sepoys improved, that under the guidance of their glorious chief, in whom they now reposed the most implicit and childlike confidence, they prepared with enthusiasm for the task.

Nothing could have proved better than the arrangements of General Pollock, who, moreover, is entitled to the entire credit of conceiving and elaborating the plan of attack; it is also not less certain that no general could have been more fortunate in the success that crowned his labour, thanks to the indomitable energy and fighting excellence of all his troops, though in carrying out these interesting and almost unique operations of war, the chief meed of praise is only justly due to that notable corps, the 9th Foot, and their gallant and chivalrous leader, Colonel Taylor.

The crowning columns quickly advanced on the right; though the precipitous nature of the ground was such that it seemed to defy the eager activity of Taylor and his men. But he stole unseen round the base of the mountain, and found a more practicable ascent than that which he had first tried. Then on both sides, the British infantry were hotly engaged with the hardy mountaineers, who contested every foot of ground with desperation. Having driven a considerable body of the enemy up the hills, which were scaled and crowned in spite of a determined opposition, the right column moved to their left, to clear the redoubts commanding the entrance to the pass, which were abandoned on their approach, the enemy suffering severely in their retreat. Major Anderson remained on the heights with his column reinforced by one company of the 9th and two companies of the 26th N. I. under Captain Gahan, whilst Colonel Taylor descended with the remainder to carry into effect the General's plan of operations, in driving off the enemy from their positions on the right of the road to Ali Musjid, which was finally accomplished in spite of obstinate resistance at several points, especially over a bridge where the enemy had concentrated in force.

The column under Major George Huish, employed to capture the hills on the left of the pass, were equally successful. Led by Captain Ferris's regiment of Jezailchees, 400 strong, the heights were speedily carried, and the summit having been gained, a smaller hill at the entrance of the pass was cleared by the fire of the column. This being effected, the post was made over to Lieut.-Col. Moseley, commanding the rear crowning column, and the troops, with the exception of two companies of the 26th N. I., descended for the purpose of continuing to scale and clear the heights on the left of the road to Ali Musjid.

While these flanking columns were at their task on the heights, the General ordered Captain Alexander, in command of the artillery, to place the guns in position, and throw shrapnel among the enemy, when opportunity afforded, which was accordingly done, and assisted much in their discomfiture.

The General, perceiving that Colonel Taylor was some time in reaching the summit of the hill to the right, owing to the sturdy opposition he met with and the extremely difficult nature of the ground, detached a party consisting of four companies of the 9th, four companies of the 26th N. I., four companies of the 64th N. I., and some Jezailchees, under the command of Brigadier Wild, to assault the position in front. The hill was, however, so extremely steep near the summit, that, notwithstanding the undaunted gallantry of the officers and men, they were for some time unable to gain a footing on the crest, and the enemy were enabled to throw stones with fatal effect upon some of the leading grenadiers of the 9th Foot; eventually the Brigadier, though wounded, gained the summit.

On the occupation of the heights by the crowning columns, the General advanced the main column to the mouth of the pass, and commenced destroying the barrier which the enemy had evacuated on finding their position turned. This task was ably performed under the direction of Lieut. John Becher . . .

. . . Acting Field Engineer, and the General was not slow in expressing to Government his high sense of the 'very essential services rendered by that officer in clearing the pass of the impediments constructed by the enemy, which he did with a degree of clarity, notwithstanding their strength and difficulty of removal, that elicited my warmest satisfaction.'

In the meantime, Col. Taylor, on the right, having been reinforced by one company of the 33rd N. I. under Lieut. Watson, directed Captain Lushington of the 9th, to move with that company and the light company of his own regiment to the right, to take the enemy's position in reverse, whilst he himself, leaving Major Anderson in command of the heights already gained, attacked the front. The enemy, drawn up in dense masses, offered a stout resistance, but the British soldiers, with the flush of victory on their brow, would not be denied, and carried everything before them. The Afreedies retreated, after having made a vigorous defence, in which many of them were slain: No further opposition was offered on this side by the enemy, who retreated on Ali Musjid.[3]

* * *

Jalalabad was besieged by Akbar Khan's tribesmen in March 1842, but defended by troops commanded by Brigadier-General Robert Sale. The sufferings of the small British garrison in this Afghan town were considerable. A Major in the infantry wrote this account:

Many stragglers from our late Cabul army (Sepoys and camp followers) have come in lately from the villages, where they have lain concealed since the massacre. Several of them have suffered miserably from the cold, having lost their toes, and in some instances, their feet. They are subsisted by the Commissariat, and despatched on rafts down the river to Peshawur. It is difficult to fancy any petty misery of a more annoying kind than what we have frequently to endure for days and nights together, when the violent wind, which blows along the valley from the west, almost buries us in dust. We are begrimed in filth; we eat it, drink it, and sleep in it, and have no comfort for a moment of our lives while this tormenting gale continues, which is generally about three days *sans intermission*. The heat, too, is increasing, and for some hours daily attains 108° in one's tent. Towards sunset the temperature becomes bearable, and the nights are not unpleasant.

'Should we remain here, all must resort to the plan of living underground, in what are called *tykhannahs*, or, in other words, we must dig holes in the earth, and take up our quarters in them; we shall, else, be likely to do so in a less voluntary manner. Jellalabad seems to be the very headquarters of earthquakes. Scarcely a day passes without one, but after the grand affair in February, we are inclined to regard a shock that will not shake down 'temple and tower' as a matter of no interest. When, however, the *tremblement* happened to be rather decided, it was diverting to see the inhabitants of *tykhannahs* all popping up their heads to look about, like rats peeping from their holes. Our life was lamentably dull and monotonous. Except with a strong escort it was unsafe to ride beyond the pickets. The inhabitants were encouraged to visit our camp, with a view to obtaining provisions, and the luxury of ice, which they brought us in abundance from the snowy mountains. These fellows lurked about, and if a soldier passed the line of sentries after nightfall, his murder was certain.[4]

Jalalabad was relieved on 16 April 1842. Pollock advanced to Kabul, where 95 prisoners were released, and destroyed the citadel and grand central bazaar. The East India Company meanwhile decided that Afghanistan would be too expensive and dangerous to garrison. British feelings of national honour having been restored, Afghanistan was evacuated in December. Dost Mohammad was allowed to rule.

Notes

1. Sir William Hay Macnaghten, quoted in Sir Henry Marion Durand, *The First Afghan War and its Causes* (1879)
2. Florentia Sale, *Journals* (1843)
3. Charles Rathbone Low, *The Life and Correspondence of Field Marshal Sir George Pollock, Bart* (1873)
4. *Ibid*

14. Their's Not to Reason Why (The Crimean War 1854–56)

It was on a bright May morning in 1833, that a cavalry regiment marched into a pretty country town and formed up in the market place directly opposite my master's shop. . . . This was the first time I had seen a regiment of cavalry with their mounted band and I became enchanted with them, particularly when I thought of what a glorious life theirs must be to mine . . . condemned to stand behind a counter from Monday morning to Saturday night. . . .[1]

The causes of the Crimean War are complex and involved. In the popular European imagination of the day, Russia was an invincible and aggressive power with the ambition to extend her domination of the world stage at every opportunity. Such an opportunity, it was thought, had arrived in 1854. According to the legendary will of Peter the Great (1672–1725) Russia was to extend westwards towards Constantinople. A dispute with local representatives of the Greek Orthodox church about responsibilities for religious observances in the Turkish capital led Czar Nicholas I to claim it was Russia's responsiblity for protecting the orthodox Christians, thus securing the entrance to the Mediterranean through the Turkish Straits. This was interpreted as the prelude to Russia's eventual expansion through Turkey into the Balkans states, as the Turkish empire was seen to be in a state of collapse (the 'sick man of Europe'). In British eyes this would be a serious threat to the overland route to India. The Emperor Napoleon III of France, as a Catholic monarch, saw it as *his* duty to protect Christians in the Ottoman empire. The Emperor of Austria resented the possible increase of Russian influence in the Balkans. The British Ambassador in Constantinople, Stratford Canning, first Viscount Stratford de Redcliffe, advised the Sultan of Turkey to refuse the Czar's demands for the protectorate over the Greek Church. (It is suggested that this policy was the result of personal animosity between the Ambassador and the Czar). The result of this crisis was that Britain and France were allied in war for the first time for two hundred years, and found themselves surprisingly engaged in a war in partnership with Turkey and Austria. Turkey rejected the Russian ultimatum. In July, 1853, Russian forces occupied parts of Turkey north of the Danube. A Russian fleet destroyed a Turkish squadron on the Black Sea. British and French policy was to defend Constantinople, and so the Crimean war began.

* * *

An expeditionary force – 57,000 strong, at that date, the largest ever sent out for war overseas – was sent to Varna. Lieutenant-Colonel Daniel Lysons, serving with the Light Division, was the first British soldier to step ashore. On 28 July 1854, he was writing to his mother to report the dreadful news that cases of cholera were already being reported, and that the supplies, especially of food, were far from sufficient:

> I was sitting one evening in Watt's tent smoking our usual evening's *chibouk*, talking of the climate and health of the men. Watt had just remarked how lucky we had been not having lost one man since we left England, when a sergeant came in and said a man had gone into the hospital tent, sick. Our assistant surgeon went up and returned shortly after, saying the man had got cholera. Before morning three men were dead; the following morning four more were buried. The General then consented to our moving our camp. We accordingly marched up here, a distance of about 5 miles, but we left many sick, several of whom died, in all sixteen

in our regiment; the Rifles, 88th, 7th, 33rd, and 19th, all lost a large number.

We were first encamped, the First Brigade on one side and the Second Brigade on the other side of the pretty village of Monastir, but our camp was found too crowded, and half of it was on the high-road, so we got leave to shift to a large grove of walnut trees, where we are now located, with a beautiful view in front of us. I luckily got between two trees, a large walnut, under which I am now writing, and a pear tree; the ground is very dusty, otherwise my house is perfect. The wind has just torn my paper. I have taken to wearing a fez and white turban, which is very comfortable.

We hear reports every day that we are going to do something in the Black Sea, and certainly great preparations are going on at Varna, and all the transports are collected for some purpose or other; time will show. I have no news to tell you. I have no doubt you will see all sorts of exaggerated accounts of the cholera in our camp in the papers; I hope it is leaving us, the men look weak, the food is very bad and insufficient. A lump of bad beef without any fat, boiled in water, and a bit of sour bread are not sufficient to keep men in good condition. We can get no vegetables whatever, and the people in the village here will not sell anything. They are a horrid set of people to be amongst, and to fight for; they are more like enemies, especially the Turks! Everybody would gladly go over to the Russians, and help them against this wretched nation if it was only the policy of England.[2]

The Russian naval base at Sebastopol had to be destroyed. The British plan, based on their observation of the map that the Crimea was a peninsula, was that the fleet should cut the Crimea off from the mainland, commanding the mainland with guns. Unfortunately, the sea on either side of the isthmus was less than three feet. Cholera, poor food supplies, incompetent planning – these were but the first signs of weak strategy, tactics and logistics which were to make the Crimean war notorious in British military history. Lord Raglan, the British Commander, had not seen service since 1815 (he referred to the enemy as the 'French' throughout the campaign) and all the generals commanding the British divisions were about seventy years old.

Fifty one thousand British, French and Turkish infantry, with a thousand British cavalry and a hundred and twenty eight guns were landed and the fleet kept pace along the coast as they advanced. The Russian forces, forty thousand strong, under General Prince Aleksander Mentschikov, blocked their advance near the Alma river. The Allies attacked on 20 September, 1854, across the river and drove the Russians up the facing slope at the point of the bayonet. The stalwart British advance impressed the French commander, General Canrobert, who said: 'They went forward as if they were in Hyde Park'. The Alma was an Allied victory, and the way to Sebastopol was now clear. However, the channel to the harbour was blocked with sunken boats, and so an assault by British naval ships was out of the question. Furthermore they lacked the base which would have enabled them properly to lay siege to Sebastopol. They did the next best thing, which was establish their base at the ports of Kamesch and Balaclava, although this involved a fifteen mile flank march round the fortress. Raglan and Canrobert then began siege operations, constructing a considerable array of batteries and earthworks for this purpose.

* * *

Bombardment and counter bombardment inflicted severe damage on both sides as the siege endured into October. On 25 October thirty thousand Russian troops attempted to divide the besieging lines at Balaclava. Turkish artillery pieces were taken. The British Heavy Cavalry Brigade under General Scarlett pushed back the attempt by Russian cavalry to exploit the breakthrough and the 93rd Highlanders stood firm, earning the celebrated comment by William Howard Russell of *The Times* 'that thin red streak topped with a line of steel'. There then followed the famous confusion which led to the Charge of the Light Brigade. Lord Cardigan, acting under a mistaken order, charged the Russian guns at the end of the valley. The confusion is well attested in this letter to his father, dated 1 December, 1854, written by Edward Cook, a young cavalry officer who took part in that notorious charge:

Our order to charge was brought by a half madman, Captain Nolan, the order was very difficult to understand rightly. On Lord Lucan asking what he was to charge, the only information was, 'there is the enemy and there is your order'. There the enemy consisted of 15,000 infantry, 4,000 cavalry protected by 10 guns, to reach them we had to go down a ravine between two hills with 10 guns on each besides a host of riflemen. Down we went very steadily, the fire was terrific, it seemed impossible to escape, we were well in range of grapeshot on each side besides the barkers in front. I got through safe up to the guns, cut down all that came within reach and then at the cavalry behind, but to our horror the heavy brigade had not followed in support and there was an alarm that we were cut off in the rear, which was true. There was nothing left for it, but to cut our way back the same way we came, the Lancers who cut us off made a very mild resistance, they seemed to be astonished at our audacity at charging them in the wretched confusion we were in, we got through them with very little loss. Just after getting through these beggars, I thought I heard a rattle behind, and by Jove, I was only just in time, we were pursued and on looking behind a Muscovite had his sword up just in my range and in the act of cutting me down, I showed him the point of my sword instantly close to his throat, he pulled his horse almost backwards and gave me an opportunity of getting more forward. I now had nothing to fear being on a good horse except going through those infernal guns again. . . .[3]

The confusion in the issuing and understanding of orders which led to this catastrophe has never really been satisfactorily explained, and no cowardice can be attached to the name of the officer who actually carried the fateful message. This is the account by William Howard Russell which appeared in *The Times*:

It appears that the Quartermaster General, Brigadier Airey, thinking that the Light Cavalry had not gone far enough in front when the enemy's horse had fled, gave an order in writing to Captain Nolan, 15th Hussars, to take to Lord

Lucan, directing His Lordship 'to advance' his cavalry nearer to the enemy. A braver soldier than Captain Nolan the army did not possess. He was known to all his arm of the service for his entire devotion to his profession, and his name must be familiar to all who take interest in our cavalry for his excellent work published a year ago on our drill and system of remount and breaking horses. I had the pleasure of his acquaintance, and I know he entertained the most exalted opinions respecting the capabilities of the English horse soldier. Properly led, the British Hussar and Dragoon could in his mind break square, take batteries, ride over columns of infantry, and pierce any other cavalry in the world, as if they were made of straw. He thought they had not had the opportunity of doing all that was in their power, and that they had missed even such chances as they had offered to them – that, in fact, they were in some measure disgraced. A matchless rider and a first-rate swordsman, he held in contempt, I am afraid, even grape and canister. He rode off with his orders to Lord Lucan. He is now dead and gone.

God forbid I should cast a shade on the brightness of his honour, but I am bound to state what I am told occurred when he reached His Lordship. I should premise that, as the Russian cavalry retired, their infantry fell back towards the head of the valley, leaving men in three of the redoubts they had taken and abandoning the fourth. They had also placed some guns on the heights over their position, on the left of the gorge. Their cavalry joined the reserves, and drew up in six solid divisions, in an oblique line, across the entrance to the gorge. Six battalions of infantry were placed behind them, and about thirty guns were drawn up along their line, while masses of infantry were also collected on the hills behind the redoubts on our right. Our cavalry had moved up to the ridge across the valley, on our left, as the ground was broken in front, and had halted in the order I have already mentioned.

When Lord Lucan received the order from Captain Nolan and had read it, he asked, we are told, 'Where are we to advance to?'

Captain Nolan pointed with his finger to the line of the Russians, and said, 'There are the enemy, and there are the guns, sir, before them. It is your duty to take them,' or words to that effect, according to the statements made since his death.

Lord Lucan with reluctance gave the order to Lord Cardigan to advance upon the guns, conceiving that his orders compelled him to do so. The noble Earl, though he did not shrink, also saw the fearful odds against him. Don Quixote in his tilt against the windmill was not near so rash and reckless as the gallant fellows who prepared without a thought to rush on almost certain death.

It is a maxim of war that 'cavalry never act without support', that 'infantry should be close at hand when cavalry carry guns, as the effect is only instantaneous', and that it is necessary to have on the flank of a line of cavalry some squadrons in column, the attack on the flank being most dangerous. The only support our Light Cavalry had was the reserve of Heavy Cavalry at a great distance behind them – the infantry and guns being far in the rear. There were no squadrons in column at all, and there was a plain to charge over before the enemy's guns were reached of a mile and a half in length.

At ten past eleven our Light Cavalry Brigade rushed to the front. They numbered as follows, as well as I could ascertain:

	MEN
4th Light Dragoons	118
8th Irish Hussars	104
11th Prince Albert's Hussars	110
13th Light Dragoons	130
17th Lancers	145
	——
Total	607 sabres

The whole brigade made one effective regiment, according to the numbers of continental armies; and yet it was more than we could spare. As they passed towards the front, the Russians opened on them from the guns in the redoubts on the right, with volleys of musketry and rifles.

They swept proudly past, glittering in the morning sun

19. Earl Roberts of Kandahar 1832-1914 "I fancy myself crossing and
recrossing the river which winds through the pass; I hear the martial
beat of drums and plaintive music of the pipes; I see riflemen and
Gurkhas, Highlanders and Sikhs, guns and horses, camels and mules..."
(of the march from Kabul to Kandahar).

20. **Mahdist Rising:** Battle of Abu Klea. General Sir Herbert Stewart's forces, 1,500 strong, defend themselves against Mahdist forces of 12,000. British square was broken when the Gardner gun jammed.

21. **Burma Campaign, 1885-87:** Officers and Senior NCOs of the 1st Battalion, King's Own Yorkshire Light Infantry.

22. 10th Bengal Lancers in Field Service (*Painting by R Simkin*).

23. Bengal Punjab Infantry on the march, 1890 (*Painting by R Simkin*).

24. **Dongola, 1896:** British Infantry on the march.

25. **Mandalay, 1895:** Wiltshire Regiment, Burma 1895.

26. Earl Kitchener of Khartoum 1850-1916: "War means risks and you cannot play the game and always win; and the sooner those in authority realise this, the better."

27. **Sudan, 1898:** Maxim machine gun

28. Battle of Omdurman, 2 September, 1898.

29. **South African War:** Magersfontein 11 December, 1899. Charge of two companies of the Black Watch in a disastrous flank assault undertaken at night against a strong Boer position — 57 officers and 700 men lost. Attack forces withdrawn. Total British losses 68 officers, 1,011 men.

30. **South African War, 1899-1902:** typical blockhouse.

31. South African War: Men of Viljoen Boer Commando, who surrendered to British Infantry in 1902.

32. South African War: Distant Drums, Bloemfontein, South Africa.
" 'Then it's Tommy this an' Tommy that, and Tommy 'ow's yer soul?'
But it's 'Thin red line of 'eroes' when the drums begin to roll."
Kipling: *Tommy*, 1892.

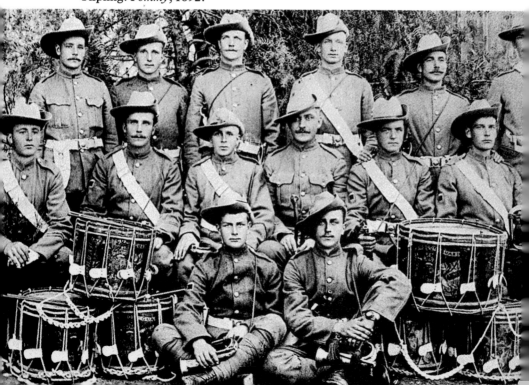

in all the pride and splendour of war. We could hardly believe the evidence of our senses! Surely that handful of men were not going to charge an army in position? Alas! it was but too true – their desperate valour knew no bounds, and far indeed was it removed from its so-called better part – discretion. They advanced in two lines, quickening their pace as they closed towards the enemy. A more fearful spectacle was never witnessed than by those who, without the power to aid, beheld their heroic countrymen rushing to the arms of death. At the distance of 1200 yards the whole line of the enemy belched forth, from thirty iron mouths, a flood of smoke and flame, through which hissed the deadly balls. Their fight was marked by instant gaps in our ranks, by dead men and horses, by steeds flying wounded or riderless across the plain. The first line was broken – it was joined by the second, they never halted or checked their speed an instant. With diminished ranks, thinned by those thirty guns, which the Russians had laid with the most deadly accuracy, with a halo of flashing steel above their heads, and with a cheer which was many a noble fellow's death cry, they flew into the smoke of the batteries; but ere they were lost from view, the plain was strewed with their bodies and with the carcasses of horses. They were exposed to an oblique fire from the batteries on the hills on both sides, as well as to a direct fire of musketry.

Through the clouds of smoke we could see their sabres flashing as they rode up to the guns and dashed between them, cutting down the gunners as they stood. The blaze of their steel, as an officer standing near me said, was 'like the turn of a shoal of mackerel'. We saw them riding through the guns, as I have said; to our delight we saw them returning, after breaking through a column of Russian infantry, and scattering them like chaff, when the flank fire of the battery on the hill swept them down, scattering and broken as they were. Wounded men and dismounted troopers flying towards us told the sad tale – demigods could not have done what they had failed to do. At the very moment when they were about to retreat, an enormous mass of lancers was hurled upon their flank. Colonel Shewell, of the 8th Hussars, saw the danger, and rode his few men straight at them, cutting his way through with fearful loss. The other regiments turned and engaged in a desperate encounter. With courage too great almost for credence, they were breaking their way through the columns which enveloped them, when there took place an act of atrocity without parallel in the modern warfare of civilised nations. The Russian gunners, when the storm of cavalry passed, returned to their guns. They saw their own cavalry mingled with the troopers who had just ridden over them, and to the eternal disgrace of the Russian name the miscreants poured a murderous volley of grape and canister on the mass of struggling men and horses, mingling friend and foe in one common ruin. It was as much as our Heavy Cavalry Brigade could do to cover the retreat of the miserable remnants of that band of heroes as they returned to the place they had so lately quitted in all the pride of life.

At twenty-five to twelve not a British soldier, except the dead and dying, was left in front of these bloody Muscovite guns.[4]

* * *

A further Russian attempt to break through the besieging allied armies – 15,000 troops under Lord Raglan and General Pelissier – was made in thick fog on 5 November at Inkerman heights. The fog played a vital part in the battle. Charles Greville, the clerk to the council at Westminster, recorded in his journal on 14 August 1856 that he was told by a Crimean veteran:

History is full of the examples of the slight and accidental causes on which the greatest events turn . . . nothing but a very thick fog which happened on the morning of Inkerman prevented the English army being swept from the positions and totally discomfited. The Russians could see nothing, lost their own way, and mistook the position of the British troops. Had the weather been clear so that they had been able to execute their plans, we could not have resisted them; a defeat instead of the victory we gained would have changed the destiny of the world, and have produced effects which it is impossible to contemplate or calculate.

As it was, Prince Mentchikov's 50,000 troops pounded away until French reinforcements arrived at 10 o'clock and saved the day. The Russian losses were over 12,000.

The armies then endured the siege throughout the Crimean winter. The Allied armies were unprepared for a winter campaign and a furious storm on 14 November wrecked shipping in Balaclava harbour which contained valuable forage, clothing and other supplies. Sir Daniel Lysons describes this storm in a letter dated 18 November 1854 to his sister:

Since I wrote to my mother we have had a terrific gale, amounting almost to a hurricane. At about two o'clock in the morning there came down a deluge of rain with heavy wind. Water literally poured through our tents; it did not drop, but actually poured on my bed. I got my greatcoat over my head and remained quiet, hoping for some time it would stop; but at dawn the wind rose, and the tent began to flap and roar like thunder. I jumped up to put something on, but before I had time to do so, a squall that was perfectly deafening struck us; our pole snapped, and away went the tent. I hustled on some boots and trousers and a shell jacket, and we then set to work to haul the tent flat over our goods and chattels and peg it firmly down. Such a scene of desolation around – all mud – ruins – only about six tents standing.

Bell and I crept into my patrol tent with the saddles and lay there for about two hours, when suddenly the wind shifted towards the west, and blew more like a Barbados hurricane than anything I can imagine. Our little tent was literally blown up into the air, leaving me sitting on a small box with a cup of tea, which the faithful Styles had managed to get for me, in my hand. I then scrambled on hands and knees back to my prostrate bell-tent and got under it. While going up I saw large, heavy boxes, hospital-stretchers, stones, and every description of article, both heavy and light, flying through the air like cannon-shot – men's chacos, camp-kettles, all went, and were being dashed to atoms.

Later it came on to hail in squalls, and the wind dropped a little. I then collected the three companies that were in camp as well as I could, got their arms and accoutrements and the colours, and we staggered down into a valley close in our front. Here we were in comparative shelter, and the men, though very wet, managed with difficulty to get some fires and cook some victuals – the first they had tasted that day.

The hail continued to fall in squalls till about three, then the wind abated, and it came on a heavy snow; by this time only two tents remained standing, and they were torn to ribbons. However, we got up a party and set to work to repair damages, and before dark got up all the tents we had poles for; they were muddy-looking things and the ground under them very wet, but better than nothing. Firelocks, knapsacks, were lying in every direction covered with snow and wet – everything perfect misery. The poor sick men – one with a mortal wound in his breast – were lying all day with the wet tent down on them; not even a crack or hole to put them into.

Next day, though cold and blustry, was pretty fine; yesterday was also fine, but cold; to-day is beautiful, wintry but clean and dry, and comparatively warm. Oh, what a blessing it is! No one that has not seen such a day as the day of the gale, without a hole to put his head in, can appreciate the real blessing of such a day as this. Everybody is cheerful; all damages are being repaired.

We have lost no men-of-war, I hear, but one or two are dismantled; our transport-service has suffered much. The *Prince*, a very large new steamer, went down with all hands, and in her all the warm clothing for the troops. The *Jason*, one of the largest steamers, and ten others are all lost; a powder-ship among the number, which was much wanted.[5]

The British difficulties, already rendered serious by the damages suffered during the November storm, were increased by the loss of the paved road from Balaclava to the encampments. It was a standing joke among the men that of the 3,000 miles between the British armies and Plymouth the most difficult to travel were the last six. By the end of the year 8,000 men were sick and less than fifty per cent of the army was fit for service. The incompetence of the administration and lack of food and medical supplies produced the situation where admittance to the hospitals only increased suffering and the likelihood of death. Captain Hedley Shafto Johnstone Vicars wrote home in early December to describe the scene at Sebastopol to his mother:

I have just returned from another night in the trenches. The rain is descending in torrents. Last night, whilst standing opposite an embrasure, serving out to my men their allowance of grog, a shell whizzed over my head within a foot. The men made a most humble salaam, but I soon got them on their legs again, by threatening to withhold the spirits. The enemy gave us a few more shots, one of which hit the burial-ground, in which the Turkish soldiers were continually burying their dead. Far away in our front was the plain with the battery beyond, in endeavouring to take which the Light Cavalry suffered so fearfully. Through our telescopes we could see the Russians moving about like bees. Our lines are very extensive and naturally strong, all the country around being hilly. I took a stroll into the country, and enjoyed the First Epistle to the Thessalonians, sitting in the dry bed of a mountain torrent. From the top of a mountain range covered with brushwood I had a fine view of the cavalry encampment.

In the afternoon I walked into Balaclava, a miserable place, the streets indescribably dirty. Many British, French, Turkish, and Tartar soldiers were moving about in all directions. I saw several men of the Guards looking very different to the appearance they present in St James's Square, with unwashed faces, tattered coats, and trousers patched with red and gray. Dead cattle were lying by the wayside, and others were quietly dying. The condition of the once beautiful horses of the Scots Greys was such, that a butcher would have been ashamed to be seen driving one in his cart.

Our things are still at Balaklava, and so are the stores! But my servant managed to get a piece of bullock for my subaltern and myself on which we fared sumptuously.

In the night we heard a sharp firing of musketry; it lasted some time, relieved occasionally by the booming of artillery. Next day we heard that Lieutenant Tryon and fifteen men of the Rifle Brigade had been killed in a brush with the enemy's advanced picquets. However, our fellows completely defeated them and took their position.

On the morning of the 22nd we received the order to march for the lines before Sebastopol, and came in sight of the white tents of the French and English, after a rough march of seven miles. Vestiges of war were to be seen all along the road. Ten dead horses were laid in one place side by side, and the ground was strewn with shell and round shot. The Zouaves turned out as we passed their camp, and cheered us most vociferously. We returned the cheer with as hearty a goodwill, and soon after reached our ground. The tents were soon pitched, and, although very wet, I never slept more soundly in my life. We were scarcely settled, when the rolling of cannon from Sebastopol and the French and English batteries began, and I may say that ever since they have been going at it continually.[6]

*　*　*

News of the scandalous conditions of the British sick and wounded was publicised by the press and the nation was deeply stirred by details of such suffering. A royal commission of enquiry was set up and a public fund opened. Florence Nightingale, who had studied hospital organisation and nursing, and had been appointed superintendent of Chandos Street Hospital, wrote to her friend Sydney Herbert, Secretary at War, to offer her services. Her request crossed a letter he had written to her:

DEAR MISS NIGHTINGALE,

You will have seen in the papers that there is a great deficiency of nurses at the Hospital at Scutari.

The other alleged deficiencies, namely of medical men, lint, sheets, etc., must, if they have really ever existed, have been remedied ere this, as the number of medical officers with the Army amounted to one to every 95 men in the whole force, being nearly double what we have ever had before, and 30 more surgeons went out 3 weeks ago, and would by this time, therefore, be at Constantinople. A further supply went on Thursday, and a fresh batch sail next week.

As to medical stores, they have been sent out in profusion; lint by the *ton* weight, 15,000 pairs of sheets, medicine, wine, arrowroot in the same proportion; and the only way of accounting for the deficiency at Scutari, if it exists, is that the mass of stores went to Varna, and was not sent back when the Army left for the Crimea; but four days would have remedied this. In the meanwhile fresh stores are arriving.

But the deficiency of female nurses is undoubted, none but male nurses having ever been admitted to military hospitals.

It would be impossible to carry about a large staff of female nurses with the Army in the field. But at Scutari, having now a fixed hospital, no military reason exists against their introduction, and I am confident they might be introduced with great benefit, for hospital orderlies must be very rough hands, and most of them, on such an occasion as this, very inexperienced ones.

I receive numbers of offers from ladies to go out, but they are ladies who have no conception of what an hospital is, nor of the nature of its duties; and they would, when the time came, either recoil from the work or be entirely useless, and consequently – what is worse – entirely in the way. Nor would these ladies probably ever understand the necessity, especially in a military hospital, of strict obedience to rule. . . .

There is but one person in England that I know of who would be capable of organising and superintending such a scheme; and I have been several times on the point of asking you hypothetically if, supposing the attempt were made, you would undertake to direct it.

The selection of the rank and file of nurses will be very difficult: no one knows it better than yourself. The difficulty of finding women equal to a task, after all, full of horrors, and requiring, besides knowledge and goodwill, great energy and great courage, will be great. The task of ruling them and introducing system among them, great; and not the least will be the difficulty of making the whole work smoothly with the medical and military authorities out there. This it is which makes it so important that the experiment should be carried out by one with a capacity for administration and experience. A number of sentimental enthusiastic ladies turned loose into the Hospital at Scutari would probably, after a few days, be *mises à la porte* by those whose business they would interrupt, and whose authority they would dispute.

My question simply is, Would you listen to the request to go and superintend the whole thing? You would of course have plenary authority over all the nurses, and I think I could secure you the fullest assistance and co-operation from the medical staff, and you would also have an unlimited power of drawing on the Government for whatever you thought requisite for the success of your mission. On this part of the subject the details are too many for a letter, and I reserve it for our meeting; for whatever decision you take, I know you will give me every assistance and advice.

I do not say one word to press you. You are the only person who can judge for yourself which of conflicting or incompatible duties is the first, or the highest; but I must not conceal from you that I think upon your decision will depend the ultimate success or failure of the plan. Your own personal qualities, your knowledge and your power of administration, and among greater things your rank and position in Society give you advantages in such a work which no other person possesses.

If this succeeds, an enormous amount of good will be done now, and to persons deserving everything at our hands; and a prejudice will have been broken through, and a precedent established, which will multiply the good to all time.

I hardly like to be sanguine as to your answer. If it were 'yes', I am certain the Bracebridges would go with you and give you all the comfort you would require, and which their society and sympathy only could give you. I have written very long, for the subject is very near to my heart. Liz is writing to Mrs Bracebridge to tell her what I am doing. I go back to town tomorrow morning. Shall I come to you between 3 and 5? Will you let me have a line at the War Office to let me know?

There is one point which I have hardly a right to touch

upon, but I know you will pardon me. If you were inclined to undertake this great work, would Mr and Mrs Nightingale give their consent? The work would be so national, and the request made to you proceeding from the Government who represent the nation comes at such a moment, that I do not despair of their consent. Deriving your authority from the Government, your position would secure the respect and consideration of every one, especially in a service where official rank carries so much weight. This would secure to you every attention and comfort on your way and there, together with a complete submission to your orders. I know these things are a matter of indifference to you except so far as they may further the great objects you have in view; but they are of importance in themselves, and of every importance to those who have a right to take an interest in your personal position and comfort.

I know you will come to a wise decision. God grant it may be in accordance with my hopes!

Believe me, dear Miss Nightingale,

ever yours,

SIDNEY HERBERT.
15 October 1854[7]

She arrived at Scutari with a staff of thirty-eight nurses early in November 1854. They were soon nursing the casualties of Balaclava and Inkerman. It is recorded that she sometimes worked twenty hours at a time, sometimes with as many as 10,000 men under her charge. In February, 1855, the death rate in the hospitals of the Bosporus was forty-two per cent. By June, her efforts and genius for organisation had reduced it to two per cent. Her main campaigns were waged against the appalling sanitation, food and medical supplies in the military hospitals, and against the hideous red-tape of the military authorities who – regarding her as a dangerous innovator – attempted constantly to thwart her efforts to render the logistics of the military hospitals more efficient. She herself was taken ill with fever, but recovered, and returned to Europe in the summer of 1855. Her efforts were universally acknowledged and she was thanked by Queen Victoria, whom she visited at Balmoral in September. With £50,000 raised in recognition of her services, she founded the training of nurses at St Thomas's Hospital. The Queen acknowledged her splendid work:

> You are, I know, well aware of the high sense I entertain of the Christian devotion which you have displayed during this great and bloody war, and I need hardly repeat to you how warm my admiration is for your services, which are fully equal to those of my dear and brave soldiers, whose sufferings you have had the *privilege* of alleviating in so merciful a manner. I am, however, anxious of marking my feelings in a manner which I trust will be agreeable to you, and therefore send you with this letter a brooch, the form and emblem of which commemorate your great and blessed work, and which, I hope, you will wear as a mark of the high approbation of your Sovereign![8]

*   *   *

Russian defence preparations grew in strength and allied assaults were renewed in June 1855 and by July the war had developed into a conflict of attrition. The battle of Traktir Ridge on 16 August turned the balance against the Russian defenders of Sebastopol, which was subjected to a well planned and co-ordinated attack by French and British forces on 8 September. This account is from a letter by Charles George Gordon – destined to become celebrated in history as 'Gordon of Khartoum' – who was a young officer serving in the Royal Engineers:

> *Sebastopol, Sept. 16, 1855.* – I must now endeavour to give you my idea of our operations from the eventful 8th of September to the present 16th. We knew on the 7th that it was intended that the French should assault the Malakoff tower at twelve the next day, and that we and another column of the French should attack the Redan and central bastion. The next day proved windy and dusty, and at ten o'clock began one of the most tremendous bombardments ever seen or heard.
> We had kept up a tolerable fire for the last four days, quite warm enough, but for two hours this tremendous fire, extending six miles, was maintained. At twelve the French

114

rushed at the Malakoff, took it with ease, having caught the defenders in their bomb-proof houses, where they had gone to escape from the shells, etc. They found it difficult work to get round to the little Redan; as the Russians had by that time got out of their holes. However, the Malakoff was won, and the tricolour was hoisted as a signal for our attack. Our men went forward well, losing apparently few, put the ladders in the ditch, and mounted on the salient of the Redan; but though they stayed there five minutes or more, they did not advance, and tremendous reserves coming up drove them out. They retired well, and without disorder, losing in all 150 officers, 2400 men killed and wounded. We should have carried everything before us if the men had only advanced. The French got driven back with great loss at the central bastion, losing four general officers. They did not enter the work. Thus, after a day of intense excitement, we had only gained the Malakoff. Lieutenant Rankin, RE, was with the ladders and in the ditch of the Redan. Anderson was in my old place with the working party. They did not leave the trenches. It was determined that night that the Highlanders should storm the Redan the next morning. I was detailed for the trenches, but during the night I heard terrible explosions, and going down to the trenches at four a.m. I saw a splendid sight, the whole town in flames, and every now and then a terrific explosion. The rising sun shining on the scene of destruction produced a beautiful effect. The last of the Russians were leaving the town over the bridge. All the three-deckers, etc., were sunk, the steamers alone remaining. Tons and tons of powder must have been blown up.

About eight o'clock, I got an order to commence a plan of the works, for which purpose I went to the Redan, where a dreadful sight was presented. The dead were buried in the ditch, the Russians with the English, Mr Wright reading the service over them. About ten o'clock Fort Paul was blown up – a beautiful sight. The town was not safe to be entered on account of the fire and the few Russians who still prowled about. The latter cut off the hands and feet of one Frenchman. They also caught and took away a sapper, who would go trying to plunder – for as to plunder, there was, and is, literally nothing but rubbish and fleas, the Russians having carried off everything else.

. . . On the 10th we got down to the docks, and a flag of truce came over to ask permission to take away their wounded from the hospital, which we had only found out that day contained 3000 wounded men. These unfortunate men had been for a day and a half without attendance. A fourth of them were dead, and the rest were in a bad way. I will not dwell any more on it, but could not imagine a more dreadful sight. We have now got into the town, the conflagration being out, and it seems quite strange to hear no firing. It has been a splendid city, and the harbour is magnificent. We have taken more than 4000 guns, destroyed their fleet, immense stores of provisions, ammunition, etc. (for from the explosions they did not appear to be short of it); and shall destroy the dockyard, forts, quays, barracks, storehouses . . .[9]

* * *

The allies took possession of Sebastopol the day after this assault. There was severe fighting on the Caucasus front, and after enduring ferocious Russian assaults and starvation conditions the Anglo-Turkish garrison at Kars, commanded by William Fenwick Williams ('Williams Pasha') surrendered on 26 November 1855:

On the 28th of November, 1855, the Turkish troops, after having laid down their arms, marched out of the beleaguered city which they had so nobly defended for nearly six months, and, accompanied by Her Majesty's Commissioner and the three English officers attached to his staff, gave themselves up as prisoners of war to the Russians.

It was a melancholy sight and one that will not be easily forgotten by those who witnessed it, and who had so lately fought by their side, to see these brave soldiers, with what little property they possessed, consisting chiefly of a change or two of linen and perhaps a few household articles belonging to their families strapped to their backs in lieu of a knapsack, dragging along their weary limbs from the scene of all their miseries, as well as of their glory, towards the camp of an enemy from whom they did not at that time know what sort of treatment they might receive.

There was not one among the poor half-starved garrison who had not, by patient endurance and resignation, shown unexampled fidelity to his sovereign; while many of his comrades, wanting in that moral courage which alone enables men to face dangers and difficulties, had deserted their posts during the blockade, and were at that moment, if not taken by the enemy while attempting to escape, enjoying comparative happiness and security in their native villages.

Nothing could exceed the feeling of depression which but too evidently pervaded all ranks as they marched slowly and heavily away, their only consolation being that they had done all that men could do, and had performed their duty nobly to the last.

The reception they met with from General Mouravieff and his army was such as might reasonably have been anticipated. The officers were received with courtesy and attention, and everything was done to make their captivity as little irksome as possible.

Preparations had been made providing for the wants of the half-famished soldiers who were reduced to such a state of weakness by want of proper nourishment that several of them fell down dead from exhaustion during the short march from Kars to the Russian camp. Many of these poor fellows, not having tasted animal food for so many weeks, could not restrain their appetites when provisions were placed before them, and fell victims to the effects of repletion.

The same kindness and good feeling, which both officers and men received on first becoming prisoners, were continued to them during the period of their captivity, in the several places to which they were conducted.[10]

*   *   *

After Allied assaults on the Alands, Sveaborg and Kronstadt, the war ground to a halt and peace conditions were drawn up in

Vienna in the Spring, 1856. The Russians had lost some 256,000 and the Allies approximately 252,000. Actual losses in battle were less – 128,000 and 70,000 respectively – the great killers were cholera and starvation. Mismanagement was the war criminal, on both sides – a fatal cocktail of indifference, incompetence and senility. Garnet Wolseley, served as a junior officer in the Crimea. In later life he recorded his views of the administration of the Crimean war:

LORD RAGLAN, as a brave soldier and a perfect gentleman in thought, word, and deed, deserves every praise – but he was not born of God to begin commanding an army when already an old man. His one great mistake was his acceptance of that command. He had been for nearly forty years leading a sedentary life in London, and I do not think he ever knew anything of war as a science. At least he had forgotten anything about it long before 1854. The Government sent him a very clever old man, Sir John Burgoyne, to coach him. But the latter was on engineering points too wedded to the ideas which held good in the days of Badajos and the Peninsula. To what extent Raglan was responsible for the selection of the Generals and Staff sent to Turkey in 1854 I know not. I was a young man in that year – just twenty-one – and in every sense one of the new school who believed in military education. We – our number was small at first – believed thoroughly in Sir Richard Airey – the ablest of the Quartermaster-Generals – in Sir Colin Campbell, in General Eyre, and a very few others of the same kidney, but we had a very low opinion of Lord Raglan and most of the Generals. The Staff was mainly composed at first of very ignorant London 'flaneurs', almost all useless. Lord Raglan, ignorant of war both in practice and in theory, was consequently very seriously handicapped. The expedition to the Crimea was one of very great risk, and to have embarked on it, as we did, without any land transport was an act of criminal folly. The few ponies we bought in Turkey were a laughable substitute for the organised transport without which the attempt on Sebastopol was a truly dangerous undertaking.

All this is, however, to be found in the pages of the Report of the Parliamentary Commission which enquired into the causes of our disasters, and which recorded so scathing a condemnation of the Government of the day.

But the knowledge of a Government is almost always what the knowledge of the educated classes is, and of war and its science no one in England knew anything. It is easy to abuse the Cabinet for going to war, when England had *no* army; but the people of England foolishly thought they had an army, and from that mistake arose all our troubles in the Crimea.

The conduct of the war was very bad. The Alma was a badly delivered battle, and when the pluck of the Regimental officer and the private soldier won it for us, we lacked both the military knowledge and the nerve to take advantage of it. We were surprised at Inkerman, and, having embarked upon a siege, we did not possess either the troops or the transport or the stores such a great undertaking demanded. Of course our having done all this is a proof that Lord Raglan was not a great general, in fact, that he was ignorant of a trade he had never learnt, indeed, I believe had never studied. He had very many fine characteristics, and I hate finding fault with him when I know how much the blame for all that took place in 1854–5 lay equally at the door of the Cabinet that urged the Crimean campaign upon him.

The fact that Lord Raglan went to the Crimea at all is to me sufficient proof that he was not fit to command an army in the field. But some of the points for which he is condemned by Lord Ellenborough cannot be directly charged against him. Indeed, Lord E., apparently anxious to find fault, has not examined his maps with sufficient care. Had he done so he would not have made the Warenzoff road run to Balaclava.

What killed our Army was want of land transport. The men who might have made a road from Col to Balaclava were employed in bringing up stores and food, and in digging up roots near Inkerman to cook that food with. I quite agree that we originally occupied too great an extent of front, but the whole expedition was a game of 'Brag', and we played it as long as we had any counters left.

Sir John Burgoyne and the other Engineer officers of rank misled Lord Raglan as regards what he could do before Sebastopol, and he was too ignorant of his trade to judge the question soundly for himself. Our victory at Inkerman – we won it, thanks to the French – destroyed all our chances of taking Sebastopol in 1854. The Russians were horribly defeated there, but their defeat secured them what they wanted, namely, either to raise the siege or to prolong it indefinitely. We very nearly did raise the siege, and it was Lord Raglan's firmness that saved the Army from embarkation after that battle. Whilst therefore I cannot endorse Lord Ellenborough's sweeping condemnation of Lord Raglan as a general, I feel that he was entirely unsuited either by experience or knowledge of war for the position the Cabinet of the day selected him for. I think he ought not to have accepted it, and that under no amount of pressure from home should he have attempted a landing in the Crimea without an ample and thoroughly efficient Land Transport service. – His only chance of effecting the object aimed at was by a victory, and then a very rapid pursuit which would have delivered Sebastopol into his hands; but he could not hope for this unless he was provided with a well-organised Land Transport service of sufficient size.[11]

Wolseley features constantly in the chapters of this book. His contribution to the Army throughout his long service was immeasurable. Having had first hand experience of the many lessons stemming from the Crimea, he devoted the rest of his service to the field of reform; serving as a staff officer with Cardwell, initiator of some of the most far-reaching reforms in the Army's history; as Adjutant General, fighting the reactionary Duke of Cambridge, the Commander-in-Chief of the Army; and later becoming Commander-in-Chief himself, though by then he was worn out and past being able to achieve all he wanted to. There can be little doubt that it was those terrible years in the Crimea that inspired his reforming spirit – so that out of evil, in the end, came good.

Notes

1. Regimental Sergeant Major Loy Smith, 11th Hussars, who took part in the Charge of the Light Brigade, 25 October, 1854
2. Sir Daniel Lysons, *The Crimean War From First to Last* (1895)
3. Edward Cook, *Letters from the Crimea* (1855)
4. William Howard Russell, *The Times* 14 November 1854. The precise truth over the misunderstanding arising from Nolan's words to Lord Lucan will probably never be established but accounts other than Russell's suggest that Nolan's words were 'There, my Lord, is your enemy and there are your [or even 'our'] guns' and that the wide sweep of his arm was meant to indicate the captured British guns in the nearby redoubts. Raglan was concerned lest the Russians should withdraw them and intended the cavalry to prevent this. Realizing that he had been completely misunderstood, Nolan galloped out in front of the advancing Brigade in an attempt to stop the advance but was killed by a Russian shell splinter.
5. Sir Daniel Lysons *op.cit.*
6. *Memorials of Captain Hedley Vicars* (1856)
7. Edward Cook, *The Life of Florence Nightingale* (1913)
8. Queen Victoria, Letter to Florence Nightingale, January 1856
9. Demetrius C. Boulger, *General Gordon's Letters from the Crimea, the Danube and Armenia* (1884)
10. Colonel Henry Atwell Lake CB, Narrative of the Defence of Kars, *Historical and Military* (1857)
11. Major General Sir Frederick Maurice and Sir George Arthur, *The Life of Lord Wolseley* (1924)

15. Victory in the Gulf
(The Persian War 1856–57)

It is impossible to say how long I may be occupied in Persia, as no one can foresee what may be the effect of our present demonstration on the Shah; but it is hardly to be expected that he will at once submit to our terms, underhandedly encouraged to opposition, as he most likely will be, by French as well as Russian advisers, for both are interested in undermining our influence in Persia. You will, I am sure, consider that I could not in honour have declined so important a trust as has been imposed on me, sole diplomatic as well as military responsibility. I only hope I may prove equal to the emergency.[1]

*

Russia's influence in Persia was strong between 1850 and 1854, her conquest of the Syr Darya Valley having enabled her to reach the central Asian border of that country. The situation between Afghanistan and Persia had remained tense during negotiations between the Shah, Nasr ed-Din and various Afghan chieftains. Persia then invaded the border and occupied Herat. Britain declared war on 1 November, 1856, and British troops occupied the port of Bushahr [Bushire] on the Persian Gulf. Sir James Outram was chosen to command two Indian Army divisions. He considered it was the Persian's aim to concentrate their forces below the passes on the North-West Frontier so as to be in position to attempt the rescue of Bushahr. They had formed a camp at Barazjan, and reinforcements were expected from Tehran. He realized that he would have to strike a blow before the enemy could summon full strength.

Outram's troops did not have an easy task. This dispatch dated 10 February 1857 gives a good idea of their serving conditions:

> The 1st Brigade, 2nd Division, which arrived on the 31st ultimo and 1st instant, was landed immediately; and on the evening of the 3rd, the troops . . . marched from this camp, without tents, or extra clothing of any sort, each man carrying his greatcoat, blanket, and two days cooked provisions; the commissariat being provided with three days addition; the protection of the camp and the town of Bushahr being duly provided for by a detachment of troops under the command of Lieutenant-Colonel Shepherd, reinforced by a party of seamen from all the ships in harbour, which the senior naval officer was so good as to place at my disposal.
>
> After a march of forty six miles in forty one hours, during which the troops were exposed to the worst of weather, cold nights, and deluging storms of rain, they reached the enemy's entrenched position on the morning of the 5th, and found it abandoned. The enemy, on hearing of our approach, had evacuated his entrenchments the previous night so precipitately that his tents and camp equipage and ordnance magazines were left behind. The former were being rapidly carried off by village plunderers, operating some hours before we arrived. I endeavoured to intercept the retreat of some of the Elkhanee's horse, who had held the camp during the night and were still in sight, and a little skirmishing took place, but eventually they made off. . . .[2]

The departing Persian forces had left behind stores and equipment, which were distributed among Outram's troops. They then began to retreat to Bushahr, only to be harassed by Persian troops. The halt was sounded and a square was formed to protect the baggage. They waited under fire all night until dawn revealed a Persian army – 7,000 strong – drawn up on their left rear:

> The order to advance was promptly given. Our cavalry and artillery swept forward, with the infantry behind them in double line. While the guns were doing their wonted duty against the Persian ranks, the Poonah Horse and the 3rd Bombay Cavalry made two dashing charges into the thick of the Persian bayonets. In one of their onsets the Bombay troopers crashed into a square of infantry, and riding through and through it, left nearly a whole regiment dead upon the spot. At sight of such slaughter the enemy broke and fled, throwing their arms away as they ran, and owing their escape from worse disaster only to the scant numbers of the British horse.
>
> The fight had taken place near the village of Khushâb. some five miles only from Burasjun. By ten o'clock the victors found themselves easy masters of a field strewn with 700 dead, besides two field-guns and many hundred stand of arms. Our infantry never came within reach of the foe. Ten killed and sixty-two wounded, many of them during the night, made up the whole of the British loss. To Major-General Stalker and Colonel Lugard, chief of the staff, was assigned by Outram himself the real credit for this achievement; their brave commander having in the first moments of the night-alarm been so stunned by the falling of his charger as to have only resumed his place in time to witness the enemy's final discomfiture. Before midnight of the following day, the 9th, most of our tired troops were back again at Bushahr, after another long march through a country in many places scarcely passable for the never-ending rain.[3]

The march back to Bushahr was undertaken in such torrential rain and across such muddy terrain that soldiers' boots were sucked off in the waterlogged soil and the entire force had to be re-equipped with new footwear. Outram now resolved to attack Mohammerah, on the north side of river Karun, close to its junction with the Shatu-l-Arab [Shatt al Arab], thirty miles from the sea. This citadel had been strongly fortified by the Persians, and plentiful supplies and transport for his forces would be found there. He also hoped that a major victory against the Persians here would compel them to abandon the conflict altogether. The fortress was stormed on 26 March 1857. Outram sent in this official report of the advance to the Commander-in-Chief, Lord Elphinstone, at Bombay:

For some months past, the Persians had been strengthening their position at Mohumra; batteries had been erected of great strength, of solid earth, twenty feet thick and eighteen feet high, with case-mated embrasures, on the northern and southern points of the banks of the Karoon and Shatool-Arab, where the two rivers join. These, with other earthworks armed with heavy ordnance, commanded the entire passage of the latter river, and were so skilfully and judiciously placed, and so scientifically formed, as to sweep the whole stream to the extent of the range of the guns up and down the river, and across to the opposite shore. Indeed everything that science could suggest, and labour accomplish in the time, appears to have been done by the enemy to effectually prevent any vessel passing up the river above their position. The banks for many miles were covered by dense date-groves, affording the most perfect cover for riflemen, and the opposite shore being neutral territory (Turkish) was not available for the erection of counter-batteries. I could have landed my troops on the Island of Abadan, which was strongly occupied by the Persians; and there is no doubt that, after defeating them, the southern battery eventually would have fallen to us; but the several batteries on the northern bank of the Karoon commanded the entire southern bank as well as the stream of the Shatool-Arab, and it would have been a serious and an extremely difficult operation to have crossed the rapid current of the Karoon in the face of the enemy, had the means existed of doing so; but until our small steamers and boats could round the southern point and join us, we should have been helpless.

After mature deliberation, I resolved to attack the enemy's batteries with the armed steamers and sloops of war, and, as soon as the fire was nearly silenced, to pass up rapidly with the troops in small steamers towing boats, land the force two miles above the northern point, and immediately advance upon and attack the entrenched camp.

I have now the very great satisfaction of announcing to your Excellency the complete success of the first two operations; the third, to the regret of the army, being frustrated by the precipitate flight of the enemy.

The Persian army, ascertained from credible report to amount to 13,000 men of all arms, with thirty guns, was commanded by the Shahzada, Prince Khanler Meerza, in person. The British force under my command composed as follows,* was the utmost I deemed it prudent to withdraw from Bushire; but with the aid of four armed steamers and two sloops of war to effect my landing, I felt confident of success, although I anticipated some loss, from what I learnt of the determination expressed by the enemy to oppose our further advance to the utmost of their power, and their extreme confidence of succeeding, as evinced by the fact of their having sent away their baggage cattle.

On the 24th instant, the steamers, with transport ships in tow, moved up the river to within three miles of the southern battery, opposite the Arab village of Hurteh; but as some of the large ships shoaled on the way, and did not reach the rendezvous until after dark, I was obliged to defer the attack for another day. During the night a reconnaissance was made in a boat to ascertain the nature of the soil of an island west of, and immediately opposite, the northern battery, where I wished to erect a mortar battery; but as it was found to be deep mud, I determined to place the mortars upon a raft. This was constructed the following day, under the superintendence of Captain Rennie, I.N., and being armed with two 8–inch and two 5½-inch mortars, with a party of artillery under Captain Worgan, was towed by the steamer 'Comet', and moored in position close to the island during the night, unobserved by the enemy,

*H.M. Light Dragoons, 89; Sind Horse, 303; H.M. 64th Foot, 704; 78th Highlanders, 830; 23rd Regiment N.I., 749; 26th do., 716; Light Battalion, 920; Bombay Sappers and Miners, 109; Madras ditto, 124; 12 guns 3rd troop Horse Artillery, 166; No. 2 Light Field Battery, 176; total, 4,886.

who, from our preparations at the rendezvous, and their confidence as to the impossibility of any vessel being able to pass above their batteries, apparently expected that we should land on the southern island (Abadan). The horses and guns of the artillery, a portion of the cavalry, and the infantry were transhipped into boats and small steamers during the day, in readiness for landing the following morning.

At break of day on the 26th, the mortars opened their fire upon both the northern and southern batteries. The range of the 5½-inch proved too short, but the 8–inch shells were very efficient, bursting immediately over and inside the enemy's works; whilst, from the position of the raft, but few of the Persian guns could be brought to bear upon the mortars.

At 7 o'clock the several vessels of war moved up into the position allotted them by Commodore Young, and by 9 o'clock the fire of the heavy batteries was so reduced, that the small steamers, with boats in tow, and one large steamer, the 'Pottinger', towing the transport, 'Golden Era', were able to pass up and land the troops above the northern battery, without a single casualty amongst the troops, although they had to run the gauntlet of both gun and musket fire. Two or three native followers only were killed, in consequence of their unnecessarily exposing themselves.

By half-past one o'clock the troops were landed and formed, and advanced without delay through the date-groves and across the plain upon the entrenched camp of the enemy, who, without waiting for our approach, fled precipitately, after exploding their largest magazine, leaving, as I have before stated, their tents and baggage, public and private stores, with several magazines of ammunition, and sixteen guns, behind. The want of cavalry prevented my pursuing them as I could have wished; but I despatched a party of Sindh Irregular Horse, under Captain Malcolm Green, to follow them up for some distance. This officer reported that he came upon their rearguard retiring in good order; but that the road in many places was strewed with property and equipments. The loss of the Persians has been estimated at 200 killed, among whom was an officer of rank and estimation, Brigadier Agha Jan Khan, who fell in the northern battery.

I beg to annex a report received from Commodore Young, with copy of a letter I had previously caused to be addressed to that officer, expressing my entire satisfaction with the naval operations. Indeed, it was impossible for my instructions to have been more ably or more successfully carried out; and the Commodore, and every officer and man under his command, have nobly earned my warmest thanks. From Commodore Young, ably seconded by Captain Rennie and the other officers of the fleet and masters of transports, I have throughout received every possible assistance.

With exception of the artillery, with the mortar battery under Captain Worgan, no portion of the military force was actively engaged with the enemy, beyond some European riflemen sent on board the war vessels; but I am not the less indebted to all for their exertions and zeal, and especially for the great order and despatch with which the landing of the troops was effected under Brigadier General Havelock, CB. The highest spirit prevailed; and had the large Persian army only awaited our approach out of the range of the ship's guns, I feel confident that it would have received a lasting lesson.

From recent information I learn that the Persian force, in a very disorganised state, is still in full retreat . . .[4]

Mohammerah was won by the warships of the Indian Navy – four steam frigates, one steam sloop and two sloops of war. British losses were minimal, ten killed and thirty wounded. The Persian forces, under Prince Mirza, were put fully to flight. This was the last major engagement of the Persian War. An armistice was followed by the Treaty of Paris, 4 March 1857, by the terms of which the Shah renounced all sovereignty over Herat, or any other Afghan province, and agreed that in any future quarrel between Persia and Afghanistan, Britain was to be the mediator.

Notes

1. Sir James Outram, letter dated 20 December 1856
2. Major General Sir F.J. Goldsmid, *James Outram: A Biography* (1880)
3. Captain Lionel J. Trotter, *The Bayard of India: A Life of General Sir James Outram, Bart.* (1903)
4. Extract from, Sir James Outram's dispatch to Lord Elphinstone after Muhamra (1857)

16. With 'Bobs' to Kandahar
(The Second Afghan War 1873–74)

I fancy myself crossing and recrossing the river which winds through the pass; I hear the martial beat of drums and plaintive music of the pipes; and I see Riflemen and Gurkhas, Highlanders and Sikhs, guns and horses, camels and mules, with the endless following of the Indian army, winding through the narrow gorges, or over the interminable boulders which made the passage of the Bolan so difficult and wearisome to man and beast.[1]

*

The Second Afghan War had its origins in internal dissensions and dynastic rivalries between Sher Ali Khan (son of Dost Mohammad) and his cousin, Abdur Rahman Khan. Sher Ali looked to Russia for support, and in proportion to the measure in which this seemed to be granted he increasingly adopted an Anti-British policy. Such news was disturbing to British foreign policy-makers, as the British Government had succeeded in obtaining from the Russian Government in 1873 a declaration that Afghanistan was beyond the Russian sphere of influence, and that the Russians recognised the Oxus as the northern Frontier of the state. Afghan hostility was increased when Sher Ali failed to gain British guarantees of his sovereignty and family succession. He refused to admit British agencies into

Afghanistan, while making celebratory fuss over the admission of a Russian mission to Kabul in July 1878. The Government of India sent an ultimatum, which Sher Ali chose to disregard, thus precipitating a British invasion.

Hostilities broke out in November 1878. The British soon occupied the Khyber Pass and Kurram Valley and by early 1879 the British entered Kandahar, Kelat-i-Ghilzai and Girishk. Sher Ali fled from Kabul and died in March 1879. His son, Yakub Khan, signed a treaty with the British by which he surrendered the Kurrum Valley, Pishin, Sibi and the control of the Khyber Pass. He further agreed to receive a British Resident at Kabul and to subordinate Afghan foreign affairs to British influence. Major Sir Pierre Louis Napoleon Cavagnari, (son of one of Napoleon's generals) who was a career diplomat and former official of the East India Company, was apparently well received. However, the Amir's control over various internal elements was insufficient to maintain civil order and on 5 September, 1879, an armed mob attacked the Residency, killing Cavagnari and his escort.

The Kurram Field Force, of 7,500 European and Indian troops and 22 guns was then assembled under Lieutenant-General Frederick Sleigh Roberts, known affectionately throughout the Army as 'Bobs'. Roberts advanced and occupied Kabul. Yakub Khan abdicated on 12 October but Roberts was then faced with a religious war waged by the Mullahs who raised an army of 100,000 Afghans and surrounded Kabul. Roberts responded by leading his troops out to attack the Afghans' flank and routed them at the battle of Sherpur on 23 December, 1879. He then recommended that the country should be politically dismembered.

Abdur Rahman was appointed Amir for the Kabul district and British influence was to be maintained under the command of Sir Donald Stewart. This done, Roberts was in the process of withdrawing his troops to India by means of the Kurram route when he received news of the total defeat of the British brigade at Maiwand on 27 July 1880 and learned that Kandahar was besieged. He then made his celebrated march with 10,000 troops and transport from Kabul to Kandahar – 313 miles over mountainous country – in twenty two days. This extraordinary achievement was only made possible by Roberts' brilliant organisation. He realised that the success of the mission was essential and that morale and endurance could only be sustained by sensible routine. In order to save weight, as much food as was possible was to be obtained locally, thereby reducing the quantity that had to be transported over long distances. Time for assembling tents and cooking meals was necessarily limited at the end of each day's march:

On the march and in the formation of the camps the same principles were, as far as possible, applied each day. The 'rouse' sounded at 2.45 a.m., and by four o'clock tents had been struck, baggage loaded up, and everything was ready for a start.

As a general rule, the Cavalry covered the movement at a distance of about five miles, two of the four regiments being in front, with the other two on either flank. Two of the Infantry brigades came next, each accompanied by a Mountain battery; then followed the field hospitals, Ordnance and Engineer parks, treasure, and the baggage, massed according to the order in which the brigades were moving. The third Infantry brigade with its Mountain battery and one or two troops of Cavalry formed the rear guard.

A halt of ten minutes was made at the end of each hour, which at eight o'clock was prolonged to twenty minutes to give time for a hasty breakfast. Being able to sleep on the shortest notice, I usually took advantage of these intervals to get a nap, awaking greatly refreshed after a few minutes' sound sleep.

On arrival at the resting-place for the night, the front face of the camp was told off to the brigade on rear guard, and this became the leading brigade of the column on the next day's march. Thus every brigade had its turn of rear guard duty, which was very arduous, more particularly after leaving Ghazni, the troops so employed seldom reaching the halting-ground before six or seven o'clock in the evening, and sometimes even later.

One of the most troublesome duties of the rear guard was to prevent the followers from lagging behind, for it was certain death for anyone who strayed from the shelter of the column; numbers of Afghans always hovered about on the look-out for plunder, or in the hope of being able to send a Kafir, or an almost equally-detested Hindu, to eternal perdition. Towards the end of the march particularly, this duty became most irksome, for the wretched followers were so weary and footsore that they hid themselves in ravines, making up their minds to die, and entreating, when discovered and urged to make an effort, to be left where they were. Every baggage animal that could possibly be spared was used to carry the worn-out followers; but notwithstanding this and the care taken by officers and men that none should be left behind, twenty of these poor creatures were lost, besides four Native soldiers.

The variation of temperature (at times as much as eighty degrees between day and night) was most trying to the troops, who had to carry the same clothes whether the thermometer was at freezing-point at dawn or at 110° Fahr. at mid-day. Scarcity of water, too, was a great trouble to them, while constant sand-storms, and the suffocating dust raised by the column in its progress, added greatly to their discomfort.

Daily reports regarding the health of the troops, followers, and transport animals were brought to me each evening, and I made it my business to ascertain how many men had fallen out during the day, and what had been the number of casualties amongst the animals.[2]

Robert's epic march ended on 31 August 1880 when his force marched into Kandahar. He was suffering from fever and unable to ride much of the way, but mounted his horse to meet the generals who came out to meet his advancing columns:

As we approached the city, the whole garrison turned out and gave us a hearty welcome; officers and men, Native and British, crowded round us, loud in their expression of gratitude for our having come so quickly to their assistance. . . .

I confess to being very greatly surprised . . . at the demoralised condition of the greater part of the garrison (1,000 British soldiers, 3,000 Native soldiers). . . . They seemed to consider themselves hopelessly defeated, and were utterly despondent; they never even hoisted the Union Jack until the relieving force was close at hand. . . .[3]

The campaign was brought to an end of 1 September in the battle of Kandahar, in which Roberts' attack totally routed the Afghan forces, capturing their camp, guns and baggage. Ayub Khan fled accompanied by a few followers and peace was restored in southern Afghanistan. This eye-witness account of the closing stage of the battle and the capture of Ayub's camp at Kandahar is by Archibald Forbes, who served with the Royal Dragoons before entering journalism. He was war correspondent of the *Morning Advertiser*, who accompanied Roberts' forces:

Considerable numbers of Ayoub's troops had earlier pushed through the Babawali Pass, and moved down toward the right front of General Burrows' Bombay brigade in position about Picquet hill. Having assured himself that Burrows was able to hold his own, Sir Frederick Roberts ordered Macgregor to move the third brigade forward toward Pir Paimal village, whither he himself rode. On his arrival there he found that the first and second brigades were already quite a mile in advance. The battle really had already been won but there being no open view to the front, General Ross, who commanded the whole infantry division, had no means of discerning this result; and anticipating the likelihood that Ayoub's camp at Mazra would have to be taken by storm, he halted the brigades to replenish ammunition. This delay gave opportunity for the entire evacuation of the Afghan camp, which when reached without any further opposition and entered at one P.M. was found to be deserted. The tents had been left standing; 'all the rude equipage of a half barbarous army had been abandoned – the meat in the cooking pots, the bread half kneaded in the earthen vessels, the bazaar with its *ghee* pots, dried fruits, flour, and corn.' Ayoub's great marquee had been precipitately abandoned, and the fine carpets covering its floor were left. But in the hurry of their flight the Afghans had found time to illustrate their barbarity by murdering their prisoner Lieutenant Maclaine, whose body was found near Ayoub's tent with the throat cut. To this deed Ayoub does not seem to have been privy. The sepoys who were prisoners with Maclaine testified that Ayoub fled about eleven o'clock, leaving the prisoners in charge of the guard with no instructions beyond a verbal order that they were not to be killed. It was more than an hour later when the guard ordered the unfortunate officer out of his tent and took his life.

The victory was complete and Ayoub's army was in full rout.[4]

* * *

History has shown us time and again that success in war depends to a great extent upon the calibre and courage of the man in command. Like Wolseley, Roberts was a deeply professional soldier who recognized that administration and logistics were as vital to the conduct of any campaign as the fighting spirit of his soldiers and that the general who could blend both aspects of command to achieve the right balance and who could in addition inspire his troops by his own example would succeed. His conduct of the great march from Kabul to Kandahar was a model of supreme generalship. Without his skill and resolution it could never have been achieved and the outcome of the war might well have been different.

Notes

1. Field Marshal Frederick Sleigh Roberts, Earl, of Kandahar, Pretoria and Waterford, describing his memories of his great march from Kabul to Kandahar in September 1872 in his *Forty-One Years in India*, Vol. 2 (1897)
2. Roberts, *op.cit.*
3. Roberts, *op.cit.*
4. Archibald Forbes, *The Afghan Wars 1839–42 and 1878–80* (1892)

AFRICA 1824–1902

17. The King's Drinking Cup
(The First Ashanti War 1824–31)

After Sir Charles McCarthy had arrived at Cape Coast, and whilst he was making great preparations for invading the country of the Ashantees, the King of Ashantee [Ashanti] sent Sir Charles his compliments, with a threat of soon having his head as an ornament to the great war drum of Ashantee! It is a singular fact that the subject of this threatening message was frequently adverted to by the late Sir Charles. When at the head of his troops, when alluding to the King of Ashantee, he once remarked in a jocular way to some officers, 'That fellow says nothing will satisfy him but my head', which created a laugh at the expense of the sable Monarch, but Sir Charles looking seriously, replied, 'You need not laugh, it might so happen'. On another occasion, two days before the fatal action of the 21 January, he said in an ironical manner to two Ashantee prisoners, who had been brought before him, 'I hear your master wants my jaw-bones for his big drum; very well, I am going to give them to him tomorrow'. Alas! how true the prediction![1]

*

West Africa had been an area of interest to Europeans since the early 18th century. The Ashanti kingdom (now part of modern Ghana) was an inland territory, north of the Gold Coast. The various tribes of the Ashanti confederation had been combined under the rule of the Kumasi, whose kingdom was founded by Osai Tutu. Traditionally his dynasty was chosen by Nyame, the god of the sky. The celebrated gold-covered throne – the Golden Stool which contained the soul of the Ashanti nation – was Nyame's direct gift. Under various succeeding monarchs the Ashanti conquered other tribes (Fanti and Assin) and extended their empire, making war on other tribes in the process.

Eventually the Ashantis collided with British trading and colonial interests while in conflict with the Assin along the Gold Coast. In 1807, after a slaughterous pitched battle with a British force at Fort Anamabo under Colonel George Torrance, Governor of the Gold Coast, the British signed an agreement with the Ashanti king, Osai Tutu Kwadwo, in which they undertook to acknowledge the conquest of Fantiland and to pay rent to the Ashanti for forts at Anabado and the Gold Coast.

Friction between the British and the Ashanti continued, as the Europeans supported first one tribe then another. Then in 1821 the government assumed control of British settlements on the Gold Coast and threw in their weight with the Fanti against the Ashanti. Sir Charles McCarthy, Governor of the Gold Coast, had an army of some 500 against the Ashanti force of over 10,000. It poured with rain incessantly for days, the climate was dreadful, and the British force was exhausted by marching through severely uncongenial territory. Poor logistics resulted in the men being issued with half the proper allowance of ammunition. When they were engaged by the Ashanti on 21 January, 1824, at Essamako they found to their cost that the Ashantis had been reinforced with 5,000 additional fresh warriors. The British were soundly defeated by Kwadwo's warriors:

About two o'clock the enemy, who were said to be considerably more than ten thousand men, instead of being divided, as it was reported, were collected together, armed with muskets, and having a large description of knives stuck in their girdles, they were heard advancing through the woods with horns blowing and drums beating, and when they came within half a mile of our party they halted, when Sir Charles ordered the band of the Royal African Corps which had accompanied him, to play 'God save the King,' and the bugles to sound, he having heard through some channel in which he placed confidence, that the greater part of the Ashantees only wanted an opportunity to come over to him. The Ashantees played in return, which was alternately repeated several times, and then a dead silence ensued, interrupted only by the fire of our men at the enemy, who had by this time lined the opposite bank of the river, which was here about sixty feet wide.

The action now commenced on both sides with determined vigour, and lasted till nearly dark. It was reported about four o'clock that our troops had expended all their ammunition, consisting of twenty rounds of ball cartridges, besides leaden slugs which were contained in small bags suspended by a sling round the men's necks, and loose powder contained in small kegs, carried also by the men themselves, application was made to Mr Brandon, who arrived in the middle of the action, for a fresh supply of ammunition, he having received his excellency's orders to have forty rounds of ball cartridges packed in kegs for each man ready to be issued. This was done to lighten the men, who had to carry respectively their own provisions for many days, as well as to preserve the ammunition from being damaged by the swamps and rain; but Mr Brandon said that it had not yet arrived, and that he had only a barrel of powder and one of ball with him, which were immediately issued.

. . . a corporal of the militia and one or two others, composing part of the escort, arrived at the place of action shortly before its conclusion, and reported that the carriers had refused to advance any further with the ammunition and that most of them had run away. On this circumstance being reported to Sir Charles, he desired to see Mr Brandon, with whom he was exceedingly angry, and if he had not suddenly disappeared either into the woods or to look after the ammunition, it is probable that if Sir Charles had had the means at the moment, he would have put his threat into execution of suspending him to a tree.

The enemy perceiving that our fire had slackened, attempted to cross the river, which at this time had become fordable and succeeded. They had often attempted it when the river was swollen by the rains that had fallen, on trees which had been previously felled across to answer as bridges, but they were repulsed with great slaughter. The enemy had dispatched a considerable force to encompass our flanks in order to prevent our retreat, and now rushed in all directions on our gallant little force, who still defended themselves with their bayonets,until they were completely overpowered by their myriads, who instantly beheaded nearly every one of those who unfortunately fell into their remorseless hands.[2]

The fate of Sir Charles McCarthy was not established for some time after the battle, though there were various reports of his severed head being held as a trophy by the Ashantee. Eventually the terrible truth was revealed by a brother of Adookoo, King of the Fanti:

A brother to Adookoo, king of the Fantees, who had been taken prisoner by the Ashantees, when they attacked and beat the Fantees in 1807, made his escape from the enemy on their retreat on the 13th, and stated that he was umbrella bearer to the king, and was with him in the action of the 11th. The Ashantee army had suffered dreadfully from small pox, dysentery, and want of provisions, which had carried off many thousands, and, in consequence, caused so much discontent and insubordination in their army, that on the night of the 11th, whole bodies had deserted from the king, who were ascertained to be Assins, and who afterwards joined our native allies. He further stated, that the heart of Sir Charles MacCarthy was eaten by the principal chiefs of the Ashantee army, that they might imbibe his bravery; that his flesh had been dried, and with his bones, divided among every man of consequence in the army, who constantly carried his respective proportion about with him, as a charm to inspire him with courage.[3]

Sir Charles' skull was used at Kumasi as a royal drinking cup. The war continued and was concluded by the signal defeat of the

Ashantis at Dodowa 7 August, 1826. A peace treaty was signed in 1831 and the Ashanti agreed to accept the Prah as their southern boundary.

Notes

1. *Gentleman's Magazine* Vol 94, 1824
2. Major H.I. Ricketts, *A Narrative of the Ashantee War; With a View of the Present State of the Colony of Sierra Leone* (1831)
3. *Ibid.*

13. The Loss of the *Birkenhead*
(The Eighth Kaffir War 1850–53)

The hostile tribes could not put into the field more than three thousand fighting men; but by betaking themselves to their fastnesses of mountains and forest they prolonged their resistance for nearly three years. The British soldier was at every disadvantage in bush-fighting, and the Kaffirs were far too cunning to encounter him in the open; yet by dint of hard work and perseverence this brave and wary enemy was at last worn down. He might have been subdued much earlier but for the constant and insane reductions of the Army since Waterloo. It is actually a fact that at this time the military power of England was strained almost to breaking point by three thousand naked savages.[1]

*

The long series of wars between the British and the Xhosa, known to history as the Kaffir Wars 1779–1877, were the result of collisions between the various tribes of the Amaxhosa from South and Central Africa moving southwards, searching for grazing lands in the southern Cape and the colonial white Europeans, who were moving north from Cape Colony. 'Kaffir' was a term given by Europeans to refer to all black tribes (Arabic, *Kaffir*, an unbeliever, an infidel). British attempts to develop

Cape Colony in the first part of the 19th Century were continually handicapped by these conflicts.

Cape Colony had scarcely absorbed the economic impact of the abolition of slavery in 1833 when the colonists suffered what was in effect the invasion of the Kaffirs. A war party swept across the frontier in December, 1834, burning farmsteads, murdering settlers, driving off cattle. Lengthy negotiations and well intentioned undertakings failed to maintain frontier security thus violated. The Dutch settlers withdrew from the Colony and made the Great Trek to found the Transvaal and the Orange Free State, recognised by the British in the Sand River (1852) and Bloemfontein (1854) Conventions. But the penetration of Bantu territory by the Boers and the failure to maintain secure eastern frontiers caused this area to suffer a long period of tribal wars. The foundations of long standing problems for the British with the native peoples and Boer communities were carefully if unwittingly laid.

The most serious of these conflicts, known as the Eighth Kaffir War, broke out in December 1850. The leading British military commander at the time was Sir Harry Smith – a household name, hero of the Penninsula War, the American War, Waterloo and brilliant commander in the Cape between 1828 and 1843. In 1847, he was made Governor of Cape Colony and High Commissioner. Sir Harry Smith believed in showing the natives a firm hand but he found himself in conflict with British policy in the Cape and its leading exponent, the British Colonial Secretary, Lord Glenelg. Troubles in the Cape frontier area, in Glenelg's view, were always the result of provocative behaviour by the European settlers, pioneers and prospectors. Towards the end of 1850, it was brought to Sir Harry Smith's notice that certain Kaffir chiefs were conspiring to foment war with the British. He deposed one of the ringleaders, Sandilli. Tension mounted and volunteers were conscripted in readiness for war. On 24 December a patrol was taken up Keiskamma Gorge, where Sandilli was rumoured to be in hiding. The troops were set upon by Kaffir warriors and a dozen soldiers were killed. Thus began the Eighth Kaffir War.

Settlers fled and the country between Grahamstown and the Orange Free State was deserted. Various tribes combined to face the British troops, a mere 1,700. The native warriors were experts in guerrilla warfare and exploited their vast knowledge of the wild terrain. Hundreds of Kaffir members of the police fled back to their tribes, taking arms and ammunition with them. The Hottentots, traditional enemies of the Kaffirs, decided to bury their differences and swelled Kaffir numbers. British estimates of their enemies' numbers were approximately 20,000. But it was not just their numerical strength that was worrying. They were well armed and had plenty of ammunition. They were fighting in country they knew well and had mobility and the ability to appear, strike, and vanish – apparently simply disappearing in the rugged bush landscape. Sir Harry Smith summed matters up well in one of his dispatches to Lord Grey, the Colonial Secretary:

> The peculiarity of the present contest must be borne in mind; it must be remembered that this Kaffir warfare is of the most completely guerrilla and desultory nature, in which neither flank, front nor rear is acknowledged, and where the disciplined few have to contend with the un-disciplined but most daring and intrepid many.

An entire day could be spent skirmishing with very little impact having been made on their elusive enemy. The terrain was dangerous and rocky, advance was made difficult by vigorous undergrowth, vines and creepers. Various tactics were evolved to draw the Kaffirs into the open where they could be assaulted – such as a false retreat – but success was extremely slow. Sir Harry Smith let it be known that in his opinion he was insufficiently supplied with troops from England. He was recalled in 1852 and replaced by Sir George Cathcart. In fact, Smith's campaigning had all but finished the Kaffir war effort. They had lost some 6,000 killed, including 80 chieftains, as well as over 80,000 cattle. Smith had actually begun to receive emissaries asking for terms. The Colonial Secretary expected an outright victory, and on 14 January, 1853, wrote to Sir Harry Smith:

> Another month of this distressing warfare has passed away and though the force at your disposal has been increased to a very considerable amount no advantage of any real importance has been gained over the enemy, while the loss of Her Majesty's troops has been exceedingly heavy. . . .

On 25 February, 1852, occurred the catastrophe for which this particular Kaffir war is remembered – the loss of the steam-transport *Birkenhead*. This troopship was carrying the additional troops so desperately needed by Sir Harry Smith in the Cape Colony. It struck a rock off Danger Point in calm water in the middle of the night when en route between Cape Town and Port Elizabeth. The *Birkenhead* stuck fast, and when the captain ordered 'Full Astern' it was ripped in two. The forward part sank with all hands. The stern remained afloat while all the troops were paraded on deck and all the women and children were loaded into the boats. As the *Birkenhead* tilted and sank the soldiers and their officers remained calmly in their ranks. Over 360 officers and men were lost:

A catastrophe of the most disastrous character has become known within weeks. Her Majesty's large steamer *Birkenhead*, which has been dispatched from England a short time back with reinforcements for the troops engaged in the Kaffir war at the Cape of Good Hope, has been lost off the coast there, and out of 638 souls on board, only 184 have been saved. . . . The speed at which she was going – eight and a half knots an hour – drove her with such force on the rocks, that within a few minutes after she struck she broke in two, and went down, carrying with her the large proportion mentioned above of the persons on board.

The coolness and steady obedience to order which the troops manifested on that awful and trying occasion present an instance of one of the noblest results of discipline. All the women and children were removed in time to secure their entire safety, and then the officers and men tried to save themselves in boats, and by whatever means they could obtain.[2]

Sir Harry Smith handed over his command to Cathcart at King William's Town and departed the Cape. Cathcart's strategy did not depart from that established by Sir Harry, and after a few months, the Eighth Kaffir War drew quietly to a conclusion.

Notes

1. Sir John Fortescue, *Military History: Lectures Delivered at Trinity College, Cambridge* (1923)
2. *Illustrated London News*, 10 April, 1852

19. The March to Magdala
(The Conquest of Abyssinia 1867–68)

So well planned, so quietly and thoroughly executed, the political part so judiciously managed, the troops so admirably handled during the long, trying march, the strength of the Anglo-Indian organisation so strikingly demonstrated, wiping out all the stories of Crimean blundering – the Abyssinian expedition stands apart, and merits, perhaps an exceptional reward.[1]

*

Britain was reaching unprecedented heights of power. A great Empire was emerging. Her people were streaming out all over the world. Her industrialisation was forging ahead. The City of London was the centre of the world's finance. The British navy ruled the waves of every ocean. The army, under General Sir Robert Napier, with supreme arrogance had marched nearly three hundred miles into unexplored parts of Abyssinia to release a few captives at Magdala; they then razed the place to the ground and returned to the coast. (The gallant Sir Robert, a great Victorian hero, was the father of nine sons and six daughters).[2]

*

The peace of Abyssinia had for centuries been subject to the tensions and rivalries between its various provinces – Tigre (northern), Amhara (central), Gojam (north western) and Shoa (southern). The centre of power had usually been situated in Amhara, the ruler of which had invariably exacted tribute from the other provinces as *negusa nagast* – 'king of kings'. These rulers invariably claimed descent in direct line from Solomon and the Queen of Sheba. Rivalry between Tigre and Amhara was always particularly fierce and brought spectacular and harrowing results in the time of Kassa, known to history as King Theodore.

Kassa was a ruler of considerable ability and ambition who achieved and maintained power by bloodshed and proclaimed himself Emperor Theodore. He campaigned vigorously and cruelly against all opponents and maintained internal order by barbarity and tyranny. Charles Duncan Cameron, who had served as an officer in South Africa, as a magistrate in Natal, and as military advisor with the Turkish army in the Crimean War, and had later become British Vice-Consul in Asia Minor, was appointed British Consul in Abyssinia in October 1862. Theodore sent him back to Britain with a letter to Queen Victoria. The letter duly arrived at the Foreign Office where it was put aside and no answer delivered. In November, dispatches were sent to Theodore but these were not regarded as in any way an answer to his letter. Theodore was further angered by the visit to Kassala, in Egypt, made by Charles Duncan Cameron. In January 1864, Theodore had Cameron and his colleagues imprisoned.

The British government now decided that an answer to Theodore's letter should be sent to him. When the British party bearing this reply arrived at the Emperor's headquarters in January 1866, they were treated hospitably. The prisoners were released and the party began the return journey to the coast. All seemed to be going well, when they were brought back and confined. At Magdala, the Europeans were put in irons and were in constant fear of their lives. One of them was released and sent back to Britain with the request for machinery and workmen to help develop the country by way of conciliation to effect the release of the prisoners. Machinery and a few artisans were dispatched but the prisoners were not released. In July, 1867, it was decided that a punitive expedition would have to be sent to Abyssinia. A force of 16,000 troops, and 12,600 transport personnel, was sent on the 400 mile march in difficult and uncharted country, inhabited by hostile tribes. Its commander was General Sir Robert Napier, who had considerable experience, having served in the Sikh Wars and in the Indian Mutiny.

Theodore's power was in fact declining as a result of serious internal difficulties with the various provinces, which he found almost impossible to contain. His army had once numbered over 100,000 but the troops were deserting. He burned his capital, Debra-Tabor, and marched to Magdala, an extremely inaccessible citadel in mountainous country, where his prisoners were being held, and which stood three hundred feet above a plateau, seven thousand feet above sea level. Here he waited the advance of Napier's army.

Initial skirmishing and the first serious exchange of hostilities convinced Theodore that he was bound to lose against the rifle fire of British and Punjabi infantry, supported by the naval rocket brigade. In the hope of conciliating the invaders, he released his prisoners. He then observed preparations for the storming of Magdala continue and in a rage he commanded hundreds of Abyssinian captives, opponents of his rule, to be thrown over the precipice in their chains. This served to stiffen the resolve of Napier's forces.

The battle began in earnest on 13 April 1868 with a ferocious twenty minute battery of artillery which was all over by three o'clock. A storming party, armed with Snider rifles, then advanced, maintaining their volley as they attacked. George Alfred Henty[3], who had served in the Crimea and was now a war correspondent for the London *Standard*, sent this account of the advance on Magdala:

> Under cover of this fire, the Engineers and the leading company advanced up the path. When they were half way up, the troops stopped firing, and the storming party dashed up at a run. All this time answering flashes came back from a high wall that extended a few yards on either side of the gateway, and from behind the houses and rocks near it. On arriving at the gateway, the troops thrust their rifles through the loopholes, and kept up a continuous fire.

There was a long pause, and then a soldier made his way down the crowded path with the astounding news that the powder bags to blow in the gate had been forgotten – an act of forgetfulness probably unparalleled in warfare. A few pioneers of the 45th were sent up with axes to cut down the gate. In the meantime, however, the men of the 33rd discovered a spot, halfway up the road, where they were able to scramble up the rock, and forcing their way through the hedge, quickly cleared away the defenders of the gate. . . . The greater portion of the regiment followed them, and blew in an inner gate at the top of a flight of steps leading up to a natural scarp thirty feet high, and wide enough for but a single man to ascend at a time. Beyond this was a flat plateau scattered over with a large number of the round native huts, with stone walls and high conical thatched roofs. At a short distance from the gate lay the body of Theodore. He had received two wounds, but death was caused by his own hand, he having discharged a pistol into his mouth. . . .

Resistance was at an end. Magdala was burned and with the flames being fanned by the wind, the entire plateau was soon on fire. All fortifications were destroyed. The prisoners were released. The campaign cost five million pounds. It was economic with the lives of the soldiers. Two officers were killed, and twenty-seven other ranks perished. Napier was awarded a British peerage. Speaking in the House of Commons Disraeli assured Members of Parliament that history would place the Abyssinian campaign on a higher level than the late war in China. All memories of the Crimean fiasco were erased, he believed. The whole thing could be compared, he ventured to add, with 'the advance of Cortez into Mexico . . .'

Notes

1. Benjamin Disraeli, recommending the ennoblement and generous pensioning of Robert Cornelis Napier, conqueror of Abyssinia
2. Brian Gardner, *The African Dream* (1970)
3. GA Henty later became a well-known author of adventure stories based upon life in India and the Colonies

20. Sir Garnet and King Koffee (The Second Ashanti War 1873–74)

Two thousand Ashantis, under the leadership of an intelligent British officer, would soon extend the power of the English from the Cape Coast across the Thogoshi Mandingo land to Benin.[1]

*

As soon as we began to move forward, it became apparent that the enemy meant to make a determined resistance. They evidently trusted in their great numerical superiority which enabled them to surround us, in the strength of their forest position and their well known fighting reputation. They all knew that their grandfathers had utterly destroyed Sir Charles MacCarthy's army in British territory, and if they reasoned at all, they must have felt how much easier it would be to cut to pieces this new army that had dared to cross the sacred Prah, to penetrate into the interior of their country.[2]

*

Kwaka Dua I was a peace-loving ruler of the Ashanti. He encouraged trade and good relations with Europeans and his neighbouring tribes. He believed the Ashantis had the right to rule of the Fanti, and this caused some tensions during his reign which lasted from 1838–67. He was succeeded by the far more belligerent Kofi Karikari ('King Koffee') who picked a quarrel after the Elmina people were transferred from Dutch to British protection, and claimed that they owed their allegiance to him. He also captured and imprisoned four Europeans. His army then began an advance southwards to the Gold Coast. In response, Sir Garnet Wolseley was dispatched with an army which included 2,400 white troops to restore the situation.

It was Wolseley's great good fortune that the Ashanti army was severely reduced by an outbreak of smallpox and fever. His expedition was supported by an additional expedition from the east led by Captain John Glover RN, the administrator of Lagos, with a band of native levies. But Wolseley faced two serious problems. One was the great difficulty in levying reliable bearers and local warriors with the courage to venture into the bush to supplement his British soldiers. The climate was also against him, as there was only a brief period of three months when military operations were possible. Their punitive expedition would have to be over before the rainy season started. A standard joke of the time has it that an engineer officer who had served on the Gold Coast was asked what one needed to take by way of kit. 'A coffin,' he replied, 'A coffin is all you will require.' Wolseley needed an early victory over the Ashanti in order to erase the memory of the British defeat at Ashanti hands in the war of 1824–31. He had an easy success in the assault on the village of Essaman and recorded in his journal:

> Our little fight had a good effect upon what would else-where be called 'public opinion'. The experience gained proved that the Ashanti powder was such poor, weak stuff, that their slugs did little harm beyond a distance of forty or fifty yards. . . . I had thus taught the Ashantees that even in the bush they were not secure from our attack, and had given the weak-hearted Fantees new life by showing them that the British were not afraid to tackle the Ashantees in the bush, and that even there we were the better men.

Instead of making a mad dash in pursuit of his retreating Ashanti enemy, which might well have exposed his troops to senseless danger and hardship, Wolseley carefully prepared for his final major assault on Kumasi, the Ashanti capital. His Engineers cut and cleared a roadway through the forests and made communication routes to secure supplies and intelligence during the final push. By the middle of December, 1873, he was nearly ready:

> The preparations along the Prahsu road for feeding and sheltering the strong, and for doctoring the sick and wounded, were now so good that I felt I might, without undue risk, land my three battalions and also the Naval brigade. . . . My plan was to concentrate them and all my fighting native forces at Prahsu, and push thence with all possible haste for Koumassie. I hoped to defeat the Ashanti army on the way, and having taken the capital and its far-famed palace, to make peace there. Should the king refuse my terms, I intended to burn both the city and palace, and then to get the white troops back on board with the least possible delay. The deadliness of the climate forbade me to calculate upon any greater military results.[3]

His native bearers and troops were convinced that the Ashantis would easily destroy them, and they deserted in large numbers as Wolseley's forces advanced in January, 1874. To make matters worse, sickness continued to ravage his British troops. When, during this advance, he received messengers from King Koffee, Wolseley gave them a free demonstration of the fire potential of his Gatling machine-guns. The news of this demonstration impressed the Ashanti sovereign who then sent more conciliatory greetings and returned some prisoners. Wolseley resolved nevertheless to maintain his advance until Koffee complied with his terms, which included reparations in gold and the release of all the Fanti prisoners.

As Wolseley's force advanced, they found empty villages in the dark, gloomy, stinkingly hot jungle. All seemed quiet. But they were conscious of being watched all the time. Letters from the King begged him to halt. Was Koffee ready to sue for peace? Then Wolseley noted that one of the interpreters had left a written message for him, recommending him to see 'Corinthians ii 2'. When Wolseley checked this in the scriptures, he read: 'Lest Satan should get an advantage of us: for we are not ignorant of his devices'. This was clearly a warning against putting any trust in the seemingly pacific intentions of King Koffee. At the village of Quarman, the force met stiff resistance and was attacked from all sides. For a time, the fighting was ferocious but gradually the numerous enemy began to give way and Wolseley advanced to Amoaful, from where Kumasi would be in easy reach. It was now early in February and the weather broke. Wolseley's army was subject to a merciless downpour of rain the night before they crossed the river to engage the waiting Ashanti armies.

After a slaughterous fire from the British rifles and artillery the Ashanti were driven back and Kumasi was taken:

The streets of Koomassee presented an odd appearance for some time after we entered, for they swarmed with armed Ashantees, who greeted every Englishman they met with 'Thank you,' the only English words they knew. I gave orders they should be treated kindly but not allowed to enter the buildings told off for the troops. It was getting late, so we had not much time to settle down well that night in our new quarters, but all of us were in houses. Big fires blazed in front of these temporary barracks, at which sat our soldiers and sailors discussing the day's events as they satisfied their hunger and quaffed hot tea.

Strict orders were issued against looting, but they were not very strictly obeyed by the Fantee carriers or by those Fantees whom we had found fastened to logs when we arrived.

We had some extensive fires in the city that night, which I attribute to the carelessness of those Fantee pillagers. This annoyed me much, but having no plans of the place, and as it was a very dark night, I could do nothing to prevent them until daybreak. I managed, however, to send a message to the King, offering to make peace and warning him of the consequences unless he did so. The house I occupied as my headquarters was not very uncomfortable, and was fairly clean inside; it had a very high-pitched roof of thatch, which, however, was not in the best repair.

I had issued a proclamation that men caught robbing would be hanged, and the police patrolled the city all through the night. One of our own Fantee police caught in the act of pillaging was hanged, and several camp-followers were flogged. On the chance of being able to treat with the

King, I did not wish him to think that I had wantonly burnt his capital.

The following morning, February 5, 1874, I issued a general order thanking the soldiers and sailors of all ranks in the Queen's name for their gallant services and their good conduct.

I sent off all my sick and wounded under a strong escort bound for Cape Coast Castle and thence for home. The sooner I could get the poor fellows into comfortable quarters on board ship the better, as the best restorative for the sick and wounded is the consciousness that each succeeding day finds them nearer home.

I again wrote to the King to warn him that I would destroy Koomassee unless he at once made a treaty upon the terms I had offered him.

During the day we had another downpour of very heavy rain. I felt the King would make no satisfactory peace and that to stay longer on the chance of his doing so would be to entail fevers and death upon many of the gallant men round me. In my heart I believed that the absolute destruction of Koomassee with its great palace, the wonder of Western Africa, would be a much more striking and effective end to the war than any paper treaty – no matter what might be its provisions – that I might possibly obtain from this brutal and deceitful monarch. But public opinion at home would have loudly condemned me had I had recourse to that extreme measure until, having done my best to make terms with King Koffee, I had absolutely failed to induce him to agree to a treaty of a nature that would be generally approved of. As a concession to what I believed to be the drift of English feeling, I had done my best to induce this Ashantee savage to make peace on reasonable terms, and in doing so I had treated him as if he were a rational being. But with this rainy season already upon us, I felt it would be to tempt Providence were I to keep my soldiers any longer in such a charnel house as Koomassee.

I visited the royal palace and was surprised to find it though not imposing in character yet well laid out, clean and fairly well kept. Some of its buildings were of substantial masonry, and most of it was solidly constructed and admirably roofed in. Its ornamentation, without and within, was decidedly Moorish in style. The Ashantees have long had much intercourse with the Mahometan tribes further north, who draw their prescribed notions of civilization, of learning, and of art from Morocco. Many of the amulets worn by the Shantees round the arm, or fastened to a necklace, contain verses from the Koran in Persian characters. . . .

The palace abounded with curious and most beautiful gold ornaments which in pattern and design were perculiar to the country. All were made from very pure gold of a deep rich and reddish yellow that I have never seen elsewhere. But if the native goldsmith's skill surprised and interested me from an artistic point of view how can I describe the horrors which sickened mind and body in the palace. The whole locality stank from the human blood with which it may be said the ground is saturated. I have been in many barbarous lands where man's life is held cheap, but here alone was the spot where men made in the image of their Maker were butchered daily in cold blood in hundreds to appease the *manes* of some cruel ancestor or in obedience to the mandate of some bloodthirsty fetish priest. There was a grove of trees hard by into which the murdered bodies were always thrown, the stench from which poisoned the surrounding atmosphere. Hating all horrors I did not venture into it, but others with stronger stomachs did so, and their descriptions of it made one sick.

Without doubt the most loathsome object my eyes have ever rested on was a sacred stool saturated with human blood, which stood near the place of execution, and which was always kept wet with the blood of victims. Great fresh clots upon it showed how recently some poor creature had been sacrificed there. Near it stood the huge 'Death Drum', some four or five feet in diameter, and decorated round its outer rim with human skulls and thigh bones.

The very heavy rain that fell during the day caused me to think seriously over our position, so far away from my base on the coast and in a country where provisions for the white man are unobtainable. The rainy season had set in earlier than usual, and I knew how flooded the river Ordah had already become. Many of the swamps we had crossed with comparative ease in the fine weather during our advance would soon be converted by such equatorial tornadoes as that we had just had into impassable quagmires. I could clearly see that although King Koffee was thoroughly frightened for his own safety and for the maintenance of his kingdom, he was not to be easily hurried into signing any formal treaty of peace. He must naturally have felt the extreme danger of his position.

King Koffee was evidently at his wits' end, not knowing what to do, nor where to turn for useful advice. Had I felt there was the least likelihood of being able, by staying a week longer at Koomassee, to obtain a better treaty I would not have quitted it on February 6. But I felt that I should not be justified in condemning my soldiers to the risk of any longer stay in such a pestiferous climate on the off chance that it might enable us to get better terms inserted in any paper treaty King Koffee might consent to. I consequently determined to quit that horrible city of blood the following morning. I named prize agents to collect all the gold and valuable articles they could during the night, and ordered the commanding Royal Engineer to mine the palace and make arrangements for setting fire to the city in several places to ensure its total destruction.

We had a succession of violent tornadoes during the night accompanied with sheets of rain which poured in freely through the roof under which I slept. I tried to keep myself dry under an umbrella, but failed and lost my rest in the effort.

We began our return march to the coast at 7 a.m. on February 6. The road was in a pitiable condition, but all ranks were too full of delight at having left Koomassee behind them, with all its foul smells and loathsome horrors, to think of so small a matter. It was a real joy to feel that every step took us nearer home. What were mud, marshes, heavy tropical rains and deep streams to men 'going home'?[4]

Wolseley had occupied Kumasi and razed it to the ground. The Ashanti armies seemed to accept their defeat, but King Koffee had fled into the bush and refused to sign the surrender. Wolseley was encumbered with so many sick and wounded and running short of supplies that he was compelled to make the return journey. After he had left, Glover's force reached Kumasi and King Koffee was finally convinced that he would have to sign the peace treaty. This he duly did on 13 February 1874.

Notes

1. Henry Morton Stanley, *Coomassie and Magdala* (1874)
2. Field Marshal Sir Garnet Wolseley, First Viscount Wolseley, *The Story of a Soldier's Life* (1903)
3. Wolseley, *op.cit.*
4. Wolseley, *op.cit.*

21. Raids, Ambushes and Skirmishes (The Ninth Kaffir War 1877–78)

The Sergeant-Instructor of Musketry of the 90th Perthshire Light Infantry killed a Kaffir by deliberate aim at 1,800 yards distance – a little over a mile! . . . one of the enemy made himself defiantly conspicuous to a party of the 2nd Battalion 24th Regiment. Several shots were fired at him, which caused the fellow gradually to increase his distance. At slightly over 1,000 yards the native appeared to consider himself safe; but an officer came upon the scene, and at his first shot the whooping dancing Kaffir received a fatal bullet between the shoulders.[1]

*

Under the terms of the Sand River Convention 1852, the British government granted the Boers independence beyond the Vaal River. Within two years, the Bloemfontain Convention granted independence to Boers living between the Orange and the Vaal. Natal remained British. These measures were not deliberately planned or intended to further the ambitions of the Boers in this part of Africa. On the contrary, they were the result of strong feeling back home in Britain that the native wars cost too many British soldiers lives and too much of the tax-payers' money. Responsibilities could be reduced, it was believed, by non-intervention – recognising the Boer republics, forming a native territory (Kaffraria) as a buffer state between Cape Colony and the Bantu, and allowing the Boers, the missionaries and the natives to settle their own differences. Some measures of self-government were granted to Cape Colony.

After the Eighth Kaffir War of 1850–53 the Xhosa nation almost allowed itself to commit suicide in 1857. Nonquanse, a Galeka girl, who was severely influenced by her witch-doctor uncle, Mdhlaka, claimed to have been granted a vision during sleep. She was told by the ghosts of deceased ancestors that if the Xhosa sacrificed all their stocks of cattle and all their crops to the tribal gods, then the great Xhosa chiefs and warriors of the past would return to life and – bringing such crops and live-stock, the like of which had never been seen before – the Xhosa would then wage the war to end all wars on the white man. The vision was acted upon and some 25,000 Kaffirs died of starvation. As numerous others drifted away, seeking food, the population of British Kaffraria fell from 105,000 to 37,000 in seven months.

Careful crop cultivation and systematic cattle breeding, together with a sensible policy of emigration helped a fairly rapid recovery. In any case, by 1877 the native population was sufficiently aroused once more to represent a serious military threat to the British colonial forces in the area.

The Ninth Kaffir War which now broke out, was, however, unlike any of the preceding Kaffir wars insofar as its causes lay in an essentially Kaffir conflict – the root causes being tribal.

It was believed by other tribes that the Fingoes always drove a hard bargain, and that they were favoured by the British. They were particularly envied by the Galekas. In September, 1877, a beer brawl near the old mission station at Butterworth, involving Fingoes and Galekas, began to spread rapidly, developing from a fight involving a mere handful of natives into a serious tribal conflict in which hundreds became readily engaged.

On 25 September 1877, a party of over 5,000 Galekas attacked their traditional enemies, the Fingoes, at Guadana Hill on the Government Reserve, where there was a troop of the Frontier Armed and Mounted Police. Inspector GB Chalmers of the Mounted Police recorded the incident in his Report:

On arrival I found the Galeka army in three divisions at the foot of the hill. On our appearance the enemy made a move towards us, and I immediately gave the order to the officer in command of the artillery – Sub-Inspector Cochrane – to open fire with the seven pounder. After the tenth round the gun became disabled, and I gave the order 'The gun will retire, under Mr Cochrane and the escort'.

Before entering into action my men were extended in skirmishing order on the brow of the hill, the horses having been left out of sight, in hand, and in charge of the usual number of men. The Fingoes . . . were placed on the left bank, between the gun and the Guadana forest, so as to command the bush; my men were placed on the right of the gun.

When the Galekas came within rifle range, I ordered the Police to commence firing, and continuous independent firing was kept up for nearly two hours, which checked the enemy until the gun retired. When the Fingoes saw this they made a general retreat, running among our horses and causing great confusion.

Finding that we were deserted, and that by remaining on the ground any longer the whole European Police would be sacrificed, I ordered the men to retire. The confusion by the Fingoes rushing about in all directions caused several of our horses to break loose, and through this unfortunate circumstance one officer and six men fell victims to the enemy. The remainder retired in order. . . . The estimated loss on the Galeka side was at least 200, besides wounded. . . .[2]

It was an intermittent war of raids, ambushes, skirmishes and few pitched small battles. The war is notable for the award of the first Victoria Cross in South Africa (to Major Moore of the Connaught Rangers) and to the first recorded use of a machine gun by the British in conflict and during an action – a Gatling. Time and again, the terrible fire-power of modern weaponry against savages however strong in number was demonstrated. Sir Bartle Frere, the Governor of the Cape, who was travelling in the area when the war broke out, wrote to Herbert Henry Howard Molyneux, Lord Caernarvon on 17 February 1878, to describe the attack on the police at Kentani, where 5,000 natives attacked the European forces (two regiments of infantry together with some cavalry – Carrington's Horse) commanded by Captain Upcher:

> They seemed to have great hopes of crushing Upcher by enveloping his position, and then of raising the Colony. They came on in four divisions very steadily and in the days of Brown Bess would certainly have closed, and being eight or ten to one would possibly have overwhelmed our people. They held on after several shells had burst among their advanced masses but they could not live under the fire of the Martini-Henry. The 24th are old steady shots and every bullet told, and when they [the Kaffirs] broke Carrington's Horse followed them up and made the success more decided than in any former action. It has been, in many respects, a very instructive action, not only as regards the vastly increased power in our weapons and organisation, but as showing the Kaffir persistence in the new tactics of attacking us in the open in masses. At present this is their fatal error, but it might not be so if they had a few renegade foreigners as drill-masters. . . .[3]

British forces were withdrawn from the Transkei. The Frontier Police were made responsible for patrolling the lands of the Galekas, whose warriors were now disbanded. There was growing fear of invasion from the Swazi or the Zulus. The latter were developing into a serious threat, with an army allegedly of half a million trained and ferociously disciplined warriors. Under an ambitious king, Cetewayo, they nurtured ambitions to reclaim the Blood River Territory they had been forced to surrender for Boer settlement on their northwest border with the Transvaal. In an attempt to stabilise the area, the British government annexed the Transvaal in April 1878. This deeply offended the Boers who continued to nurse their grievances and who found a leader and spokesman in Paul Kruger. It further alarmed the Zulus who now found themselves confronted by white imperialism in the north, and in the south. The British were soon to learn the severe cost of offending Zulus and Boers in southern Africa.

Notes

1. General Sir Arthur Augustus Thurlow Cunynghame, Commander-in-Chief in South Africa, on the effects of the new Martini-Henry rifle, used by the British Army for the first time in the Ninth Kaffir War.
2. James Grant, *British Battles on Land and Sea* (1897)
3. John Martineau, *Life and Correspondence of Sir Bartle Frere* (1895)

22. Tragedy and Triumph for the 24th Foot (The Zulu War 1879)

I do kill, but do not consider that I have done anything in the way of killing yet. Why do the white people start at nothing? I have yet to kill; it is the custom of our nation and I shall not depart from it ... My people will not listen unless they are killed; and while wishing to be friends with the English I do not agree to giving my people over to be governed by laws sent by them. Have I not asked the English to allow me to wash my spears since the death of my Mpande, and they have kept playing with me all this time, treating me like a child? I shall now act on my own account.... The Governor and I are in like positions: he is Governor of Natal and I am Governor here.[1]

*

A ZULU VICTORY: On the 21st inst. a British column, consisting of a portion of the 24th Regiment (South Wales Borderers) and 600 natives with one battery, was defeated with terrible loss by an overwhelming force of Zulus, who numbered 20,000. A valuable convoy of supplies, consisting of 102 wagons drawn by 1,000 oxen, two guns, 400 shot and shell, 1,000 rifles, 250,000 rounds of ammunition, and 60,000 lb. of commissariat stores, and the colours of the 24th Regiment fell into the hands of the enemy. The engagement occurred about 10 miles beyond Rorke's

Drift on the Tugela River. The number of Zulus killed and wounded is estimated to have been 5,000, while our force was completely annihilated.[2]

*

Traditionally, Zululand was the north-eastern part of the province of Natal, in south-east Africa (latterly part of modern South Africa). During the last century the peace of southern Africa had been handicapped continually by various tribal wars, wars with Europeans and civil wars – the Kaffir War 1850–53, the Basuto Wars 1858–68, the Transvaal Civil War 1862–64 and the Zulu-Boer border conflicts of 1854–77. Britain had renounced her sovereignty over the Transvaal in 1852 and recognised the Orange Free State in 1854. Diamonds were discovered along the Orange River in 1867 and Britain then annexed the Hopetown region in 1871. The following year the Zulus achieved a new king, Cetewayo became Zulu ruler. His rule was tyrannic and bloody. He began to revive the military spirit of his people, using the methods of his formidable uncle, Chaka. The Zulu army was organised almost in regimental fashion, with all males having to serve stipulated periods of military training and activity. He was soon in serious border disputes with the Transvaal. After the Kaffir War of 1877–78 Britain had annexed all of Kaffraria and now found herself having to deal with the problems of border definitions and responsibilities.

In July, 1878, a Commission appointed by the Lieutenant Governor of Natal, published its findings in support of nearly all the Zulu claims. The High Commissioner of South Africa, Sir Bartle Frere, considered the award one-sided and unfair to the Boers and was personally convinced that the upsurging power of the Zulu nation under Cetewayo would have to be checked.

To this end, Frere demanded among other things that a British Resident should be accepted as part of plans which amounted to the establishment of a virtual protectorate over Zululand. The demands were made to Zulu deputies on 11 December, 1878, and a reply was required by 31 December. When no answer was received, a state of war was presumed and on 11 January the British invaded Zululand. General Frederick Augustus Thesiger, Viscount Chelmsford, led an army of 5,000 British and 8,200 native troops, which entered Zululand in three columns, with the intention of converging on the Royal Kraal at Ulundi.

The centre column – 1,600 European and 2,500 native troops – had advanced from Rorke's Drift and camped near Isandhlwana on 22 January 1879. That morning General Thesiger left with a reconnaissance party, leaving the camp under the command of Colonel Anthony Durnford. The camp was surprised by a Zulu army of 10,000 men and terrible casualties were inflicted upon the defenders – 806 Europeans killed and 471 natives – and Colonel Durnford himself was killed while covering the retreat. 'An assagai has been thrust into the belly of the nation' was Cetewayo's comment after Isandhlwana. This account of the aftermath of the slaughter at Isandhlwana is by Commandant George Hamilton-Browne of the Natal Native Contingent, an irregular force raised to serve in this campaign:

At about 11 o'clock I was on ahead and looking through my glasses when I saw a puff of smoke rise from the hills on the left of the camp. It was followed by another. They seemed to come from a huge black shadow that lay on the hills. Presently another puff and in a moment I knew they were bursting shells. Not a cloud was in the sky, and I knew that the black shadow resting on the hills must be the Zulu army moving down to attack the camp. . . .

I could now see the troops lying down and firing volleys, while the guns kept up a steady fire. The Zulus did not seem able to advance. They were getting it hot, and as there was no cover they must have suffered very heavy losses, as they shortly afterwards fell back. The guns and troops also ceased firing. At about midday I was looking back anxiously to see if the mounted men and guns were coming up, when I heard the guns in camp reopen again; and riding forward, we were then about four miles from the camp, I saw a cloud of Zulus thrown out from their left and form the left horn of their army. These men swept round and attacked the front of the camp, and I saw the two right companies of the 24th and one gun thrown back to resist them. There was also plenty of independent firing going on within the camp, as if all the wagon men, servants, and in fact everyone who could use a rifle was firing away to save his life. . . .

The defenders fought desperately and I could see through the mist the flash of bayonet and spear together with the tossing heads and horns of the infuriated cattle, while above the bellowing of the latter and the sharp crack of the rifles could be heard the exulting yells of the savages and the cheers of our men gradually dying away. Of course I saw in a moment everything was lost and at once galloped back to my men.

There was no time to write, but I said to Captain Develin, a fine horsemen and a finer fellow, 'Ride as hard as you can, and tell every officer you meet, "For God's sake come back, the camp is surrounded and must be taken."'

Then getting my officers together, I said to them, 'Our only chance is to retreat slowly,' and ordered them to form their companies into rings, after the Zulu fashion, and retire, dismounting themselves and hiding all the white men among the natives. This we did, and although there were large parties of the enemy close to us, they took no notice of us, and we gradually retired out of their vicinity. When we had got to a place, about five miles from the camp, where I thought my white men and Zulus could put up a bit of a fight in case we were attacked, I halted and determined to await the course of events. During the retreat I had often looked back and seen that the fighting was over in the camp, but that one company, in company square, was retreating slowly up the hill surrounded by a dense swarm of Zulus. This was Captain Younghusband's company. They kept the enemy off as long as their ammunition lasted, then used the bayonet until at last overcome by numbers they fell in a heap like the brave old British Tommy should.

We sat and lay where we were. There was nowhere to go, nothing to be done, we had no food, and very little ammunition, but we had some water and tepid and muddy as it was it was thankfully used as there was no shade and the sun shone like a ball of fire. As soon as I had made what few arrangements I could I told the men to get some rest, as I was convinced that later on, we should be called upon to retake the camp, as through that camp was the only possible retreat for the General's party and ourselves. . . .

The long afternoon passed slowly away, and towards evening I saw a small body of horsemen riding towards us. On using my glasses I discovered it was the General and his staff and I at once mounted and rode to meet him.

He looked very surprised when he saw me and said, 'What are you doing here, Commandant Browne. You ought to have been in camp hours ago.' I replied. 'The camp has been taken, sir.'

He flashed out at once, 'How dare you tell me such a falsehood? Get your men into line at once and advance.' I did so and led my 700 miserables supported by the staff against the victorious Zulu army.

We moved on about two and a half miles until we had opened out a good view of the camp, when he called me to him and said, in a kindly manner, 'On your honour, Commandant Browne, is the camp taken?' I answered, 'The camp was taken at about 1.30 in the afternoon, and the Zulus are now burning some of the tents.'

He said, 'That may be the quartermaster's fatigue burning the debris of the camp.' I replied, 'QM's fatigue do not burn tents, sir,' and I offered him my glasses. He refused them, but said, 'Halt your men at once,' and leaving me, rode back to the staff and dispatched an officer to bring up the remainder of the column.

I had just halted my men and placed them in the best position I could, when to my utter astonishment I saw a man on foot leading a pony, coming from the direction of the camp, and recognised him as Commandant Lonsdale.

He had had the most wonderful escape. As I have said before he was still suffering from sunstroke and having somehow lost the battalion he was with, had ridden towards the camp. More than half stupefied by the great heat, he rode into it, and all at once awoke to the fact that the camp was full of Zulus, some of them wearing soldiers' tunics, and that the ground was littered with dead men. He then realised the situation at a glance and in less time than words can tell, he turned his pony's head and rode as hard as he could away. He was pursued, but the ground was good-going, and his pony 'Dot' a *very* smart one, so he got clear away and joined us.

Well, again a weary halt. As we lay we could see long lines of Zulus marching along the hills on our right flank. They had with them many of our wagons, most probably loaded with their wounded men, or plunder out of the camp.[3]

*   *   *

After their triumph as Isandhlwana, the Zulu forces moved on to Rorke's Drift, where a garrison of about eighty men, with about forty men in the hospital accommodation there, all under the command of Lieutenant Chard and Lieutenant Bromhead. The Zulu force – 4,000 strong – attacked the stockade six times, and six times were repulsed (at times in hand to hand combat). At dawn the Zulus withdrew, leaving over 350 dead. British losses totalled 17 dead and 10 wounded. The Victoria Cross was awarded to eleven soldiers for this battle – more than for any other single engagement. This is the eye-witness account of Henry Hook VC:

> . . . there was a commotion in the camp, and we saw two men galloping towards us from the other side of the river, which was Zululand. Lieutenant Chard of the Engineers was protecting the ponts over the river and, as senior officer, was in command at the drift. The ponts were very simple affairs, one of them being supported on big barrels, and the other on boats. Lieutenant Bromhead was in the camp itself. The horsemen shouted and were brought across the river, and then we knew what had happened to our comrades. They had been butchered to a man. That was awful enough news, but worse was to follow, for we were told that the Zulus were coming straight on from Isandhlwana to attack us. At the same time a note was received by Lieutenant Bromhead from the Column to say that the enemy was coming on, and that the post was to be held at all costs.
>
> 'For some time we were all stunned, then everything changed from perfect quietness to intense excitement and energy. There was a general feeling that the only safe thing

was to retire and try and join the troops at Helpmakaar. The horsemen had said that the Zulus would be up in two or three minutes; but luckily for us they did not show themselves for more than an hour. Lieutenant Chard rushed up from the river, about a quarter of a mile away, and saw Lieutenant Bromhead.

Orders were given to strike the camp and make ready to go, and we actually loaded up two waggons. Then Mr Dalton, of the Commissariat Department, came up and said that if we left the drift every man was certain to be killed. He had formerly been a sergeant-major in a line regiment and was one of the bravest men that ever lived. Lieutenants Chard and Bromhead held a consultation, short and earnest, and orders were given that we were to get the hospital and storehouse ready for defence, and that we were never to say die or surrender.

Not a minute was lost. Lieutenant Bromhead superintended the loop-holing and barricading of the hospital and storehouse, and the making of a connection of the defences between the two buildings with walls of mealie-bags and waggons. The mealie bags were good big heavy things, weighing about 200 pounds each, and during the fight many of them were burst open by assegais and bullets, and the mealies (Indian corn) were thickly spread about the ground.

The biscuit boxes contained ordinary biscuit. They were big, square, wooden boxes, weighing about a hundredweight each. The meat boxes, too, were very heavy, as they contained tinned meat. They were smaller than the biscuit boxes. While these preparations were being made, Lieutenant Chard went down to the river and brought in the pont guard of a sergeant and half-a-dozen men, with the waggons and gear. The two officers saw that every soldier was at his post, then we were ready for the Zulus when they cared to come.

They were not long. Just before half past four we heard firing behind the conical hill at the back of the drift, called Oskarsberg Hill, and suddenly about five or six hundred Zulus swept around, coming for us at a run. Instantly the natives – Kaffirs who had been very useful in making the barricade of waggons, mealie-bags and biscuit boxes around the camp – bolted towards Helpmakaar, and what was worse their officer and a European sergeant went with them. To see them deserting like that was too much for some of us, and we fired after them. The sergeant was struck and killed. Half-a-dozen of us were stationed in the hospital, with orders to hold it and guard the sick. The ends of the building were of stone, the side walls of ordinary bricks, and the inside walls or partitions of sun-dried bricks of mud. These shoddy inside bricks proved our salvation, as you will see. It was a queer little one-storeyed building, which it is almost impossible to describe; but we were pinned like rats in a hole, because all the doorways except one had been barricaded with mealie-bags and we had done the same with the windows. The interior was divided by means of partition walls into which were fitted some very slight doors. The patients' beds were simple rough affairs of boards, raised only about half a foot above the floor. To talk of hospitals and beds gives the idea of a big building, but as a matter of fact this hospital was a mere little shed or bungalow, divided up into rooms so small that you could hardly swing a bayonet in them. There were about nine men who could not move, but altogether there were about thirty. Most of these, however could not help to defend themselves.

As soon as our Kaffirs bolted, it was seen that the fort as we had first made it was too big to be held, so Lieutenant Chard instantly reduced the space by having a row of biscuit-boxes drawn across the middle, about four feet high. This was our inner entrenchment, and proved very valuable. The Zulus came on at a wild rush, and although many of them were shot down they got to within about fifty yards of our south wall of mealie-bags and biscuit boxes and waggons. They were caught between two fires, that from the hospital and that from the storehouse, and were checked; but they gained the shelter of the cookhouse and ovens, and gave us many heavy volleys. During the fight they took advantage of every bit of cover there was, ant-hills, a tract of bush that we had not had time to clear away, a garden or sort of orchard which was near us, and a ledge of rock and some caves (on the Oscarsberg) which were only about a hundred yards away. They neglected nothing, and while they went on firing, large bodies kept hurling themselves against our slender breastworks.

But it was the hospital they assaulted most fiercely. I had charge with a man that we called Old King Cole of a small room with only one patient in it. Cole kept with me for some time after the fight began, then he said he was not going to stay. He went outside and was instantly killed by the Zulus, so that I was left alone with the patient, a native whose leg was broken and who kept crying out, 'Take my bandage off, so that I can come.' But it was impossible to do anything except fight, and I blazed away as hard as I could. By this time I was the only defender of my room. Poor Old King Cole was lying dead outside and the helpless patient was crying and groaning near me. The Zulus were swarming around us, and there was an extraordinary rattle as the bullets struck the biscuit boxes, and queer thuds as they plumped into the bags of mealies. Then there was the whizz and rip of the assegais, of which I had experience during the Kaffir Campaign of 1877–8. We had plenty of ammunition, but we were told to save it and so we took careful aim at every shot, and hardly a cartridge was wasted. Private Dunbar, shot no fewer than nine Zulus, one of them being a Chief.

From the very first the enemy tried to rush the hospital, and at last they managed to set fire to the thick grass which formed the roof. This put us in a terrible plight, because it meant that we were either to be massacred or burned alive, or get out of the building.

All this time the Zulus were trying to get into the room. Their assegais kept whizzing towards us, and one struck me in front of the helmet. We were wearing the white tropical helmets then. But the helmet tilted back under the blow and made the spear lose its power, so that I escaped with a scalp wound which did not trouble me much then, although it has often caused me illness since. Only one man at a time could get in at the door. A big Zulu sprang forward and seized my rifle, but I tore it free and, slipping a cartridge in, I shot him point-blank. Time after time the Zulus gripped the muzzle and tried to tear the rifle from my grasp, and time after time I wrenched it back, because I had a better grip than they had. All this time Williams was getting the sick through the hole into the next room, all except one, a soldier of the 24th named Conley, who could not move because of a broken leg. Watching for my chance I dashed from the doorway, and grabbing Conley I pulled him after me through the hole. His leg got broken again, but there was no help for it. As soon as we left the room the Zulus burst in with furious cries of disappointment and rage.

Now there was a repetition of the work of holding the doorway, except that I had to stand by a hole instead of a door, while Williams picked away at the far wall to make an opening for escape into the next room. There was more desperate and almost hopeless fighting, as it seemed, but most of the poor fellows were got through the hole.

... All this time, of course, the storehouse was being valiantly defended by the rest of the garrison. When we got into the inner fort, I took my post at a place where two men had been shot. While I was there another man was shot in the neck, I think by a bullet which came through the space between two biscuit boxes that were not quite close together. This was at about six o'clock in the evening, nearly two hours after the opening shot of the battle had been fired. Every now and then the Zulus would make a rush for it and get in. We had to charge them out. By this time it was dark, and the hospital was all in flames, but this gave us a splendid light to fight by. I believe it was this light that saved us. We could see them coming, and they could not rush us and take us by surprise from any point. They could not get at us, and so they went away and had ten or fifteen minutes of a war-dance. This roused them up again, and their excitement was so intense that the ground fairly seemed to shake. Then, when they were goaded to the highest pitch, they would hurl themselves at us again. We could sometimes, by the light of the flames, keep them well in sight, so well that we could take aim and fire coolly. When we could do this they never advanced as far as the barricade, because we shot them down as they ran in on us. But every now and then one or two managed to crawl in and climb over the top of the sacks. They were bayoneted off.

All this time the sick and wounded were crying for water. We had the water-cart full of water, but it was just by the deserted hospital, and we could not hope to get at it until the day broke, when the Zulus might begin to lose heart and to stop their mad rushes. But we could not bear the cries any longer, and three or four of us jumped over the boxes and ran and fetched some water in.

The long night passed and the day broke. Then we looked around us to see what had happened, and there was not a living soul who was not thankful to find that the Zulus had had enough of it and were disappearing over the hill to the south-west. Orders were given to patrol the ground, collect the arms of the dead blacks, and make our positions as strong as possible in case of fresh attacks.[4]

* * *

Between January and April, 1879, one of General Thesiger's three columns, commanded by Colonel Pearson was besieged at Eshowe. Eshowe was relieved at the battle of Ginginhlove by a force under Thesiger himself. A further column commanded by Sir Evelyn Wood at Kabula fended off a fierce assault by 20,000 Zulus – who suffered losses of 1,000. By the beginning of May, reinforcements had arrived from Britain. International attention was focused on the Zulu conflict after the Prince Imperial, son of the Emperor Napoleon III of France, who was serving as a volunteer with the British, was killed in an ambush. The war now moved swiftly to an end. Sir Garnet Wolseley had been sent out to supersede Thesiger (Lord Chelmsford). The British forces reached the vicinity of Ulundi with 4,200 European and 1,000 native troops. Here on 4 July they were attacked by Cetewayo's army – 10,000 strong. They formed a hollow square, with cavalry inside. The series of Zulu assaults were repulsed with musket fire and bayonets and finally the Zulus were put to flight by a cavalry charge. British losses were 100 but the Zulus had 1,500 killed. Cetewayo fled, but was captured on 27 August. He was deposed and the country was ruled by eleven Zulu chiefs, who referred to a British Resident.

Notes

1. Cetewayo, the Zulu King, to Sir Harry Bulwer, Lieutenant Governor of Natal
2. *The Times* 11 February 1879
3. George Hamilton-Browne, *A Lost Legionary in South Africa* (1912)
4. Henry Hook, 'Survivor's Tales of Great Events – How They Held Rorke's Drift', *The Royal Magazine*, February 1905

23. The Transvaal Revolt
(The First Boer War 1880–81)

I cannot conceive what can have so suddenly caused the Boers to act as they have'.[1]

*

A dirty, unkempt-looking fellow, with long hair and beard. The chances are he has one spur on upside down, his head covered with a broad-brimmed felt hat, high in the crown, and a dirty flannel shirt.[2]

*

The first Boer War 1880–81, sometimes called the 'Transvaal Revolt', came about as the result of the discovery of gold and diamonds in this area of Africa, combined with dithering and bungling on the part of the British Government at home and its diplomatic, administrative and military representatives in the Cape. Diamonds had been discovered near the Orange River – in an oblong area with the Orange River to the south, the Hart River to the west, the Vaal to the north and the Orange Free State to the east – and gold was discovered at Kimberly in 1870. There was considerable dispute about the conflicting rights of the Boers and the British, as well as continuing border troubles with the native black population. The forward, imperial policy followed by Disraeli was discontinued by his successor, Gladstone, who became Prime Minister in 1880. It was hoped that matters might be resolved by a confederation of the British colonies and the Dutch republics, but this suggested union was not popular in the Cape parliament (despite the united front of white Europeans which it would have demonstrated). Nevertheless, the Transvaal was annexed in 1877. The British government justified this act on the grounds of alleged Boer ill-treatment of the natives – cruelty, slavery and traffic in 'black ivory'.

The Union Jack was raised on 12 April, 1877, by the secretary of Sir Theophilis Shepstone, a young man named Rider Haggard. The timing was excellent, as world news was dominated by the Balkan crisis, the Russo-Turkish war and the sensational archeological discoveries at Mycenae. The British failed to comprehend the depth of Boer feelings at the insult of annexation. In Boer eyes the British had contravened their own undertaking enshrined in the Sand River Convention not to encroach north of the Vaal. The Boers regarded themselves as God's Chosen People and this was their Promised Land. The British were the enslaving Egyptians. Kimberly, made a boom town by diamonds and gold, a city of booze and prostitution, was a latter-day Sodom and Gomorrah.

The Boer leader, Paul Kruger, travelled to London a month after annexation to plead the Transvaal cause, to no avail. Boer discontent increased, expressed in endless petitions. The British continued to underestimate Boer feelings and had little regard for their capacity to stand up for their own rights. In the opinion of Sir Garnet Wolseley: 'They are given to more boasting and tall talk than the Americans, but at heart they are cowards, and cowards that would be relentless to a fallen foe. They have all the cunning and cruelty of the Kaffir without his courage or his honesty. They know they could not stand up to our troops for an hour'. The Boers hoped that the British Government would listen to their plea for self government. They were to be disappointed. The British Government, they were told, was fully committed towards the native population of the Transvaal. The Transvaal treasury was in deficit. The British Government had only granted a mere £100,000, which was soon exhausted in salaries and communications. There was no civil hospital, no bridges, no modern roads. The Boers were counselled to be patient, pay taxes and wait. They must be content with Crown Colony status. The new legislative council opened in Pretoria during the spring of 1880 contained no Boer representatives. The Boers now prepared for armed resistance. On Saturday 10 December, 1880, they hoisted the *Vierkleur*, their national flag. A proclamation was drafted, which restored legitimacy to the restored Boer government of the Transvaal. The independence of the Transvaal was declared and an ultimatum dispatched to the British.

The Boers had several initial advantages. They could raise a force of some 7,000, which outnumbered Major General Sir George Colley's Natal and Transvaal troops by three to one (but the British would be swift to send reinforcements). The Boers were expert in veld campaigning and guerrilla war. They were well armed, the majority with Martini-Henry rifles. After a few skirmishes, some 2,000 Boers invaded Natal on 28 January, 1881. They were commanded by General Paul Joubert. They were met by 1,400 British under Colley at Laing's Nek in the Drackensberg Mountains. This was a Boer victory, but nothing compared to the rout they achieved the following month.

Colley resolved on a daring plan by means of which he hoped to gain the advantage. He resolved on a secret night march to take the heights of Majuba, which overlooked the main past through the mountains and towered over the main area of the conflict. If the British occupied this position, he believed, they would have the strategic advantage. Theoretically Colley's plan was reasonable. There are classic examples in the annals of warfare demonstrating the advantage of such a position, particularly in being able to fire down upon an advancing army. But in executing the plan Colley made several catastrophic errors. He took no guns, Gatlings or rockets with which he could fire upon the laager below. The troops he took were a selection from his various regiments, instead of seasoned campaigners from, say, one Highland regiment. He must have considered a battle unlikely and wanted all units to share the glory of his escapade. The results were catastrophic. The mixing of a variety of units seriously reduced the familiar comradeship which is such a feature of the British regimental system. The men were not ordered to dig in. As daylight developed a few British took pot-shots at the Boers below them in the valley, thus alerting the enemy to their manoeuvre. The Boers then decided to come and get them.

The line of experienced marksmen maintained a ferocious fire on the British mountainside positions, while assault troops put into practice some of the hard learned lessons gained from fighting natives, and zig-zagged their way up three sides of the mountain under cover of the comrades' relentless rifle fire. They continued slowly to climb Majuba all the day, while the fusillade was maintained. The British were so confident that Colley actually took a long nap at one o'clock in the afternoon. The defenders could not believe their eyes when the impossible happened – Boers appeared at the summit. This account is by John Alexander Cameron, the war correspondent of the *Illustrated London News:*

> Major Fraser, and myself were discussing the situation, when we were startled by a loud and sustained rattle of musketry, the bullets of which shrieked over our heads in a perfect hail. Lieutenant Wright, of the 92nd, rushed back, shouting out for immediate reinforcements. The General, assisted by his Staff, set about getting these forward, and then for the first time it dawned upon us that we might lose the hill, for the soldiers moved forward but slowly and hesitatingly. It was only too evident they did not like the work before them. By dint of some hard shouting and even pushing they were most of them got over the ridge, where they lay down, some distance behind Hamilton and his thin line of Highlanders, who, although opposed to about five hundred men at 120 yards, never budged an inch.
>
> It seems that the advance of the enemy had been thoroughly checked, when one of our people – an officer, I believe – noticing the Boers for the first time, ejaculated, 'Oh, there they are, quite close,' and the words were hardly out of his lips ere every man of the newly arrived reinforcements bolted back panic-stricken. This was more than flesh and blood could stand, and the skirmishing line under Hamilton gave way also, the retreating troops being exposed, of course, to the Boer fire with disastrous effect.
>
> I was on the left of the ridge when the men came back on us, and was a witness of the wild confusion which then

prevailed. I saw McDonald, of the 92nd, revolver in hand, threaten to shoot any man who passed him; and, indeed, everybody was hard at work rallying the broken troops. Many, of course, got away and disappeared over the side of the hill next to the camp; but some hundred and fifty good men, mostly Highlanders, blue-jackets, and old soldiers of the 58th, remained to man the ridge for a final stand.

Some of the Boers appeared, and the fire that was interchanged was something awful. Three times they showed themselves, and three times they as quickly withdrew, our men, when that occurred, at once stopping their fire. I could hear the soldiers ejaculate, 'We'll not budge from this. We'll give them the bayonet if they come closer,' and so on, but all the time dropping fast, for Boer marksmen had apparently got to work in secure positions, and every shot told, the men falling back hit, mostly through the head.

It was a hot five minutes, but nevertheless I thought at the time we should hold our own. I expected every minute to hear the order given for a bayonet charge. That order unfortunately never came, although I am sure the men would have responded to it. But our flanks were exposed, and the enemy, checked in front, were stealing round them; across the hollow on the side of the hill facing the camp we had no one, and as the men were evidently anxious about that point, frequently looking over their shoulders, Colonel Stewart sent me over to see how matters were going on. There I reported all clear, and, indeed, if the enemy had attempted to storm the hill on that face he would have been decimated by the fire of his own people aimed from the other side.

We were most anxious about our right flank. It was evident that the enemy were stealing round it, so men were taken to prolong the position there. They were chiefly blue-jackets, led by a brave young officer, and, as I watched them follow him up, for the third time that day, the conviction flashed across me that we should lose the hill. There was a knoll on the threatened point, up which the reinforcements hesitated to climb. Some of them went back over the top of the plateau to the further ridge, others went round.

By-and-by there was confusion on the knoll itself. Some

of the men on it stood up, and were at once shot down; and at last the whole of those who were holding it gave way. Helter skelter they were at once followed by the Boers, who were able then to pour a volley into our flank in the main line, from which instant the hill of Majuba was theirs. It was *sauve qui peut*. Major Hay, Captain Singleton, of the 92nd, and some other officers, were the last to leave, and these were immediately shot down and taken prisoners.

The General had turned round the last of all to walk after his retreating troops, when he also was shot dead, through the head. A minute or two previously Lieutenant Hamilton, requesting the General to excuse his presumption, had asked for a charge, as the men would not stand the fire much longer. Sir George Colley replied, 'Wait until they come on, we will give them a volley and then charge,' but before that moment arrived it was too late.

To move over about one hundred yards of ground under the fire of some five hundred rifles at close range is not a pleasant experience, but it is what all who remained of us on the hill that day had to go through. On every side, men were throwing up their arms, and with sharp cries of agony were pitching forward on the ground. At last we went over the side of the hill.

The Boers were instantly on the ridge above, and for about ten minutes kept up their terrible fire on our soldiers, who plunged down every path. Many, exhausted with the night's marching and the day's fighting, unable to go further, lay down behind rocks and bushes, and were afterwards taken prisoners: but of those who remained on the hill to the very last probably not one in six got clear away. The Boers were everywhere assisting our disabled men. Dr Landon, who, when the hill was abandoned by our panic-stricken troops, had steadily remained by his wounded, was lying on the ground with a shot through his chest. The Boers, as they rushed on the plateau, not seeing or not caring for the Geneva Cross, had fired into and knocked over both him and his hospital assistant; so there was only one, Dr Mahon, left to look after a great number of very bad cases.[3]

Colley himself was killed, along with 91 of his men, 134 were wounded and 59 taken prisoner. The Boers were hardly scratched. It was a disaster. On 5 April the Treaty of Pretoria granted independence to the South African Republic, under British suzerainty. Paul Kruger became the Boer president.

Notes

1. Major General Sir George Colley, Governor of Natal, 1880
2. Description of an Afrikaner mounted rifleman by an anonymous British regimental officer
3. John Alexander Cameron, 'The Fight on Majuba Hill', *Illustrated London News*, 24 April 1881

24. War on the Nile
(Egypt and the Sudan 1881–98)

TEL-EL-KEBIR: THE VICTORY IN EGYPT – In all parts of the country the news of the victory in Egypt created great excitement yesterday, information being awaited with anxiety and received with enthusiasm. At Her Majesty's Theatre the playing of 'Rule Britannia' before the commencement of the performance was received by a crowded house on their feet with cheering. At Balmoral, where an arch had been erected by the Tenantry to welcome the Duchess of Albany on her first visit to Deeside, there was immense excitement. Cheer after cheer was raised for Sir Garnet Wolseley and the British Soldiers, and General Ponsonby, who was present on behalf of Her Majesty, expressed the Queen's gratitude for the strong display of loyalty. Bonfires were lit, and the dark hills round Lochnagar and Balmoral presented a weird appearance. The Duke of Albany expressed great gratification at the hearty reception accorded him, and much pleasure at the intelligence from Egypt.[1]

*

NOW MARK THIS, if the Expeditionary force, and I ask for no more than two hundred men, does not come in ten days, the town may fall; and I have done my best for the honour of our country. Good-bye.[2]

No nation was prouder of its military heroes than Victorian Britain, and no military hero was so admired, so loved, as General Gordon. He seemed to embody the very qualities of the Christian hero, the saint in arms, the soldier of Christ and the pious servant of Empire. The political-military escapades in Egypt and the Sudan are inextricably bound up with national memories of Gordon. 'I would sooner live like a Dervish with the Mahdi, than go out to dinner every night in London,' Gordon wrote in his Khartoum journal in 1883. He said that if he had been in command he would never have employed himself, as he was 'incorrigible'. His reading was confined almost exclusively to the Bible, where he believed all truth was to be found. But in the opinion of Sir Evelyn Baring, 'A man who habitually consults the prophet Isiah when he is in difficulty is not apt to obey the orders of anyone.' Controversy still rages about Gordon's last expedition, and his interpretation of his purposes. Shortly before he was killed, he wrote in his journal: 'It is not the fear of death, that is past, thank God, but I fear defeat and its consequences. I do not believe in the calm, unmoved man'. But he told the people of the besieged city of Khartoum: 'When God was portioning out fear to all the people in the world, at last, it came to my turn, and there was no fear left to give me'. He told the authorities that if help did not arrive, the town would fall. His last message to Sir Garnet Wolseley was 'Khartoum is all right. Could hold out for years'. The English speaking world seemed to watch the dreadful events in Khartoum as they unfolded and perceived them as the battle between Good and Evil.

*   *   *

For years it had been British policy to avoid entangling itself with Egypt. In 1857 Lord Palmerston had stated the British position:

> While it is very possible that many parts of the world would be better governed by France, England, and Sardinia than they are now . . . we do not want to have Egypt. . . . We want to trade with Egypt and to travel through Egypt, but we do not want the burden of governing Egypt.

But gradually Britain was to find itself drawn willy-nilly into Egyptian affairs. Nominally, Egypt was part of the Ottoman Empire. During the latter part of the 19th Century, attempts were made to modernise the country. A railway was built from Alexandria to Cairo and in 1856 Ferdinand de Lesseps obtained the concession to construct the Suez Canal. The British got the right to start the Telegraph Company and the Bank of Egypt. These modernising measures were encouraged during the reign of Khedive Ismail, 1863–79, but his extravagance brought the nation to the verge of bankruptcy. A controlling proportion of the Suez Canal shares was bought by Disraeli for the British government with money he raised from the French bankers, Rothschild. Thus British and French interests were strongly focused in Egypt.

The Sultan then deposed Ismail and replaced him with Tewfik, his son. The British now began seriously to contemplate the need to have some control over the area. Lord Salisbury, Secretary for Foreign Affairs, commented: 'The geographical situation of Egypt, as well as the responsibility which the English Government have in past times incurred for the actual conditions under which it exists as a state, make it impossible to leave it to its fate. They are bound, both by duty and interest, to do all that lies in their power to arrest misgovernment before it results in the material ruin and almost incurable disorder to which it is evident by other oriental examples that such misgovernment will necessarily lead'. In 1879, the British and French secured dual control of Egypt.

Feelings were raised against Turkish, British and French interference in Egypt's affairs. A revolt was concocted among the Arab troops, led by Ahmed Arabi. There was a massacre of 'foreigners' in Alexandria on 11 June, 1882. British and French naval squadrons arrived at Alexandria and on 11 July the British bombarded the port (the French declined to assist Admiral Sir Frederick Beauchamp Paget Seymour) and 25,000 British troops were landed under Sir Garnet Wolseley. The revolt was ended by the Egyptian defeat at Tel-el-Kebir on 13 September, 1882. After a night march across the desert, Wolseley's troops attacked Arabi's entrenchments, defended by 38,000 men with 60 guns. Arabi lost 2,000 killed and 500 wounded. British losses were 58 killed, 379 wounded and 22 missing. The British now controlled Egypt.

However, their troubles were not at an end. In the Sudan, a religious rebellion broke out led by Mohammed Achmet, who called himself the Mahdi, as foretold by Mohammed. He asserted he had a divine mission to reform Islam, to establish a universal equality, a universal law, a universal religion and a community of goods. All who did not believe in him should be destroyed, be they Christian, Mohammedan or Pagan. He called upon Mohammed Saleh, a learned fakir of Dongola, directing him to collect his Dervishes (followers) and friends to join him. But Mohammed Saleh, considering him mad, informed the Government.

Colonel William Hicks ('Hicks Pasha'), in command of an Egyptian army, was sent out with a force of 11,000. He was led by a treacherous guide into a trap at El-Obeid, 225 miles south west of Kartoum. Here, on 3 November, 1883, at the battle of Kashgal, they were massacred to a man by the Mahdi's forces. This comment on the massacre of Hicks' expedition is by Bennet Burleigh, War Correspondent of the *Daily Telegraph*:

I was a fellow-passenger with Colonel Hicks, a retired Indian [Army] officer, who was then going out to take service under the Khedive for the purpose of fighting the Mahdi. The acquaintanceship I formed at that time with him led me to conclude that no more gallant soldier or energetic officer could have been selected to send against the fanatics led by the False Prophet. He certainly did not underrate his enemy, nor the work before him; and it must have been because of some exceptional wrench of circumstances that any command under his leadership was forced to accept destruction at the hands of an uncivilised foe.

I knew several members of Hicks Pasha's Staff, and a more efficient body of officers never accompanied any Egyptian force afield. What the real cause was of the fate that befell Hicks Pasha's army near El Obeid, we shall possibly never know. Perhaps it was due to the one fatal defect that pertains to all Egyptian troops composed of fellaheen – want of courage, or martial ardour. There is no disguising the fact, that as a soldier the Egyptian fellah is worthless. He cowers at alarms, and shrinks from a contest involving physical suffering to himself. For any practical purpose an Egyptian army is useless, and their maintenance is but a waste of money. No amount of personal example and European officering will prevail upon them to offer stubborn and desperate battle even in a situation where their lives are the forfeit.[3]

* * *

Osman Dinga, the Mahdi's lieutenant, defeated another Anglo-Egyptian force at El Teb near Suakin on 4 February 1884. This led Gladstone's government to evacuate the Sudan. General Gordon, who was preparing for service to King Leopold of Belgium in the Congo, was picked as the ideal commander to supervise the British withdrawal:

It will come as a welcome surprise to the country to learn that General Gordon started last night, not for the Congo, but for Egypt. Hastily summoned from Brussels by the Government, he reached London yesterday, was received by Lord Hartington and other members of the Cabinet in the afternoon at the War Office, and was there and then intrusted with a special mission, and left England at night by the mail for Brindisi. . . . His appointment will be received by the country with a certain sense of relief, as showing that the Government has been willing to seek the best advice and to select the mos competent agent for the development of its policy in the Sudan.[4]

Gordon's instructions from the government seem quite unambiguous:

Her Majesty's Government are desirous that you should proceed at once to Egypt, to report to them on the military situation in the Soudan, and on the measures it may be advisable to take for that country, and for the safety of the European population of Khartoum. You are also desired to consider and report on the best mode of effecting the evacuation of the interior of the Soudan.

However, the surviving evidence suggests that Gordon resolved quite early during this mission that he would attempt to establish a settled government in the area, with a Governor-General appointed by the British. This was hardly surprising as Gordon had put forward Rahama Zobeir, an Egyptian war-lord and notorious ivory and slave trader, as his successor after the British withdrawal. This proposal was singularly unpopular in Britain. Gordon believed that once evacuation had been achieved, the country would be at the mercy of the Mahdi, it was obviously his opinion that Rahama Zobeir would be the very man to deal ruthlessly with the Mahdi. (His view was shared by Sir Evelyn Baring, Gladstone and Queen Victoria, but they feared British public opinion). Gordon wrote to the British Consul-General in Egypt, Sir Evelyn Baring:

> Of course my duty is evacuation . . . but if Egypt is to be quiet, the Mahdi must be smashed up. The Mahdi is most unpopular, and with care and time could be smashed. Remember that, once Khartoum belongs to the Mahdi, the task will be far more difficult. . . . If you decide on smashing the Mahdi, then send up another £100,000 and send up 200 Indian troops to Wadi Halfa. . . . Leave Suakim [Suakin] and Massawa alone. I repeat that evacuation is possible, but you will feel the effect in Egypt and will be forced to enter into a far more serious affair in order to guard Egypt. At present it would be comparatively easy to destroy the Mahdi. . . .

The situation was difficult to control partly because communication between Gordon and his superiors was of necessity so slow but was certainly not helped by Gordon's own peculiar temperament. Although an admired and experienced commander and administrator with a curious saintly reputation, he was acknowledged as an eccentric visionary who frequently changed his opinion and tended to act unilaterally.

The situation deteriorated dramatically. Gordon was convinced that with the refusal of his proposal that Rahama Zobeir should take over, all hope of an orderly and peaceful retreat of the Egyptian garrisons had evaporated. Various tribes began to desert to the Mahdi. The Mahdi's rebel forces advanced on Khartoum. There was a revolt in eastern Sudan. Egyptian troops in Suakin were defeated. Gordon requested that the road between Suakin and Berber be kept open. The necessary forces were denied him. British troops were withdrawn from Suakin, and Berber surrendered. Khartoum was now wholly isolated. Gordon had only one British officer to support him, the town was badly fortified and there was a food shortage. Khartoum was besieged early in March, 1884. British public opinion clamoured for Gordon's rescue, but it was not until November that the relief expedition under Sir Garnet Wolseley was ready to depart from Wadi Halfa. Khartoum had held out for nearly a year, but on 26 January, 1885, the Mahdi's forces breached the city and the entire population was butchered. Wolseley's relief force arrived two days later. Wolseley was shattered by the death of a professional colleague he so greatly admired. He wrote to Gordon's brother:

> I have postponed writing to you from week to week, hoping I might have, if not good news, at least some definite information to give you about your heroic brother. By and by we shall be able to ascertain more particulars about his death, for dead there can be little doubt that he is. Had Mohammed Ahmed caught him alive he would, I think, have kept him a prisoner for his own political purposes, but he was killed before that fellow could catch him. Besides, I don't think he would ever have allowed himself to be taken alive. . . . I have read through the six volumes of his journal which came into my hands, and it was indeed sad reading for me to think that, if Mr Gladstone had sent us out a month, aye, a week earlier, your brother would now in all probability be alive and well . . . picture to yourself our horror when Wilson returned with the news that Khartoum had been taken and your brother killed. Sorrow and rage was in every man's heart; sorrow for the gallant soul who had striven with might and main to save the place, and rage with the Minister whose folly had prevented the effort to reach Khartoum from being undertaken earlier. Well, he is gone from amongst us, and I shall never know his like again; and, indeed, many generations may come and go without producing a Charlie Gordon. His example will be one that every father will hold up to their sons in England, and as long as any faith in God remains to us as a nation, and that we continue to be manly enough to revere the

highest form of courage and devotion to duty, so long will your brother be quoted and referred to as the luminous embodiment of all manly and Christian virtue.

*   *   *

The Mahdi died on 21 June, 1885, but the conquest of the Sudan by the dervishes was completed by his successor, Kalifa Abdulla. The 'Scramble for Africa' was now at its height. During the following decade, the British government watched with some anxiety the increasing French and Italian influence in the Nile Valley. The British then decided to reoccupy the Sudan in 1896.

The campaign was commanded by General Sir Horatio Kitchener, who took a force of British and Egyptian troops on a well planned and logistically well supported expedition up the Nile, supported by a flotilla of gunboats and the construction of a railway from Wadi Halfa to Abu Hamed – and eventually as far as Atbara – a distance of 385 miles. Aby Hamed was captured on 7 August, 1897, Dongola on 21 September and at Atbara on 8 April, 1896, Kitchener's army of 14,000 utterly routed 18,000 Mahdists, killing at least 5,000 in battle and many more in pursuit. Over 1,000 prisoners were taken. Osman Dinga, the Mahdist commander, concentrated his forces at the fortress of Omdurman, northwest of Khartoum.

Kitchener's troops, reinforced with soldiers from Britain, now numbered 25,000. The brigade of artillery was the most formidable Africa had ever seen. Winston Churchill saw service here with the 21st Lancers. Six miles from Omdurman on 2 September, 1898, the British infantry was arranged in a line, one rank kneeling, one standing. They heard the enemy shouting at a distance as 40,000 of them advanced. Then they saw banners. The artillery opened fire, then rifles, then machine guns. Tactics in this battle were minimal and consisted of lines and lines of reckless dervishes hurling themselves against the most ferocious fire power then possible. Kitchener then counterattacked towards Omdurman. The dervishes attacked the British right flank and rear, but were eventually swept from the field by a traditional cavalry charge by the 21st Lancers. Dervish losses totalled 10,000 killed, 20,000 wounded and 5,000 prisoners. Kitchener's losses were 500 in all.

This account of Omdurman is from Winston Churchill's dispatch, dated 6 September, 1898, to the *Morning Post* which he later used as the basis for his book, *The River War* (1899).

The bugles all over the camp by the river began to sound at half-past four. The cavalry trumpets and the drums and fifes of the British division joined the chorus, and everyone awoke amid a confusion of merry or defiant notes. The moon was full, and by its light and that of lanterns we dressed ourselves – many with special care. Those who were callous, who had seen much war, or who were practical, set themselves to deliberately eat a substantial meal of such delicacies as 'porrig', 'sausig', ration biscuits, and 'bully' beef. Then it grew gradually lighter, and the cavalry mounted their horses, the infantry stood to arms, and the gunners went to their batteries, while the sun rising over the Nile displayed the wide plain, the dark rocky hills, and the waiting army. It was as if all the preliminaries were settled, the arena cleared, and nothing remained but the final act and the rigour of the game.

As soon as it was light enough to move, several squadrons of British and Egyptian cavalry were pushed swiftly forward to feign contact with the enemy and to learn his intentions. It was my fortune to be sent with an advanced patrol of the 21st Lancers.

At half-past five the British and Egyptian army was drawn up in line, with its back to the river. Its flanks were secured by the gunboats, which were moored in the stream. Before it was the rolling sandy plain. To the right were the rocky hills of the Kerreri portion, near which the nine squadrons of Egyptian cavalry were massed. On the left the 21st Lancers were trotting towards Heliograph Hill, with their advanced patrols already cantering up its lower slopes. My patrol was, I think, the first to reach the top of the ridge and to look into the plain beyond. I had expected that the Dervish army would have retired to their original position, and could not believe that they would advance to the attack in daylight across open ground. Indeed, it seemed more probable that their hearts might have failed them in the night and that they had melted away into the deserts of Kordofan. But these anticipations were immediately dispelled by the scene which was visible from the crest of the ridge.

It was a quarter to six. The light was dim, but growing stronger every minute. There in the plain lay the enemy, their numbers unaltered, their confidence and intentions apparently unshaken. Their front was nearly five miles long, and composed of great masses of men joined together by thinner lines. Behind and to the flanks were large reserves. They looked from where I stood dark blurs and streaks, relieved and diversified with odd-looking gleams of light from the spear points. After making the necessary reports I continued to watch the strange and impressive spectacle. As it became broad daylight, that is to say about ten minutes to six, I suddenly realised that all the masses were in motion and advancing swiftly. Their Emirs galloped about, among and before their ranks scouts and patrols began to scatter themselves all over the front. Then they began to cheer. They were still a mile away from the hill when a tremendous roar came up in waves of intense sound, like the tumult of the rising wind and sea before a storm.

The advance continued. The Dervish left began to stretch out across the Kerreri Plain – as I thought to turn to our right flank. Their centre, over which the black flag of the Khalifa floated high and remarkable, moved directly towards the hill. Their right pursued a line of advance south of Heliograph Hill, and would, I saw, pass over the ground on which I stood. This mass of men was the most striking of all. They could not have mustered less than seven thousand. Their array was perfect. They displayed a great number of flags – perhaps five hundred – which looked at the distance white, though they were really covered with texts from the Koran, which by their admirable alignment made the divisions of the Khalifa's army look like the old representations of the Crusaders in the Bayeux Tapestry. I called them at the moment 'the white flagmen' to distinguish them from the other masses, and that name will do as well as any other.

The attack developed. The left, under a famous Emir, appeared to have mistaken the squadrons of the Egyptian Cavalry for our main position. Ten thousand strong they toiled right up to the Kerreri hills, and did not come into action until later in the day. The centre deployed across the plain and marched straight towards the zareba.[5]

The Dervish advance could not get close to the lines of infantry which poured forth fire, supported by the machine guns and artillery. But the lines of charging tribesmen were propelled by their own impetus directly into the onslaught. The ground in front of the infantry became white with dead men's drapery. The rifles became red-hot. Soldiers seized them by the slings and dragged them back to the reserve to have them changed for cool weapons. This was not a battle. It was an execution. After an hour, the Dervishes withdrew, leaving 2,000 dead and numerous wounded. It was then that Kitchener decided to drive the enemy before him into Omdurman. Churchill continues:

The second phase of the action, or, as an excitable correspondent called it, 'the second battle,' now began. Disregarding the presence of the Dervish left on and among the Kerreri Hills, the Sirdar gave the order for the army to march on towards Omdurman. The 21st Lancers moved out of the zareba and trotted over the ridge near Heliograph Hill. The whole of the British division made a left wheel, and faced south, their left on the river at right angles to the enemy's centre, and to their former front. The Egyptian and Sudanese divisions were echeloned on the right by brigades. Thus the army presented its flank to the Dervish centre, and its right rear to the Dervish left. Probably Sir Herbert Kitchener was anxious above all things to gain a moral advantage, and realised that if he could enter Omdurman the resistance of the enemy would collapse. Events, however, proved the movement to be premature. The Dervish left, who had started out in the morning confident of victory, and who had vainly toiled after the elusive cavalry and Camel Corps among the Kerreri Hills, now returned an exasperated but undefeated ten thousand. Infusing into the centre the encouragement of a reinforcement, they fell on

General MacDonald's Sudanese Brigade, which was the rearmost of the echelon. That officer, who by personal prowess and military conduct has passed from the rank of private to that of general, faced about, and met the attack with a skill and determination which excited the admiration of all. General Lewis, with the Egyptian Brigade, also swung round, and thus the army assumed an A-shaped formation, the apex pointing west and away from the Nile, four brigades looking north-west towards the Dervish attack.

This was the critical moment of the engagement. The Sirdar, not the least disconcerted by the discovery of his mistake, immediately proceeded to rectify it. The movement of bringing up the right shoulders of the army ceased. Pivoting on the two brigades who were now hotly engaged, the British division and the whole south front of the A swung round until it became a straight line facing nearly west. Advancing in that direction the army steadily drove the Dervishes before them, away from the river, and as the left began to come up more and more threatened to cut their line of retreat.

Of all this I had but fleeting glances, for an event was taking place on the southern slopes of Heliograph Hill which absorbed my whole attention, and may perhaps invite yours. I will describe it at length and in detail, because I write as an eye witness, perhaps even as more, and you may read with interest. Everyone describes an action from his own point of view. Indeed, it is thence that we look at most things, human or divine. Why should I be or make an exception?

At about a quarter past eight the 21st Lancers moved out of the zareba, and occupied a position on the ridge of Heliograph Hill, whence a view of the ground right up to the walls of Omdurman was obtainable. Here we waited, dismounting a few troops to fire at the Dervish skirmishers on the higher slopes. At 8.40 orders reached us to advance, harass the enemy's right, and endeavour to cut him off from Omdurman. In pursuance of these orders Colonel Martin advanced his regiment in line of squadron columns slowly down the southern slopes of the ridge and hill, and continued across the plain in a south-westerly direction. In the distance large numbers of the enemy could be seen retreating into Omdurman. The whole plain was crossed by a continual stream of fugitives.

In the foreground about two hundred Dervishes were crouching in what appeared to be a small khor or crease in the plain. The duty of the cavalry to brush these away and proceed at once to the more numerous bodies in rear was plain. With a view to outflanking them the squadrons wheeled to the left into columns of troops, and, breaking into a trot, began to defile across their front. We thought them spearmen, for we were within three hundred yards and they had fired no shot. Suddenly, as the regiment began to trot, they opened a heavy, severe, and dangerous fire. Only one course was now possible. The trumpets sounded 'right-wheel into line,' and on the instant the regiment began to gallop in excellent order towards the riflemen. The distance was short, but before it was half covered it was evident that the riflemen were but a trifle compared to what lay behind. In a deep fold of the ground – completely concealed by its peculiar formation – a long, dense, white mass of men became visible. In length they were nearly equal to our front. They were about twelve deep. It was undoubtedly a complete surprise for us. What followed probably astonished them as much. I do not myself believe that they ever expected the cavalry to come on. The Lancers acknowledged the unexpected sight only by an increase of pace. A desire to have the necessary momentum to drive through so solid a line animated each man. But the whole affair was a matter of seconds.

At full gallop and in the closest order the squadron struck the Dervish mass. The riflemen, who fired bravely to the last, were brushed head over heel in the khor. And with them the Lancers jumped actually on to the spears of the enemy, whose heads were scarcely level with the horses' knees.

It is very rarely that stubborn and unshaken infantry meet equally stubborn and unshaken cavalry. Usually, either the infantry run away and are cut down in flight, or they keep their heads and destroy nearly all the horsemen by their musketry. In this case the two living walls crashed together with a mighty collision. The Dervishes stood their ground manfully. They tried to hamstring the horses. They fired their rifles, pressing their muzzles into the very bodies of their opponents. They cut bridle-reins and stirrup-leathers. They would not budge till they were knocked over. They stabbed and hacked with savage pertinacity. In fact, they tried every device of cool determined men practised in war and familiar in cavalry. Many horses pecked on landing and stumbled in the press, and the man that fell was pounced on by a dozen merciless foes.

The regiment broke completely through the line everywhere, leaving sixty Dervishes dead and many wounded in their track. A hundred and fifty yards away they halted, rallied, and in less than five minutes were reformed and ready for a second charge. The men were anxious to cut their way back through their enemies. But some realisation of the cost of that wild ride began to come to all of us. Riderless horses galloped across the plain. Men, clinging on to their saddles, lurched hopelessly about, covered with blood from perhaps a dozen wounds. Horses streaming from tremendous gashes limped and staggered with their riders. In one hundred and twenty seconds five officers, sixty-six men, and one hundred and nineteen horses out of less than three hundred had been killed or wounded.

The Dervish line, broken and shattered by the charge, began to reform at once. They closed up, shook themselves together, and prepared with constancy and courage for another shock. The 21st, now again drawn up in line of squadron columns, wheeled and, galloping round the Dervish flank, dismounted and opened a heavy fire with their magazine carbines. Under the pressure of this fire the enemy changed front to meet the new attack, so that both sides were formed at right angles to their original lines. When the Dervish change of front was completed they began to advance against the dismounted men. But the fire was accurate, and there can be little doubt that the moral effect of the charge had been very great, and that these brave enemy were no longer unshaken. Be this as it may, the fact remains that they retreated swiftly, though in good order, towards the ridge of Heliograph Hill, where the Khalifa's black flag still waved, and the 21st Lancers remained in possession of the ground – and of their dead.

I have told you the story of the charge, but you will perhaps care to hear a few incidents. Colonel Martin, busy with the direction of his regiment, drew neither sword nor revolver, and rode through the press unarmed and uninjured. Major Crole Wyndham had his horse shot from under him by a Dervish who pressed his muzzle into the very hide. From out of the middle of that savage crowd the officer fought his way on foot and escaped in safety. Lieutenant Wormald, of the 7th Hussars, thrust at a man with his sword, and that weapon, by a well-known London maker, bent double and remained thus.

I myself saw Sergeant Freeman trying to collect his troops after the charge. His face was cut to pieces, and as he called on his men to rally, the whole of his nose, cheeks, and lips flapped amid red bubbles. Surely some place may be found in any roll of honour for such a man.

Lieutenant Nesham, of the 21st Lancers, had an even more extraordinary escape. Amid a crowd of men slashing and stabbing he remained in his saddle throughout. He left hand was nearly severed from his body by a single stroke. He managed to twist the reins round his right wrist. The near bridle rein and the off stirrup-leather were both cut. The wounded officer reeled. His enemies closed around him. He received another deep cut in his right leg and a slighter one in his right arm. Yet his horse, pressing forward, carried him through the Dervishes to fall fainting among the rallying Squadrons.

I have written thus of others. You would ask me of my own experiences. You know my luck in these things. As on another occasion in the Indian Frontier, I came safe through – one of the very few officers whose saddlery, clothes, or horse were untouched, and without any incident that is worth while putting down here.

One impression only I will record. I remember no sound. The whole event seemed to pass in absolute silence. The yells of the enemy, the shouts of the soldiers, the firing of many shots, the clashing of sword and spear were unnoticed by the senses, unregistered by the brain. Others say the same. Perhaps it is possible for the whole of a man's faculties to be concentrated in eye, bridle-hand, and trigger-finger, and withdrawn from all other parts of the body.[5]

⁕   ⁕   ⁕

The Dervishes then fled to El Obeid. After fourteen years the bones of General Gordon were given a Christian funeral. This account is by George Warrington Steevens, War Correspondent of the *Daily Mail*:

The troops formed up before the palace in three sides of a rectangle – Egyptians to our left as we looked from the river, British to the right. The Sirdar, the generals of division and brigade, and the staff stood in the open space facing the palace. Then on the roof – almost on the very spot where Gordon fell, though the steps by which the butchers mounted have long since vanished – we were aware of two flagstaves. By the right-hand halliards stood Lieutenant Staveley, RN, and Captain Watson, KRR; by the left hand Bimbashi Mitford and his Excellency's Egyptian ADC.

The Sirdar raised his hand. A pull on the halliards: up ran, out flew, the Union Jack, tugging eagerly at his reins, dazzling gloriously in the sun, rejoicing in his strength and his freedom. 'Bang!' went the 'Melik's' 12½-pounder, and the boat quivered to her backbone. 'God Save our Gracious Queen' hymned the Guards' band – 'bang!' from the 'Melik' – and Sirdar and private stood stiff – 'bang!' – to attention, every hand at the helmet peak in – 'bang!' – salute. The Egyptian flag had gone up at the same instant; and now, the same ear-smashing, soul-uplifting bangs marking time, the band of the 11th Sudanese was playing the Khedivial hymn. 'Three cheers for the Queen!' cried the Sirdar: helmets leaped in the air, and the melancholy ruins woke to the first wholesome shout of all these years. Then the same for the Khedive. The comrade flags stretched themselves lustily, enjoying their own again; the bands pealed forth the pride of country; the twenty-one guns banged forth the strength of war. Thus, white men and black, Christian and Moslem, Anglo-Egypt set her seal once more, for ever, on Khartum [Khartoum].

Before we had time to think such thoughts over to ourselves, the Guards were playing the Dead March in 'Saul.' Then the black band was playing the march from Handel's 'Scipio,' which in England generally goes with 'Toll for the Brave'; this was in memory of those loyal men among the Khedive's subjects who could have saved themselves by treachery, but preferred to die with Gordon. Next fell a deeper hush than ever, except for the solemn minute guns that had followed the fierce salute. Four chaplains – Catholic, Anglican, Presbyterian, and Methodist – came slowly forward and ranged themselves, with their backs to the palace, just before the Sirdar. The Presbyterian read the Fifteenth Psalm. The Anglican led the rustling whisper of the Lord's Prayer. Snow-haired Father Brindle, best beloved of priests, laid his helmet at his feet, and read a memorial prayer bareheaded in the sun. Then came forward the pipers and wailed a dirge, and the Sudanese played 'Abide with me.' Perhaps lips did twitch just a little to see the ebony heathens fervently blowing out Gordon's favourite hymn; but the most irrestible incongruity would hardly have made us laugh at that moment. And there were those who said the cold Sirdar himself could hardly speak or see, as General Hunter and the rest stepped out according to their rank and shook his hand. What wonder? He has trodden this road to Khartum for fourteen years, and he stood at the goal at last.

Thus with Maxim-Nordenfeldt and Bible we buried Gordon after the manner of his race. The parade was over, the troops were dismissed, and for a short space we walked in Gordon's garden. Gordon has become a legend with his countrymen, and they all but deify him dead who would never have heard of him had he lived. But in this garden you somehow came to know Gordon the man, not the myth, and to feel near to him. Here was an Englishman doing his duty, alone and at the instant peril of his life; yet still he loved his garden. The garden was a yet more pathetic ruin than the palace. The palace accepted its doom mutely; the garden strove against it. Untrimmed, unwatered, the oranges and citrons still struggled to bear their little, hard, green knobs, as if they had been full ripe fruit. The pomegranates put out their vermilion star-flowers, but the fruit was small and woody and juiceless. The figs bore better, but they, too, were small and without vigour. Rankly overgrown with dhurra, a vine still trailed over a low roof its pale leaves and limp tendrils, but yielded not a sign of grapes. It was all green, and so far vivid and refreshing after Omdurman. But it was the green of nature, not of cultivation: leaves grew large and fruit grew small, and dwindled away. Reluctantly, despairingly, Gordon's garden was dropping back to wilderness. And in the middle of the defeated fruit-trees grew rankly the hateful Sodom apple, the poisonous herald of desolation.

The bugle broke in upon us; we went back to the boats. We were quicker steaming back than steaming up. We were not a whit less chastened, but every man felt lighter. We came with a sigh of shame: we went away with a sigh of relief. The long-delayed duty was done. The bones of our countrymen were shattered and scattered abroad, and no man knows their place; none the less Gordon had his due burial at last. So we steamed away to the roaring camp and left him alone again. Yet not one nor two looked back at the mouldering palace and the tangled garden with a new and a great contentment. We left Gordon alone again – but alone in majesty under the conquering ensign of his own people.[6]

* * *

Kitchener was elevated to the peerage and awarded £30,000 by a grateful nation. The Mahdi's tomb was blown up and his bones tossed into the Nile. The whole campaign cost a mere £2,500,000. Sir Garnet Wolseley recorded in his diary:

'God be praised. We can once more hold up our heads in the Soudan . . .'

On receiving the news Queen Victoria wrote in her journal: 'Surely, he is now avenged'.

Notes

1. *Daily News*, 14 September, 1882
2. Charles George Gordon, *Journal*, Khartoum, 14 December, 1884
3. Bennet Burleigh, *Desert Warfare: Being the Chronicle of the Eastern Soudan Campaign* (1884)
4. *The Times*, 19 January, 1884
5. Winston S. Churchill, *The River War* (1899)
6. G.W. Steevens, *With Kitchener to Khartum* (1898)

25. The Death of a Noble King (The Matabele War 1893)

You have said that it is me that is killing you: now here are your masters coming. . . . You will have to pull and shove wagons; but under me you never did this kind of thing. . . . Now you be joyful because here are your future rulers . . . the white people are coming now. I didn't want to fight with them . . .[1]

٭

We have already seen how the discovery of gold and diamonds led to unrest in the eastern provinces of South Africa and ultimately to war between the Afrikaner Boers and the British. It also brought a flood of fortune hunters – known to the Boers as *Uitlanders* – who began to compete with the Boers for control of the Transvaal. International interest too was stirred and the Germans, who were already taking an active interest in South West Africa now came to regard all land north of the borders of the British Protectorate of Bechuanaland as a likely area of expansion for their activities, perhaps even spreading their influence right through to the East African coast.

The British had established their Protectorate in Bechuanaland in 1885, ostensibly to protect the so-called 'Missionary Route' to the interior. Sensing the Germans' growing interest in expansion, they proclaimed Matabeleland – the land of King Lobengula – as a British sphere of interest in 1888.

One year later, Cecil Rhodes, a former diamond digger from Kimberley, who had become a very powerful political figure in South Africa, formed the British South Africa Company under royal charter to take over various mining concessions from Lobengula, for he saw the acquisition of Matabeleland to be not only essential for his company but as a positive, patriotic duty. Knowing that the Boers, too, had an eye on Matabeleland, Rhodes recognised the need for prompt action. In the following year, he became Prime Minister of Cape Colony and at once established a policy of British domination of what he saw to be potentially one of the richest areas of the world. Thus he planned to keep the Boers firmly in check. Realising this, the Boers developed a deep distrust of the British and suspicion of any move that looked like a British attempt to establish further control.

* * *

Rhodes had learned a great deal about the Matabele people. They were called 'matabele', which means vanishing or invisible people, because of their appearance in battle behind an enormous oxhide shield. They were of Zulu origin, having been driven northwards out of the Transvaal by the Boers in the late 1830's. They survived as herdsmen and had incorporated many of the Mashona tribe whom they had conquered. Rhodes realized their territory was potentially rich in gold and diamonds and had negotiated certain digging rights in Matabeleland as early as 1888 with the Matabele King. Thus his action in forming the British South African Company had been a logical development of those negotiations. In 1890 a pioneer expedition was sent up to take possession of these rights in Mashonaland, an area east of Matabeleland but under King Lobengula's control. The first settlement was established and named Salisbury.

The series of events which led up to the Matabele War reflect little credit on Rhodes and his colleagues and supporters, or on the British Government. It is obvious that Lobengula did not fully understand the subtleties of English law which while observing his 'sovereignty' over his kingdom, granted 'rights' and 'concessions' to the minerals found in his land. The British, for their part, did not make much effort to understand Matabele and Mashona culture, customs, laws and agreements.

Nevertheless, the story is plain enough. Rhodes knew the Germans continued to be interested in African colonial expansion, particularly a German belt from South-West Africa to Tanganyika. It was his ambition to make sure that the Germans did not expand into Matabeleland. Rhodes further knew that the Boers still harboured designs on the Transvaal, and claimed that a concession to parts of Mashonaland had been granted to a Boer named Adendorff by a native chief. But on the face of it Rhodes' intentions were compromised by his knowledge that neither the South Africa Company nor the British Government had sovereign rights over Lobengula's territories, they were no more than tenants of the mineral rights. Lobengula had been extremely amenable, in fact, and had given a promise that he would not cede any part of his kingdom without the sanction of the British Government. Tension began between Lobengula and the British South Africa Company, possibly deliberately fanned by Rhodes' seeking an excuse to 'deal with' the Matabeles once and for all. The Matabeles were a warrior nation, and it was difficult for Europeans to turn them into wage slaves. The Mashona tribe, on the other hand, were quite happy to be employed by the Company.

The Company recognised Lobengula as ruler of the Matabele, together with other tributary tribes including the Mashona. The Company's officials provoked Lobengula, firstly by denying his right to levy tribute from these tribes. Secondly, they sought to subject the Mashonas to the Company's authority, if necessary by force. Understandably, the Matabele King saw this as insupportable interference with his rightful authority. This, in spite of the fact that, since 1888, both the Company and the British government had recognised the King of Matabeleland as 'Ruler of the tribe known as the Amandabele (Matabele) together with the Mashona and Makalaka, tributaries of the same. . . .' What Rhodes was trying to engineer was a situation which would provide a pretext to enter Matabeleland 'to restore order' – but, in effect, to seize it.

The tribute claimed and unpaid was made the excuse for the Company's agents to raid native kraals. When native chiefs attempted to intervene, they were arrested. Early in 1892, a local chief was slain and his dwelling set in flames. Lobengula protested. In a further incident over twenty natives and a chief were machine gunned to death. Several hundred yards of the Company's telephone wires were cut by Mashona tribesmen. The Company demanded that either a severe fine be paid, or the guilty snippers be handed over for punishment. The chief decided to pay the fine – in cattle as requested. But in Lobengula's view, the cattle actually belonged to the King of the Matabele. After assuring the white authorities he meant no harm to white men, Lobengula sent a party of warriors to sort out his erring Mashona. A Company force escalated the situation beyond redemption. The Matabele warriors were ordered off and in fact were leaving when they were fired on. Thirty two of them were killed.

Even now, Lobengula remained patient. He wrote to the authorities in Cape Town, begging them to understand that he wanted no trouble, but complaining of the behaviour of the Company's troops. But the decision had now been taken to deal with Lobengula. The timing was excellent, as a large part of the King's forces were in action sorting out tribal problems in neighbouring Barotseland.

Seven hundred Company troops were ordered to march on Bulawayo. Each of them was promised 6,000 acres of land and twenty gold claims in Matabeleland. These troops were supported by nine hundred Mashona tribesmen. The settlers of Salisbury and Victoria gave this expedition of bandits the appearance of acting in the general good by voting to put an end to the 'Matabele threat'. The *casus belli* was a strongly worded note to the King demanding reparations which it was known Lobengula would never grant. As the Company's troops moved into Matabeleland they were fired on. This served to increase their determination to deal with Lobengula once and for all. Rhodes declared that the Company's forces were being deployed to 'eliminate ruthless barbarism in South Africa'. To make sure of their victory, they were assisted by the entry into Matabeleland of four hundred Bechuanaland Border Police and one thousand eight hundred armed native troops.

The column of wagons was drawn by oxen. If attacked they were prepared to form the wagons into a square to form a laager from which cover they could unleash rifle and machine-gun fire on attacking natives. Lobengula's warriors were equipped with a few rifles but they were not fully trained or experienced riflemen. Many of them had muzzle-loading weapons and the rest simply fought with spears and shields. Europeans armed with automatic weapons could inflict the most fearsome casualties on such warriors in a matter of minutes. And so it proved. By 24 October 1893 the expedition was camped a mile from the Shangani river. There Lobengula's army of about 6,000 attacked them in the early morning before break of day:

> At about half-past two in the morning, a shot and wild yell from the camp of the 'friendlies' roused the whole force. Then came several scattering shots followed by the terrific war cry of the Matabele as they rushed our laager, and the battle of the Shangani began. This was one of the most spectacular night fights I have ever taken part in; what with the double line of fire from the men laying on top of the large African trek-wagons and those crouching under the wheels, the roar of the Maxims, and the continuous crack of several hostile rifles that rimmed our entire laager. Over and above all the din of the firing rose the shrieks and yells of the friendly natives as they were stabbed and slaughtered by the onrushing Matabele. It was on this occasion that some of the unfortunate friendlies got mixed up with the enemy and were swept against our laager willy-nilly, to be shot down by our own Maxim guns. The firing continued until the light of day brought deadly accuracy to our rifles and enabled us to open the laager and with our mounted men sweep the grass and timber free of the enemy in the direction of Bulawayo.[2]

The Matabele withdrew leaving five hundred killed or wounded. They were so unused to fighting modern armies that whenever a shell burst near them they would fire their weapons into the explosion, because they believed a shell was full of little white men who would run out after the explosion and kill them all. The armies continued their advance to Bulawayo, harassed at all times by the natives. On 1 November, close to the Imbembesi river, the Matabele attacked again, but were driven off in a battle lasting less than three quarters of an hour, suffering considerable losses. Bulawayo was entered and burned. King Lobengula fled into the bush. Efforts were made to capture him and he, for his part, tried to buy off his pursuers. He sent a bag of 1,000 sovereigns and a message: 'Take this and go back. I am conquered'. But the search continued. Early in December, a patrol came across the King's wagons by the Shangani river. But the patrol of thirty four men were attacked by Matabele warriors and hacked to death. This comment by Major PW Forbes of the Matabele expedition has been preserved:

> My sincere sorrow at the loss of gallant Major Wilson and his brave band . . . the story of how these thirty-four . . . stood and fell, shoulder to shoulder, rather than desert two of their number who could not escape with them, will not only remain for ever in our history, but will be handed down through generations of the native tribes of Africa as an instance of how Englishmen can and will die, and the effect of their heroism on the natives, who above all else honour personal bravery, cannot be over estimated. . . .[3]

Taking the remnants of his army with him, Lobengula fled to the north. Gradually his supporters surrendered to the European armies. Feeling that all was truly lost, he resolved to take his own life. He sent one last message to his peoples:

> You have said that it is me that is killing you: now here are your masters coming. . . . You will have to pull and shove wagons; but under me you never did this kind of thing. . . . Now you be joyful because here are your future rulers . . . the white people are coming now. I didn't want to fight with them. . . .

He poisoned himself and died in the company of his chief counsellor. He was buried wrapped in the skin of a black ox, sitting in a cave, with his counsellor at his feet. Rhodes' victory had not been expensive – about fifty white lives and fifty thousand pounds. The South Africa Company was saved from economic ruin. The new country would be named after Rhodes. But the conquerors made the mistake of believing their troubles with the Matabele were over:

Almost every page of South African history is stained with the blood shed in a long series of wars undertaken to establish the supremacy of the white races, and – it sounds paradoxical, but is none the less true – to secure that 'Pax Britannica', which is our true tradition. It is therefore no small thing to say that it seems quite possible that the war lately concluded has finally removed the need for another. The Matabele nation constituted the last unbroken military power which menaced the general peace of South Africa; and, as we have already found before in that country, so it proved to be now, a trial of strength was inevitable. Apart altogether from Matabeleland, the moral effect of the object lesson among the other native races had been striking. . . .[4]

The peace would not endure.

Notes

1. Lobengula, King of the Matabele, in his last speech to his people before his suicide, December 1893
2. F.R. Burnham, *Scouting on Two Continents* (1927)
3. W.A. Wills and L.T. Collingridge, *The Downfall of Lobengula* (1894)
4. Wills and Collingridge, *op.cit.*

26. Prempeh Deposed
(The Third Ashanti War 1895–96)

In 1895–96 we waged the third serious Ashanti war within half a century. The cost in blood and treasure, in valuable lives, felt so heavily by the august head of the nation, as well as by the nation at large, and in valued money, should be a very special concern to the representatives of the people. The ultimate unit, the tax-payer – whether at home or colonial – looks for two groups of results as his reward. On the one hand, he hopes to see Christianity and civilization pro tanto *extended; and, on the other, to see some compensating development of industry and trade. Unless he, or 'his servants the Government', secure either or both these results, the question must be plainly asked, has he the right, and is he right, to wage such wars?*[1]

*

King Prempeh of the Ashanti was failing to keep to the provisions of the 1874 treaty and the British were anxious that the Ashanti awkwardness should not handicap the passage of trade through West Africa.

There were two reasons for the punitive expedition against the Ashanti which left the Cape Coast on 27 December 1895 under the command of Colonel Sir Francis Scott. The first was Prempeh's continuing refusal to accept the British Protectorate and the second was the Ashanti practice of raiding neighbouring tribes in order to capture slaves. It was not so much the issue of slavery as the use that the Ashantis made of these unfortunate natives which they caught. Slaves in some parts of the world are a kind of currency. This was not the case here, as gold dust was the medium of exchange. They were not needed for food as the Ashanti diet was mainly vegetables and fruit, which grew naturally and in abundance. They were needed for ritual human sacrifice. Other tribes lived in terror of Prempeh's raids. The British had tried to end these troubles by putting various tribes under their protection but it was finally resolved to put an end to slavery problems at source. Human sacrifice would be forcibly put down by an invasion of the Ashanti kingdom. King Prempeh had refused to deal with the Governor of the Gold Coast, Sir William Edward Maxwell, and sent informal agents to England, with whom the British Government declined to negotiate. Invasion and the subsequent appointment of a British Resident at Kumassi was seen as the only answer. This is how the situation was described in the House of Commons by Joseph Chamberlain, Secretary for the Colonies:

> The king said he had sent his messengers to see the Queen of England and make known his wishes. Lord Ripon sent word to the Governor of the Gold Coast to tell the messengers if they came to England that they would not be received by the Queen or her representatives. He actually forbade their coming to England, although he did not feel justified in preventing them by force. On what grounds did Lord Ripon take this course? He had many grounds. In the first place, that their character was bad; in the second place, that they were representatives of a king who indulged in human sacrifice, and that the representatives of such a potentate were not to be received by the Queen of England (cries of 'Oh, oh!'); and, in the third place, that in dealing with these subject tribes under the circumstances which I have detailed, it would be absolutely ruinous to the governor on the spot if, at any moment you chose, you could pass him by and claim to be received directly in London. We place a great responsibility upon the heads of the governors whom we send out to those distant places, and who have to act

very often on the spur of the moment; and if we ourselves reduce their authority in the eyes of these subjects, there would be simply no end to the representations with which we should have to deal in this country, and to the tricks by which these savage rulers would escape from their responsibility. When I came to office the matter came before me, having been already decided by my predecessor. I do not want on that account in the slightest degree to lessen my responsibility. If I had occupied office at the time Lord Ripon did, I should have taken exactly the same course. These persons came to England, and I refused to receive them. Representations were made to me on their behalf by a member of this House: and I said I would be most happy to receive him, but I refused to recognise him as their representative. He did not desire to be recognised as their representative, but wished on his own account to place before me some statements which he had heard from them. Their statement was to the effect that they had credentials from the King of Ashanti; that they had plenipotentiary authority from him to deal with me as the representative of the Government; and, finally, that they were prepared to accept the terms which I informed the gentleman who saw me it was our intention to demand. Well, I told them I accepted their assurances for what they were worth (laughter); but that Her Majesty's Government would not on that account countermand the expedition. It is very easy, of course, to say we should have stopped the expedition; that we would have saved the expenditure and attained the same result. That is a hypothetical statement. I confess I have not the remotest belief that we should have attained the same result, or anything like it. And I think I have some reason for saying that when I had to make my decision, of course, I did not know all the facts, but what I did know was that if the expedition was held back, and if, thereafter, these so-called envoys were repudiated by the King of Ashanti, not only would great expenditure have been incurred for no purpose, but we should have to repeat the expedition at a time when, owing to the difficulties of season and climate, the loss of life would have been very much greater. I thought the risk too great. What justification has come to hand of the action which we took in this matter? In the first place, these so-called envoys had absolutely no authority whatever to make the terms to which they gave their signature; their credentials were forged credentials, the seal of the King of Ashanti was manufactured in London after they came here (laughter); they had no power whatever to accept the conditions imposed upon them by Her Majesty's Government; and the only authority they had was authority which they themselves had sought to obtain redress from Her Majesty's Government for the grievances of the Ashanti people. And it is perfectly clear that what I feared would have taken place, and that if they had gone back without an expedition, they would have been repudiated, and properly repudiated, by the Ashanti king. Then it is said, 'Why this display of force?' In order to avoid bloodshed. (Cheers.) It is also said that all this might have been done by a small force, and I believe that is true, but it would not have been done without bloodshed. If we had gone there with a small force, we should have tempted the Ashantis to war. Do not let it be supposed that the Ashanti king had no idea of resistance. You will find that he sent an embassy to Samory, who is a powerful chief, inviting him to join in resisting the British attack; and nothing but the sense of his own impotence prevented a collision which must have resulted in a very considerable amount of bloodshed.

This Ashanti campaign was brilliantly planned and professionally executed. Loss of life was limited and in spite of the climate and terrain, conditions for the European and native troops were congenial. Kumasi was occupied by 17 January, 1896, and on the 20 January Prempeh was compelled, in a curious ceremony, to show submission to the Queen's representative, Governor of the Gold Coast, Sir William Edward Maxwell. The Governor's party sat on a raised platform hastily made for this occasion with stacks of biscuit boxes. Prempeh and the Queen Mother were compelled to demonstrate their submission in the tradition of the Ashantis, namely, bowing to their conqueror and embracing his knees. This humiliating ceremony was enacted and the British would have been satisfied had the required additional tribute in gold dust been forthcoming. Unfortunately only a twentieth part was forthcoming and consequently Prempeh, the Queen Mother and a few chiefs were arrested and imprisoned at Elmina. (They were eventually exiled to the Seychelles). A few leading buildings in Kumasi were burned. Among the few casualties was Prince Henry of Battenberg, who was married to Princess Beatrice, youngest daughter of Queen Victoria. He had volunteered to attend the campaign in the capacity of military secretary to Sir Francis Scott. He caught fever and died at sea. Among the British officers serving in this Ashanti campaign was Robert Baden-Powell, a Major in the 13th Hussars. He was already seasoned by experience in India and Afghanistan, later to achieve fame as the defender of Mafeking. He described the ceremony at Kumasi and the close of the expedition:

... the king was carried forth in his state cradle with a small following, and, escorted by the troops, he proceeded hurriedly to the palaver-ground. The queen-mother, similarly escorted, followed shortly after, as well as all the chiefs. They were then marshalled in a line, with a limited number of attendants each, in front of the Governor, Mr Maxwell, CMG, who was seated on a dais, together with Colonel Sir Francis Scott, KCB, and Colonel Kempster, DSO.

A square of British troops was formed all round, backed by Houssas and the native levy.

Then the doom of the nation was pronounced in a set-scene, and amid dramatic incidents such as could not fail to impress both natives and Europeans alike.

The first of these was that Prempeh should render submission to the Governor, in accordance with the native form and custom signifying abject surrender. This is a ceremony which has only once before been carried out between the Ashantis and a British Governor, namely, Governor Rowe. On that occasion the king deputed officers of his court to perform the actual ceremony; but in this case it was insisted that the king must himself personally carry it out.

Accordingly, with bad enough grace, he walked from his chair, accompanied by the queen-mother, and, bowing before Mr Maxwell, he embraced his knees. It was a little thing, but it was a blow to the Ashanti pride and prestige such as they had never suffered before.

Then came the demand for payment of the indemnity for the war. Due notice had been previously given, and the Ashantis had promised to pay it; but unless the amount, or a fair proportion of it, could now be produced, the king and his chiefs must be taken as guarantee for its payment.

The king could produce about a twentieth part of what had been promised. Accordingly, he was informed that he, together with his mother and chiefs, would now be held as prisoners, and deported to the Gold Coast.

The sentence moved the Ashantis very visibly. Usually it is etiquette with them to receive all news, of whatever description, in the gravest and most unmoved indifference; but here was Prempeh bowing himself to the earth for mercy, as doubtless many and many a victim to his lust for blood had bowed in vain to him, and around him were his ministers on their feet, clamouring for delay and reconsideration of the case. The only 'man' among them was the queen.

In vain. Each chief found two stalwart British non-commissioned officers at his elbow, Prempeh being under charge of Inspector Donovan. Their arrest was complete. . . .

There had been reports of the palace being undermined, and it was natural to expect that if this was so, the main entrance would be the spot selected for the mine, and that at any rate the place where the inmates were collected would be safe. Accordingly, making its way through the deserted garden, this company proceeded to the back entrance, and burst open the door. This opened into a large courtyard. Not a soul to be seen! Everything silent. Two painted doors in a side wall were kicked in by soldiers, and immediately after Tommy Atkins' persuasive voice was sounding, 'Come out of that, you blather-skiting idiot; d'ye think I want to eat you?' and so on, as a frightened flock of natives were dragged out into the daylight. They were placed in the courtyard under sentries, while the remainder of the company proceeded to search every corner of every court and alley of the palace – and these were many – for further occupants. A hundred or two of these were taken, and then the work of collecting valuables and property was proceeded with.

There could be no more interesting, no more tempting work than this. To poke about in a barbarian king's palace, whose wealth has been reported very great, was enough to make it so. Perhaps one of the most striking features about it was that the work of collecting the treasures was entrusted to a company of British soldiers, and that it was done most honestly and well, without a single case of looting. Here was a man with an armful of gold-hilted swords, there one with a box full of gold trinkets and rings, another with a spirit-case full of bottles of brandy, yet in no instance was there any attempt at looting.

It need not be supposed that all the property found in the palace was of great value. There were piles of the tawdriest and commonest stuff mixed indiscriminately with quaint, old, and valuable articles, a few good brass dishes, large metal ewers, Ashanti stools, old arms, etc. But a large amount of valuables known to belong to the king had disappeared, probably weeks previously – such as his celebrated dinner service of Dutch silver, his golden hat, his golden chair of state, and, above all, the royal stool, the emblem *par excellence* of the King of Ashanti.

These were all probably hidden, together with his wives, in various hamlets in the remote bush. The 'loot' which we collected was sold by public auction, excepting golden valuables, which were all sent home to the Secretary of State.

Finding so little of real value in the palace, it was hoped that some treasure might be discovered in the sacred fetish-houses at Bantama, the burial-place of the kings of Ashanti, about a mile out of Bantama. This place had also been piqueted, but all its priests had disappeared previously, and when we broke in, only one harmless old man was found residing there. No valuables – in fact, little of any kind was found in the common huts that form the sacred place. In the big fetish building, with its enormous thatched roof, when burst open, we only found a few brass coffers – all empty! The door, which was newly sealed with mortar, showed no signs of having been quite freshly closed up, and it may therefore be inferred that the treasure had been removed some weeks previously.

Then, in accordance with orders, we set the whole of the

fetish village in flames, and a splendid blaze it made. The great fetish-tree, in whose shade hundreds of victims have been sacrificed, was blown up with gun-cotton, as also were the great fetish-trees on the Kumassi [Kumasi] parade-ground. Among the roots of these there lie the skulls and bones of hundreds, and possibly of thousands, of victims to the *régime* which to-day has so dramatically been brought to a close.[2]

Prempeh's reign of terror was extinguished.

Notes

1. Sir George Smyth Baden-Powell, Conservative MP for Kirkdale (Manchester) 1885–98
2. Robert Stephenson Smyth Baden-Powell, *The Downfall of Prempeh* (1896)

27. And so, Rhodesia . . .
(The Matabele Uprising 1896)

When the British South Africa Company laid armed hands upon the Matabele nation, they merely surprised them into an apparent submission and, believing the effect of the coup d'état *to be final, proceeded to administer the land upon the basis of a white dominant race and a heliot nation of conquered blacks. Was it to be expected that a race like the Matabele, with the warlike instincts of their Zulu forefathers, would, after one taste of defeat, submit to whatever conditions their victors, the white men, might think fit to impose? It says much for their cunning and self-restraint that they should have lulled all suspicion by apparently accepting the force of circumstances as* kismet. . . . *The fire, however, was smouldering. It was soon to break out more fiercely than before, with results disastrous to those settlers, traders and prospectors who had no inkling it was even alight.*[1]

*

Although usually catalogued as yet another small 'colonial' war, the Matabele uprising of 1896 has considerable historical importance as the earliest major native revolt by a subject nation against the British. Several reasons combined to bring matters to such an explosive head in the spring of that year.

Although the colonial masters remained in apparent oblivion

of it, native resentment had been simmering for a very long time. Thousands of acres of land had been appropriated and an ancient (if primitive) economic and social system swept away. Each volunteer who served in the adventure of 1893 had been rewarded with 6,000 acres of land. The veldt was transformed into numerous white-run farms. Forced labour was the method used physically to encompass this transformation. The pro-warrior caste, unused to labouring, because their way of life had rested on the work of captured slaves, was now cheaply and brutally exploited to dig, fence, fetch and carry. Blacks had been born to work for the white man, and if wages were insufficient incentive, then the whip made up the balance. This fuelled the deep resentment already conceived by the theft of their land and cattle. Bulawayo was rebuilt and became a thriving boom town. Within two years it had a population of over a thousand whites, three quarters of whom were British. (The remainder were Boers, Germans or Americans). Law and order were maintained by the South Africa Company's police.

Peace was maintained but several natural catastrophes combined to create the explosion of 1896. The agricultural economy was wrecked by a plague of locusts, drought and rinderpest. Famine stared the country in the face. What probably caused the explosion was the news – which spread rapidly amongst the black population – that the Company's police force was in serious disarray. This situation was due to the fiasco of the raiding party into the Transvaal led by Rhodes's partner, Jameson, at the end of December, 1895 (See Chapter 28 page 230). There was virtually no police presence in Matabeleland. A general insurrection broke out in which at least 200 white men, women and children were slaughtered in the most brutal fashion. Two thousand surviving settlers barricaded themselves in the various townships – Bulawayo, Gwelo, Bellingwe and Mangwe.

For a time, the rebels had victory in their grasp. They were well armed (with two thousand modern rifles) and took the whites wholly by surprise. But planning and strategy were both lacking and the advantage they had achieved by surprise was soon lost. The Matabele rebels were joined by the neighbouring tribe of Mashonas. The whites raised a volunteer defence force and began mercilessly to defend their new homeland. Major Herbert Plumer took command of the Matabeleland Relief Force with the intention of joining up with Rhodes' volunteers. The government sent relief officers, among them General Sir Frederick Carrington, with thirty years experience of imperial wars, and Colonel Robert Baden-Powell (who was serving with the 13th Hussars and hoped he was not too late to join in the 'fun' which gave him experience that proved valuable later when he founded the Scout movement). His record of the campaign is full of interesting insight into contemporary attitudes:

> Of course this was a very one sided fight, and it sounds rather brutal to anyone reading in cold blood. . . . Lord Wolseley says 'when you get niggers on the run, keep them on the run'. . . . our only chance of bringing the war to a speedy end is to go for them whenever we get the chance, and hit as hard as we can: any hesitation or softness is construed by them as a sign of weakness, and at once restores their confidence and courage. They expect no quarter, because as they admit themselves, they have gone beyond their own etiquette of war, and have killed our women and children. We found one wounded man who had hanged himself after the fight. This is not an uncommon occurrence in these fights . . .
>
> Don't think from these remarks that I am a regular nigger-hater, for I am not. I have met lots of good friends among them – especially among the Zulus. But, however good they may be, they must, as a people, be ruled with a hand of iron in a velvet glove; and if they writhe under it, and don't understand the force of it, it is of no use to add more padding – you must take off the glove for a moment and show them the hand. They will then understand and obey. In the present instance they had been rash enough to pull the glove for themselves, and were now beginning to find out what the hand was made of.[2]

The rising took a serious turn when it spread to the Mashonas as they were informed by fleeing Matabele that Lobengula was not dead, but was hiding in the north, ready to join and lead them all to victory. In the event, the rebels were no match for ruthless, well-armed and professionally trained volunteers, and at the beginning of December 1896 the rising was declared over and the troops withdrew. The whole country was then named Rhodesia.

The commander of the Matabeleland Relief Force, the volunteer army recruited for this emergency, wrote an extremely interesting account of the campaign of 1896. This book provides fascinating details which include information about the men who served, how they were equipped and how they were knocked into shape in such a short space of time to face the rigors of action:

Every effort of course was made to secure young men, but of sufficient maturity and stamina to withstand the hardships and privations that might have to be endured, as it was especially desirable that there should be in the ranks a sufficient proportion of men who had had some little military training and experience. Every recruit was questioned closely as to his riding and shooting capabilities, and very rarely was any man accepted who could not produce some testimonial or certificate of character; but notwithstanding all these precautions much had necessarily to be taken on trust. Amongst the applicants, however, there were a good many who had had previous service in the Bechuanaland Border Police, the Cape Mounted Rifles, or in one or other of the Volunteer Corps of Cape Colony or Natal, and a few old soldiers. Every candidate was examined by a doctor, and was certified by him to be physically fit for a campaign before he was finally approved.

The following rates of pay were fixed for non-commissioned officers and men, viz.:–

Staff-Sergeant	.	.	11/- per diem.
Troop Sergeant-Major	.	.	10/- ” ”
Sergeant	.	.	9/- ” ”
Corporal	.	.	8/- ” ”
Trooper	.	.	7/6 ” ”

As regards the officers it was arranged that inspectors in the B.S.A. Company's Police should rank as captains in the corps, and sub-inspectors as lieutenants, and that their pay should be:–

Captain	.	.	17/- per diem.
Lieutenant	.	.	13/- ” ”

The Imperial officers serving with the corps received 15/- a day each, in addition to their regimental pay.

Men were enrolled for no definite period, but for such time as their services might be required in Matabeleland.

By Part II. of the Colonial Forces Act of 1892, under which they took service, a commanding officer has power to—

(*a*) Award imprisonment, with or without hard labour, for any period not exceeding seven days.

(*b*) For the offence of drunkenness, order the offender to pay a fine not exceeding £1.

(*c*) In addition to or without any other punishment, order the offender to suffer any deduction from his ordinary pay to an amount not exceeding five days' pay.

(*d*) In the case of a non-commissioned officer, sentence the offender to be reduced to any lower grade or to the ranks.

(*e*) In the case of persons subject to this Act, not in receipt of ordinary military pay, to inflict a fine not exceeding £2.

Serious offences could be referred to ordinary or special courts of officers. Ordinary courts, which could be convened by any commanding officer, must consist of at least three members, and had the power of inflicting a fine of £15 and of awarding imprisonment, with or without hard labour, for any period not exceeding six months; they had no power to try offenders above the rank of non-commissioned officers.

Special courts, which could try officers, must be convened by the Governor, or by persons authorized by warrant to convene them; they could dismiss officers and others from the service; award imprisonment, with or without hard labour, for any period up to one year; and inflict a fine of £25.

Such were the powers placed in our hands for enforcing discipline. As a matter of fact, by the terms of the engagement any man was liable to discharge whose services were not required; and during the earlier days of the corps the punishment of dismissal was the one usually meted out to men who by their behaviour showed they were unlikely to be of service to us.

By Monday night, the 6th April, we had approved 65 recruits who had passed the doctor at Kimberley, and these were enrolled at 7 a.m. on the 7th and despatched at 9 a.m., under Lieutenant Cashel, by train to Mafeking. . . .

. . . A good many men were found who had some knowledge of the working of Maxim guns, and no very great difficulty was experienced in getting together a detachment for them; but we found very few signallers, and though we had a complete set of signalling equipment from the Ordnance Stores at Cape Town, it was some time before Lieutenant Dent could get together any number of men sufficiently trained.

We had secured as medical officers to the corps Doctors Michell and Morris. The former served throughout all the operations, and did excellent work; the latter only remained a short time after our arrival in Matabeleland. Dr Michell was appointed senior medical officer, and brought with him five or six men with some medical knowledge, who acted as hospital orderlies, and others were appointed from the corps after our concentration.

During the next two or three days recruits were coming in freely, and it was soon evident that with the Johannesburg contingent we should have no difficulty in obtaining the numbers we required; in fact, there were many desirable men who came up late for whom we had no vacancies, though, in view of the considerable 'waste' the long march would probably entail, a good many were enrolled in excess of the authorized establishment.

A few men possessing special qualifications were enrolled by the B.S.A. Company at Cape Town, and a small but very useful detachment, recruited by Major Nesbitt of Grahamstown, was taken from the Eastern Province; but with these exceptions, and the Johannesburg contingent, all men made their own way to Kimberley or Mafeking for enrolment.

Altogether more than 1000 were on the rolls at various times, but of these only some 850 can be really said to have served in the campaign, and the following particulars as to the nationality, previous occupation, etc., of these men will perhaps be found interesting:—

English born, who had arrived in the Colony within three years (about)				300
English born, who had been resident in the Colony over three years (about)				290
Afrikanders	English .	(about)		150
”	Dutch .	(about)		50
Australians	.	.	.	22
Canadians	.	.	.	5
Americans	.	.	.	5
Germans	.	.	.	4
Spanish	.	.	.	2
Others	.	.	.	17

Statistics as to their previous occupations are more difficult to compile, so many having tried more than one kind of employment; but they may be roughly classified as under:—

Miners and Engineers	.	.	.	100
In employment of De Beers Co.	.	.		50
Farmers	.	.	.	120
Clerks	.	.	.	100
Old Soldiers	.	.	.	50
From Colonial Corps	.	.	.	30

The remaining 400 had served before either in the Bechuanaland Border Police or the B.S.A. Company's Police, as in addition to those of the latter who came out from England many men gradually joined us who had not gone home after the incursion into the Transvaal, and others were picked up on the road or arrived later in Rhodesia.

There was considerable variety in the ages of the men, a good many exceeding forty, while a few were quite young. The average age was probably between twenty-five and twenty-seven years.

After careful consideration I had come to the conclusion that the best means of getting the corps up to Bulawayo as rapidly as possible, and at the same time of ensuring that they were an efficient body of men on arrival, was to start them off from the base at Mafeking in small detachments, following each other daily, and concentrating to whatever extent the movements and dispositions of the enemy might render necessary, either at Macloutsi or Mangwe; and I fixed the number of non-commissioned officers and men for each detachment at fifty.

The corps was composed of men who were being hurriedly collected together from various parts of the Colony, many of whom had had no knowledge of military life or discipline, who were unknown to the officers and non-commissioned officers who were to be placed in authority over them, and to each other; while a large proportion of the officers themselves, though all were as anxious and willing as possible, had had very little previous military experience of any kind, certainly none of handling troops in the field. It would, I considered, have been utterly unreasonable to expect such material to form itself or to be formed at once into an efficient fighting unit, more especially as the first duty which would devolve upon it would be such a difficult and arduous undertaking as the long march from Mafeking to Bulawayo. On the other hand, in each small detachment the officers had a fair chance of becoming acquainted with their men, and of selecting those likely to become non-commissioned officers, and they were not handicapped at starting by the responsibilities of a command beyond their powers, while the men in their turn had far more opportunities of acquiring a knowledge of their duties and of settling down gradually into this new mode of life, the daily routine with a small party being more elastic and less irksome to novices than that of a large force; and finally, I should be able to judge, from the state of efficiency in which I found each detachment at the end of the march, what were the capabilities of the officers and non-commissioned officers with it.

Then as regards the march itself. The water supply along the road was, as we all know, far from plentiful, and there was far less chance of its failure altogether at any particular point if it was drawn on for small numbers day by day than if parties of 200 or 300 men, with a correspondingly large number of animals, came together.

Further, it was foreseen that there must necessarily be many difficulties with the transport wagons, most of the mules having been just bought, and the conductors and drivers only recently engaged. It was hoped that with a succession of small parties, each accompanied by only two or three wagons, any breakdown in the transport of any particular detachment could be repaired with the co-operation and assistance of the succeeding one when they overtook them, and that even under the most adverse circumstances the failure of any one party would not entail the interruption of the steady and continuous flow of reinforcements for Bulawayo, which it was of vital importance to keep up.

I am fully convinced that the fact that so few *contretemps* and delays were experienced on the road, and that immediately on arrival in Matabeleland the corps was fit for active operations in the field, was due in no small measure to the march having been carried out by small detachments.[3]

Such was the rapidly formed volunteer army, with an officer corps chiefly borrowed from the British South Africa Company Police, which put down the Matabele and Mashona revolt, while the Colonial Secretary, Joseph Chamberlain, attempted in the British parliament to explain away involvement in the Jameson Raid into the Transvaal. His performance became known as the 'Lying in State'. The reputation of the disgraced and resigned Prime Minister of the Cape was marked by the name given to the territories to which peace had so energetically been restored – Rhodesia.

Notes

1. Frank W Sykes, *With Plumer in Matabeleland* (1897)
2. Robert Stephenson Baden-Powell, *The Matabele Campaign 1896* (1897)
3. Lieutenant Colonel Herbert Plumer, *An Irregular Corps in Matabeleland* (1897). Plumer would soon gain a reputation as an outstanding commander of mounted infantry in the Second Boer War and, later, become a highly competent, well-liked and trusted Army Commander under Sir Douglas Haig on the Western Front in the First World War.

28. The Last of the Small Wars
(The Second Boer War 1899-1902)

The Boers are certainly a peculiar people. . . . They are very relig-ious, but their religion takes its colour from the darkest portions of the Old Testament; lessons of mercy and gentleness are not at all to their liking, and they seldom care to read the Gospels. What they delight in are the stories of wholesale butchery by the Israelites of old; and in their own position they find a reproduc-tion of that of the first settlers in the Holy Land. Like them they think they are entrusted by the Almighty with the task of exter-minating the heathen native tribes around them, and are always ready with a scriptural precedent for slaughter and robbery . . .

It is difficult to agree with those who call the Boers cowards, an accusation which the whole of their history belies. A Boer does not like fighting if he can avoid it, because he sets a high value on his own life; but if he is cornered, he will fight as well as anybody else.[1]

*

It is our business in all these new countries to make smooth the paths for British commerce, British enterprise, the application of British capital, at a time when . . . other outlets for the commercial energies of our race are being gradually closed by the commercial principles which are gaining more and more adhesion. Everywhere we see the advance of commerce checked by the enormous growth which the doctrines of Protection are obtaining. We see it with our three great commercial rivals, France, Germany and America. The doctrines of protection are stronger and stronger, and operate to the exclusion of British commerce . . . it is the duty of the government to spare no opportunity of opening fresh outlets for the energy of British commerce and enterprise.[2]

*

As Prime Minister of Cape Colony, it was Cecil Rhodes' ambition that eventually the British and Dutch interests should combine and South Africa should be harmoniously melded together under the British Crown. To this end he made it his aim in the Cape Parliament to extend British influence whenever and wherever possible, and to support British endeavours in East Africa, Uganda and Egypt as and when he could. The main obstacle to his ambitions lay in the Transvaal, then ruled by President Kruger, who had a lifelong distrust of the English. In order to render the Transvaal independent of the hated British at the Cape and in Natal, he built a railway from the Portuguese port at Delgoa which was eventually to connect with his own port at Kosi Bay. But the British quashed his hopes by annexing Kosi Bay. Kruger further failed to drum up overt support from Germany, and was further aggravated by the immense influx of prospecting foreigners – Germans, Jews, French and British – who flocked to his country after the discovery of gold at Witwatersrand in the Transvaal in 1885. His actions then fertilised the seeds of discontent so abundant in the political soil. The foreign population in the Rand (as Witwatersrand was popularly known) now outnumbered the Boers by four to one. There were over 80,000 of them, mostly British. Kruger resolved to make life difficult for them. The tax and revenue system ensured that these *Uitlanders* (foreigners) contributed nineteen twentieths of the public revenue. They had no say in the government, state or local, and were exploited by the monopolies of the supply of dynamite and other necessaries which Kruger granted to Dutch and German traders. The *Uitlanders* looked to the Colonial Secretary, Joseph Chamberlain, and the British Government for support.

The situation simmered and Rhodes plotted a reckless solution. The matter would be resolved, he believed, if Britain could annex the Transvaal. But such an act could not be achieved without a credible reason. If only the political situation were to errupt into chaos, then an armed force could be dispatched to 'restore law and order'. The scheme was to be effected by Dr Leander Starr Jameson, a close associate of Rhodes, who was ordered to concentrate a force of some 500 armed and mounted men at Pitsani, some fifty miles north of Mafeking, on the Transvaal frontier. Becoming impatient, Jameson sent a message to Rhodes saying that, unless he had orders to the contrary, he intended to ride into Johannesburg to prod the 'Reform Committee' (who were behind the rising tide of revolt against the Boers) into action. Rhodes vehemently forbade him to do so, but the message arrived too late and, on 29 December, 1895, what became known to the world as 'the Jameson Raid' was launched. After a short battle at Krugersdorp, on 2 January, 1896, Jameson and his force were compelled to surrender to an overwhelming force of Boers. Rhodes was forced to resign from the Cape Parliament. Jameson was handed over to the British authorities and sentenced to 15 months imprisonment (he was released after less than six months).

The problems of the *Uitlanders* continued unresolved. In June 1899 negotiations took place between Kruger's government and the British, represented by Alfred, First Viscount Milner, British High Commissioner and Governor of the Cape. Kruger refused to grant the foreigners any franchise. Both sides knew a showdown was impending. The British were strengthening reinforcements in Natal. On 9 October, 1899, President Kruger issued the British Government an ultimatum – all British military preparations were to be disbanded within forty eight hours. This was refused. The Orange Free State announced its alliance with the South African Republic, and Boer forces advanced rapidly east and west. Within two weeks Mafeking was besieged – and defended with some vigour by Colonel Baden-Powell. Free State troops besieged Kimberley.

This second Boer War continues to be of considerable military interest. It was by no means typical of the small wars fought by the British overseas during the highwater mark of Victorian imperialism. Baden-Powell was fresh from his triumphs over the

Matabele, but the Boers were an entirely new kind of enemy. The Boer effort relied mainly on extremely mobile mounted infantry. Boer troops were brilliant marksmen and experienced huntsmen – they knew the terrain well. From positions not easily visible to the British they could inflict massive casualties on close ranks of slow-manoeuvring forces. They could appear and disappear with ease. They had little artillery, but what they had was of excellent modern French and German manufacture. The Boer command had little understanding of military strategy. But they were fighting a commando war. As Conan Doyle wrote so memorably:

> Take a community of Dutchmen of the type of those who defended themselves for fifty years against all the power of Spain at a time when Spain was the greatest power in the world. Intermix with them a strain of those inflexible French Hugeunots who gave up home and fortune and left their country forever at the time of the Revocation of the Edict of Nantes. The product must obviously be one of the most rugged, virile, unconquerable races ever seen upon earth. Take this formidable people and train them for seven generations in constant warfare against savage men and ferocious beasts, in circumstances under which no weakling could survive, place them so that they acquire exceptional skills with weapons and in horsemanship, give them a country which is eminently suited to the tactics of the huntsman, the marksman, and the rider. Then, finally, put a finer temper upon their military qualities by a dour fatalistic Old Testament religion and an ardent and consuming patriotism. Combine all these qualities and all these impulses in one individual and you have the modern Boer – the most formidable antagonist who ever crossed the path of Imperial Britain. . . .[3]

George Warrington Steevens, writing from the border of the Orange Free State in early October, 1899, gives this account of the atmosphere just before the outbreak of the conflict:

> The most conspicuous feature of the war on this frontier has hitherto been its absence.

The Free State forces about Bethulie, which is just over the Free State border, and Aliwal North, which is on our side of the frontier, make no sign of an advance. The reason for this is, doubtless, that hostilities here would amount to civil war. There is the same mixed English and Dutch population on each side of the Orange river, united by ties of kinship and friendship. Many law-abiding Dutch burghers here have sons and brothers who are citizens of the Free State, and therefore out with the forces.

In the mean time the English doctor attends patients on the other side of the border, and Boer riflemen ride across to buy goods at the British stores.

The proclamation published yesterday morning forbidding trade with the Republics is thus difficult and impolitic to enforce hereabouts.

Railway and postal communication is now stopped, but the last mail brought a copy of the Bloemfontein 'Express', with an appeal to the Colonial Boers concluding with the words:—

'We shall continue the war to the bloody end. You will assist us. Our God, who has so often helped us, will not forsake us.'

What effect this may have is yet doubtful, but it is certain that any rising of the Colonial Dutch would send the Colonial British into the field in full strength.

Burghersdorp, through which I passed yesterday, is a village of 2000 inhabitants, and, as I have already put on record, the centre of the most disaffected district in the colony. If there be any Dutch rising in sympathy with the Free State it will begin here.

Later Steevens wrote:

And so there's warlike news at last.

A Boer force, reported to be 350 strong, shifted camp today to within three miles of the bridge across the Orange river. Well-informed Dutch inhabitants assert that these are to be reinforced, and will march through Aliwal North tonight on their way to attack Stormberg Junction, sixty miles south.

The bridge is defended by two Cape policemen with four others in reserve.

The loyal inhabitants are boiling with indignation, declaring themselves sacrificed, as usual, by the dilatoriness of the Government.

Besides the Boer force near here, there is another, reported to be 450 strong, at Greatheads Drift, forty miles up the river.

The Boers at Bethulie, in the Free State, are believed to be pulling up the railway on their side of the frontier, and to be marching to Norvals Pont, which is the ferry over the Orange river on the way to Colesberg, with the intention of attacking Naauwpoort Junction, on the Capetown-Kimberley line; but as there are no trains now running to Bethulie it is difficult to verify these reports, and indeed, all reports must be received with caution.

The feeling here between the English and Dutch extends to a commercial and social boycott, and is therefore far more bitter than elsewhere. Several burghers here have sent their sons over the border, and promise that the loyal inhabitants will be 'sjambokked' (you remember how to pronounce it?) when the Boer force passes through.

So far things are quiet. The broad, sunny, dusty streets, fringed with small trees and lined with single-storeyed houses, are dotted with strolling inhabitants, both Dutch and natives, engrossed in their ordinary pursuits. The whole thing looks more like Arcady than revolution.

The Boers across the Orange river so far make no sign of raiding. Many have sent their wives and families here into Aliwal North, on our side of the border, in imitation, perhaps, of President Steyn, whose wife at this moment is staying with her sister at King William's Town, in the Cape Colony.

Many British farmers, of whom there are a couple of hundred in this district, refuse to believe that the Free State will take the offensive on this border, considering that such aggression would be impious, and that the Free State will restrict itself to defending its own frontier, or the Transvaal, if invaded, in fulfilment of the terms of the offensive and defensive alliance.

Nevertheless there is, of course, very acute tension between the Dutch and English here. No Boers are to be seen talking to Englishmen. The Boers are very close as to their feelings and intentions, which those who know them interpret as a bad sign, because, as a rule, they are inclined to irresponsible garrulity.[4]

* * *

The war divides itself into three phases. The conflict opened with the Boer invasion which ends with the relief of Ladysmith (28 February, 1900). The second stage ends with the flight of President Kruger. The final phase consisted of the commando war fought by the Boers, during which period Boer resistance was broken down by British blockhouses and the massive infusion of British and imperial forces (by the end of the war in May 1900 nearly half a million soldiers had been brought to South Africa).

After investing Mafeking and Kimberley, the Boer's main forces (15,000 strong, commanded by General Joubert) met poor resistance from the Natal Defence Force at Laing's Nek (12 October) and after three further brushes with the British, they bottled up Sir George White's forces at Ladysmith (2 November). A British relief force under Sir Redvers Buller, the Commander-in-Chief, diffused its efforts by attempting to deal with several Boer units at the same time. With minimum casualties, Boer forces were able to maul General Lord Paul Methuen's forces severely at the Modder River while en route to relieve Kimberley. During one terrible week in December, 1899 – 'Black Week' – British forces were beaten with terrible losses at Stormberg, Magersfontein and at Colenso, where Buller was leading a force of 21,000 to relieve Ladysmith. As they were crossing the Tugela River, Buller attempted to turn General Louis Botha's Free State forces' left flank. The British attack was subject to horrendous small arms fire and British batteries were ambushed by a concealed Boer force.

The British were driven back with losses of 143 killed, 756 wounded and 220 men and 11 guns captured. Boer losses scarcely totalled 50 men. Buller was relieved of supreme command and was succeeded by Field Marshall Lord Roberts. General Lord Kitchener became his Chief-of-Staff.

British strategy was now revised. While Lord Roberts concentrated on building up British strength in mounted infantry to combat the Boers' great strength, Major General John French kept the Boers busy with a campaign in the Free State. In January 1900 the British again sustained severe losses in unsuccessful attempts to cross the Tugela at Spion Kop and Vaal Kranz. This is an account by the Boer commando leader Deneys Reitz of the close of the battle at Spion Kop (British losses 87 officers and 1,647 men):

The hours went by; we kept watch, peering over and firing whenever a helmet showed itself, and in reply the soldiers volleyed unremittingly. We were hungry, thirsty and tired; around us were the dead men covered with swarms of flies attracted by the smell of blood. We did not know the cruel losses that the English were suffering, and we believed that they were easily holding their own, so discouragement spread as the shadows lengthened.

Batches of men left the line, openly defying Red Daniel, who was impotent in the face of this wholesale defection, and when at last the sun set I do not think there were sixty men left on the ledge.

Darkness fell swiftly; the firing died away, and there was silence, save for a rare shot and the moans of the wounded. For a long time I remained at my post, staring into the night to where the enemy lay, so close that I could hear the cries of their wounded and the murmur of voices from behind their breastwork.

Afterwards my nerve began to go and I thought I saw figures with bayonets stealing forward. When I tried to find the men who earlier in the evening had been beside me, they were gone. Almost in a panic I left my place and hastened along the fringe of rocks in search of company, and to my immense relief heard a gruff '*werda*.' It was Commandant Opperman still in his place with about two dozen men. He told me to stay beside him, and we remained here until after ten o'clock, listening to the enemy who were talking and stumbling about in the darkness beyond.

At last Opperman decided to retreat, and we descended the hill by the way which we had climbed up nearly sixteen hours before, our feet striking sickeningly at times against the dead bodies in our path. When we reached the bottom most of the horses were gone, the men who had retired having taken their mounts and ridden away, but our own animals and those belonging to the dead or wounded were still standing without food or water where they had been left at daybreak.

The first thing to do was to quench our raging thirst and that of our horses at a spring near by. We then consulted as to our next move. Most of the wounded had been taken off in the course of the day, but we found a few serious cases that would not bear transport collected in charge of an old man, who, by the dim light of a lantern, was attending to their wants. We could get no coherent information and stood discussing what to do next, for we did not know that the English had also been fought to a standstill, and that they in turn were at that very moment retreating down their own side of Spion Kop. We fully believed that the morning would see them streaming through the breach to the relief of Ladysmith, and the rolling up of all our Tugela line.

While we were talking, Mr Zeederberg came out of the dark. I had lost sight of him during most of the day, but he had been on the hill all the time, and had only come down shortly before us. He had seen nothing of Isaac Malherbe and the rest of our Pretoria men, and had no idea of what had become of them. A few more stragglers joined us and we agreed to lead our horses to the Carolina wagon-laager that, as we knew, lay not far off. We foraged for food in the saddle-bags of such horses as were left, and then went off. When we reached the laager we found everything in a state of chaos. The wagons were being hurriedly packed, and the entire Carolina Commando was making ready to retire. They had borne the brunt of the day's battle and had fought bravely, but, now that the struggle was over, a reaction had set in and there was panic in the camp. Fortunately, just as the foremost wagons moved away and the horsemen were getting ready to follow, there came the sound of galloping hoofs, and a man rode into our midst who shouted to them to halt. I could not see his face in the dark, but word went round that it was Louis Botha, the new Commandant-General, appointed in place of Piet Joubert, who was seriously ill. He addressed the men from the saddle, telling them of the shame that would be theirs if they deserted their posts in this hour of danger; and so eloquent was his appeal that in a few minutes the men were filing off into the dark to reoccupy their positions on either side of the Spion Kop gap. I believe that he spent the rest of the night riding from commando to commando exhorting and threatening, until he persuaded the men to return to the line, thus averting a great disaster.

As for Commandant Opperman and our party, now that the Carolina burghers were returning we led our horses back to the foot of Spion Kop, to wait there.

We woke with the falling of the dew and, as the sky lightened, gazed eagerly at the dim outline of the hill above, but could make out no sign of life.

Gradually the dawn came and still there was no movement. Then to our utter surprise we saw two men on the top triumphantly waving their hats and holding their rifles aloft. They were Boers, and their presence there was proof that, almost unbelievably, defeat had turned to victory – the English were gone and the hill was still ours.

Leaving our horses to fend for themselves, we were soon hastening up the slope past the dead until we reached yesterday's bloody ledge. From here we hurried across to the English breastworks, to find them abandoned. On our side of the fighting-line there had been many casualties, but a worse sight met our eyes behind the English *schanses*.

In the shallow trenches where they had fought the soldiers lay dead in swathes, and in places they were piled three deep.

The Boer guns in particular had wrought terrible havoc and some of the bodies were shockingly mutilated. There must have been six hundred dead men on this strip of earth, and there cannot have been many battlefields where there was such an accumulation of horrors within so small a compass.[5]

On 15 February, 1900, French relieved Kimberley. Three days later, 5,000 Boers under Cronje were retreating across the Modder River, and French's troops, returning from Kimberley, held back their crossing. Several British infantry brigades and artillery batteries, commanded by Kitchener, tried to dislodge the Boers from their refuge in the Tugela river. The Boers were then besieged but their resistance was ferocious. The British advance was handicapped by lack of cover. The British lost 98 officers and 1,437 men – 1,100 were killed during the first day of the action. Boer prisoners numbered 4,100. Cronje could have broken through but only at the terrible cost of abandoning his sick and wounded. The Boers were finally driven by starvation to surrender on 27 February. It was a black day for the Boers. They had surrendered nearly 10 per cent of the Boer field force. The day was traditionally celebrated by the Boers to commemorate their victory over the British at Majuba Hill. When he learned of the surrender President Kruger exclaimed: 'The English have taken our Majuba Day away from us!'

During this action Buller was making a further advance to relieve Ladysmith. Some idea of the conditions endured by the besieged may be gathered from this letter written by Lieutenant-General Sir George White, VC, who commanded at Ladysmith:

> I think I may commence a letter to you as Sir Redvers Buller is approaching the Tugela and we may reasonably expect some hard fighting within the next week, the result of which I hope will be the relief of Ladysmith, and the opening of our communications with the outside world from which we have been so long cut off. I have been in good health all the time but it has been weary work. I fought in the open as long as I could with a superior enemy on both sides of me. I was heartbroken over the loss of the Gloucestershire Regiment, the Royal Irish Fusiliers and the Mountain Battery and of course I now wish with all my heart I had not sent them out, but two regiments and a battery ought to have been able to hold their own against the number of Boers sent against them which, as far as I can make out, were only 750 men.

We occupy a very large position here. It is some 13 miles round. This is rendered necessary by the immense range of the enemy's guns. One big 6–in gun which annoyed us for a very long time threw a shell into our lines to a distance of over 10,000 yards from the gun. When this is repeated north, south, east and west of us, it makes it hot for us but it is remarkable how few casualties there have been. The soldiers spend the days in shelters which save them from the shells. Most of the officers and civil residents have also dug themselves shelters underground. The escapes have been marvellous. I have over and over again seen shells bursting amidst groups of soldiers and horses without hurting anyone.

There are several women and children still in Ladysmith. Thank goodness none of the children has been hit and only one woman. A 6–in shell burst actually in the room in which this woman was sitting and blew everything to ribbons and the whole side out of the house.

Sometimes the Boer guns bombard us at night and this is distressful. The night before last my Chief of Staff, Major-General Sir Archibald Hunter led a party of 600 picked men and made a raid on Gun Hill, one of the enemy's positions round Ladysmith. He surprised the post and took three guns including one of the enemy's largest (6–in) guns.

I am so pleased not only because that gun was doing us much harm but also because Hunter is such a delightful fellow and has done so well all through the siege and previous operations. You will like to hear of our mess and manner of life. All the Headquarter Staff live in the same house which we have commandeered . . .

We have had plenty to eat and to drink and we keep very early hours. I am up about 4 o'clock every morning and we generally retire between 9 and 10 o'clock. At one time before our defences were as strong as they are now I used always to sleep in my clothes ready to turn out in a second; but now a large proportion of the Boer Army has gone south to face the relieving force on the Tugela and I turn in regularly. Most of the Regimental officers, however, have to sleep in the open with their men in strong points built of stones heaped together. There is no dearth of this class of building material in Natal. The climate is very variable; some days are very hot, about as hot as Simla in mid-June, or perhaps a little hotter. We then have a severe thunderstorm with most vivid lightning and this cools the weather down greatly.

Ladysmith is a nasty place and I fear there will be a terrible plague of enteric if we are kept much longer. Already there are 80 cases and the numbers are increasing rapidly. We had more enteric fever here last year than in any other station of the British Army and I dread the result of siege conditions this year far more than the shells and bullets of the enemy.

We have also a bad prospect of horse sickness which is very bad at Ladysmith and usually sets in about this time. The flies are a terrible nuisance. The number of horses, mules, cattle, etc., bring them in myriads. In our dining room, which is very small, we catch them on fly papers and in wire domes in millions but it does not seem to decrease their numbers. They get into everything left uncovered.[6]

Buller's advance was checked initially and then, finally, at Pieter's Hill, he gained command of the Tugela river, which the British crossed on 21 February. Their advance was hampered by terrible losses from concentrated Boer fire (they lost nearly half their number during the advance on the Boer trenches). Eventually a general advance was secured on 27 February. The British force of 12,000 under Sir George White had been besieged by the Boers under General Joubert from 2 November 1899 until 27 February 1900. If there was a particular moment in this second Boer War when the tide turned, it was here. Winston Churchill describes the courageous advance of the Irish Brigade under General Hart on 23 February 1900:

At half-past twelve on the 23rd General Hart ordered his brigade to advance. The battalions, which were sheltering among stone walls and other hastily-constructed cover on the reverse slope of the kopje immediately in front of that on which we stood, rose up one by one and formed in rank. They then moved off in a single file along the railroad, the Inniskilling Fusiliers leading, the Connaught Rangers,

Dublin Fusiliers and the Imperial Light Infantry following in succession. At the same time the Durham Light Infantry and the 2nd Rifle Brigade began to march to take the place of the assaulting brigade on the advanced kopje.

Wishing to have a nearer view of the attack, I descended the wooded hill, cantered along the railway – down which the procession of laden stretchers, now hardly interrupted for three days, was still moving – and, dismounting, climbed the rocky sides of the advanced kopje. On the top, in a little half-circle of stones, I found General Lyttleton, who received me kindly, and together we watched the development of the operation. Nearly a mile of the railway was visible, and along it the stream of infantry flowed steadily. The telescope showed the soldiers walking quite slowly with their rifles at the slope. Thus far, at least, they were not under fire. The low kopjes which were held by the other brigades shielded the movement. A mile away the river and railway turned sharply to the right; the river plunged into a deep gorge, and the railway was lost in a cutting. There was certainly plenty of cover; but just before the cutting was reached the iron bridge across the Onderbrook Spruit had to be crossed, and this was evidently commanded by the enemy's riflemen. Beyond the railway and the moving trickle of men the brown dark face of Inniskilling Hill, crowned with sangars and entrenchments, rose up gloomily and, as yet, silent.

The patter of musketry along the left of the army, which reached back from the advanced kopjes to Colenso village, the boom of the heavy guns across the river, and the ceaseless thudding of the field artillery making a leisurely preparation, were an almost unnoticed accompaniment to the scene. Before us the infantry were moving steadily nearer to the hill and the open ground by the railway bridge, and we listened amid the comparatively peaceful din for the impending fire storm.

The head of the column reached the exposed ground, and the soldiers began to walk across it. Then at once above the average fusillade and cannonade rose the extraordinary rattling roll of Mauser musketry in great volume. If the reader wishes to know exactly what this is like he must drum the fingers of both his hands on a wooden table, one after the other as quickly and as hard as he can. I turned my telescope on the Dutch defences. They were no longer deserted. All along the rim of the trenches, clear-cut and jet black against the sky stood a crowded line of slouch-hatted men, visible as far as their shoulders and wielding what looked like thin sticks.

Far below, by the red ironwork of the railway bridge – 2,000 yards at least from the trenches – the surface of the ground was blurred and dusty. Across the bridge the infantry were still moving, but no longer slowly – they were running for their lives. Man after man emerged from the sheltered railroad, which ran like a covered way across the enemy's front, into the open and the driving hail of bullets, ran the gauntlet and dropped down the embankment on the further side of the bridge into safety again. The range was great, but a good many soldiers were hit and lay scattered about the ironwork of the bridge. 'Pom-pom-pom,' 'pom-pom-pom,' and so on, twenty times went the Boer automatic gun, and the flights of little shells spotted the bridge with puffs of white smoke. But the advancing infantry never hesitated for a moment, and continued to scamper across the dangerous ground, paying their toll accordingly. More than sixty men were shot in this short space. Yet this was not the attack. This was only the preliminary movement across the enemy's front.

The enemy's shells, which occasionally burst on the advanced kopje, and a whistle of stray bullets from the left, advised us to change our position, and we moved a little further down the slope towards the river. Here the bridge was no longer visible. I looked towards the hilltop, whence the roar of musketry was ceaselessly proceeding. The artillery had seen the slouch hats too, and forgetting their usual apathy in the joy of a live target, concentrated a most hellish and terrible fire on the trenches.

Meanwhile the afternoon had been passing. The infantry had filed steadily across the front, and the two leading battalions had already accumulated on the eastern spurs of Inniskilling Hill. At four o'clock General Hart ordered the attack, and the troops forthwith began to climb the slopes.

The broken ground delayed their progress, and it was nearly sunset by the time they had reached the furthest position which could be gained under cover. The Boer entrenchments were about 400 yards away. The arête by which the Inniskillings had advanced was bare, and swept by a dreadful frontal fire from the works on the summit and a still more terrible flanking fire from the other hills. It was so narrow that, though only four companies were arranged in the firing line, there was scarcely room for two to deploy. There was not, however, the slightest hesitation, and as we watched with straining eyes we could see the leading companies rise up together and run swiftly forward on the enemy's works with inspiring dash and enthusiasm.

But if the attack was superb, the defence was magnificent; nor could the devoted heroism of the Irish soldiers surpass the stout endurance of the Dutch. The artillery redoubled their efforts. The whole summit of the hill was alive with shell. Shrapnel flashed into being above the crests, and the ground sprang up into dust whipped by the showers of bullets and splinters. Again and again whole sections of the entrenchments vanished in an awful uprush of black earth and smoke, smothering the fierce blaze of the lyddite shells from the howitzers and heavy artillery. The cannonade grew to a tremendous thundering hum. Not less than 60 guns were firing continuously on the Boer trenches. But the musketry was never subdued for an instant. Amid the smoke and the dust the slouch hats could still be seen. The Dutch, firm and undaunted, stood to their parapets and plied their rifles with deadly effect.

The terrible power of the Mauser rifle was displayed. As the charging companies met the storm of bullets they were swept away. Officers and men fell by scores on the narrow ridge. Though assailed in front and flank by the hideous whispering Death, the survivors hurried obstinately onward, until their own artillery were forced to cease firing, and it seemed that, in spite of bullets, flesh and blood would prevail. But at the last supreme moment the weakness of the attack was shown. The Inniskillings had almost reached their goal. They were too few to effect their purpose; and when the Boers saw that the attack had withered they shot all the straighter, and several of the boldest leapt out from their trenches and, running forward to meet the soldiers, discharged their magazines at the closest range. It was a frantic scene of blood and fury.

Thus confronted, the Irish perished rather than retire. A few men, indeed, ran back down the slope to the nearest cover, and there savagely turned to bay, but the greater part of the front line was shot down. Other companies, some from the Connaught Rangers, some headed by the brave Colonel Sitwell, from the Dublin Fusiliers, advanced to renew – it was already too late to support – the attack, and as the light faded another fierce and bloody assault was delivered and was repulsed. Yet the Irish soldiers would not leave the hill and, persuaded at length that they could not advance further, they lay down on the ground they had won, and began to build walls and shelters, from behind which they opened a revengeful fire on the exulting Boers. In the two attacks both colonels, three majors, 20 officers and 600 men had fallen out of an engaged force of scarcely 1,200. Then darkness pulled down the curtain, and the tragedy came to an end for the day . . .[7]

*　*　*

Ladysmith was relieved on 28 February. The 22,000 inhabitants were very near the last stages of resistance. They had endured few casualties from shellfire but had heavy losses from sickness. Buller's total losses in the relief operations were considerable – at Colenso 1,100 men, Spion Kop 1,700, Vaalkranz 400 and in the final onslaught over 1,600. But the Natal invaders now retreated to the mountains to the north of the colony. Signs of failure in the Boer war effort were discernible in the offer now made to the British Government (a restoration of the pre-war status quo). These overtures were rejected by Lord Salisbury.

Between March and September the British, now reinforced, began the final phase of the war. Bloemfontein, the capital of the Orange Free State, fell to Roberts on 13 March and in early May he had reached Kroonstad. Buller was sweeping away Boer resistance in Natal. The Orange Free State was annexed by Britain on 24 May, 1900. Mafeking was relieved on 18 May after a siege of over seven months. This was followed by the invasion of the Transvaal in late May. All formal Boer resistance was at an end by 4 July. President Kruger fled to Portuguese and Dutch protection. But the war was not over. The last terrible stages were now to be enacted. Lord Roberts went home and the campaign was left in Kitchener's hands.

The Boers now continued the war by other means. The manner adopted by them for this stage of the war – guerilla tactics – suited them and the terrain perfectly. They concentrated on using small, highly mobile bands of mounted militiamen, who could appear suddenly from nowhere, inflict immediate and considerable damage to personnel, equipment, communications or transport systems, and then evaporate. Railways were a frequent target. Isolated posts, troop convoys, supplies – nothing seemed safe. The ground they covered was impressive in its scope – Brandwater Basin, through the Transvaal, Frederikstad, Bothaville, Bloemfontein, the Orange River, Bethuile, Dewetsdorp and even as far as the Atlantic coast, where they exchanged shots with a British warship. By the beginning of 1901, Kitchener called for reinforcements and adopted a new plan for dealing with the Boer commandos. He concentrated his troops in a few main depots, secured his railway communications, and attempted to depopulate whole areas by putting the women and children from Boer homesteads into camps. He believed that he was thereby denying the Boer guerrillas food and shelter.

On 10 February a Boer force of 3,000 under Christian De Wet invaded Cape Colony. The invasion failed but demonstrated that there was still plenty of fight left in the enemy. British armies under John French and Bindon Blood dealt severe defeats on the Boers in the northern Transvaal and the Swaziland border. A heavy defeat at Lichtenburg on 3 March brought the Boers to the negotiating table, but the peace talks broke down on the issue of the treatment of the Cape rebels. Boer strength bled away but their resistance continued. By 1902 they still had 25,000 men in the field.

Kitchener's final plan was the blockhouse system – a series of well placed pill-boxes so arranged that they were a series of blockhouses and barbed wire stretching like a vast net to entrap the enemy. Each pill-box would be filled with infantry armed with automatic small arms. Each little fort would be in rifle range of the next. The British columns would then drive the Boers into these traps. It was not a cheap method of dealing with the particular enemy he was fighting, but Kitchener could see no alternative. By the end of Autumn 1901 ten thousand square miles of the Transvaal and Northern Orange River Colony as well as 4,200 square miles round Bloemfontein had been cleared by this system. By May, 1902, there were eight thousand of these blockhouses, covering 3,700 miles, guarded by 50,000 British and 16,000 African scouts. The entire network was kept fairly well in touch by telephone communication and Kitchener's troops were thus able to drive the remaining Boers into the inhospitable wastelands of the extreme west and north west. The remaining strong Boer resistance was left in the north east corner and the semi-desert area of the Transvaal. Gradually, Kitchener reduced resistance by sweeping these areas. The Boers eventually realised that further resistance was pointless and 23 Boer representatives came to Pretoria to negotiate terms to bring the war to an end. The articles of peace were signed on 31 May, 1902.

This last major imperial war cost 5,774 British lives and 22,829 wounded. Boer losses included 4,000 killed and untold wounded. At the conclusion of the war, the British held 40,000 Boer prisoners. By the Treaty of Vereeniging, all burghers in the field, together with arms and ammunition, were surrendered; all those who surrendered and declared themselves subject of King Edward VII were to be repatriated; none of those who surrendered were to be deprived of their property or liberty; there were to be no reprisals for acts of war; Dutch was to be taught in schools at the request of parents; Dutch was to be allowed in courts of law; licences were to be required for sporting guns; military administration to be replaced by civil administration as soon as possible; the matter of the native franchise was not to be considered until after the introduction of self-government and compensation for damage to farmlands and other property was to be assessed by a commission.

* * *

The closing years of the last century – the Jubilee parades, departing troopships, redcoats triumphing over thousands of natives, a vast overseas Empire willed by the Almighty and ruled from London, the benefits of Christianity as made in England and the representative parliamentary democracy promised in due course – perceived from this distance in a Technicolor haze of mythology with an Elgarian soundtrack – seem to us to be the highwater mark of British Imperialism. Joseph Chamberlain, the Colonial Secretary, speaking at the Imperial Institute on 11 November 1895, only a month before the Jameson Raid, seemed to be speaking for the nation when he said:

> I venture to claim two qualifications for the great office which I hold, which to my mind . . . is one of the most important that can be held by any Englishman (cheers); and those qualifications are that, in the first place, I believe in the British Empire (cheers), and in the second place, I believe in the British race. (Cheers) I believe that the British race is the greatest of governing races that the world has ever seen. (Cheers) I say that not merely as an empty boast, but as proved and shown by the success which we have had in administering vast dominions which are connected with these three small islands . . . I think a man who holds my office is bound to be sanguine, is bound to be confident. Then I have those two qualifications. (Laughter and cheers).[8]

But, all of a sudden, this blaze of imperial glory was over and done with. The South African War is now seen not only as the last of the gentlemen's wars (whatever they might have been) but the very last of the small wars. The new century brought the era of major international conflicts. For the first time Britain had fought an enemy trained and experienced in rifle and small arms fire. It took the nation (with help from the Empire) over two and half years to defeat a Boer army of scarcely more than 83,000 men. By the end of war, the British had troops numbering 500,000. The new century brought warfare of the new age – mass armies, extended front lines, artillery fire-power resulting from the application of modern science, technology and engineering to the armaments industry, rapid and wide ranging communications, rapid troop movement and deployment. The continuity which was seemingly maintained by the service in the

Great War of such Boer War heroes as Sir John French, Douglas Haig, Herbert Plumer and Edmund Allenby (all cavalrymen and all believers in the importance of rapidly achieved frontal assault) was an illusion. To a very serious extent, they were figures out of their time.

Notes

1. Henry Rider Haggard, *The Last Boer War*, (1899)
2. Lord Salisbury in a speech in the House of Lords, 14 February, 1895
3. Sir Arthur Conan Doyle, *The Great Boer War* (1900)
4. George Warrington Steevens, *From Capetown to Ladysmith: An Unfinished Record of the South African War* (1900)
5. Deneys Reitz, *Commando: A Boer Journal of the Boer War* (1929) Reitz was General Jan Smuts's son-in-law. He fought in the British Army in the First World War and later became Minister for Defence in the South African government
6. M. Durand, *Sir George White* (1914). White's letter was dated 10 December, 1899
7. Dispatch from Winston Churchill dated 5 March, 1900. From Frederick Woods (Ed.), *Young Winston's Wars: The Original Dispatches of Winston S. Churchill, War Correspondent 1897–1900* (1972)
8. *The Times*, 12 November 1895, reporting a speech at the Imperial Institute.

Epilogue

Those echoes of our Imperial past live with us still. To some, mostly those of older generations, they are perhaps more evocative than to people of the late Twentieth Century – and understandably so. Yet, in a very changed world, their significance should not be lost even though, as Baden-Powell was to put it, the story of Empire was very much one of the iron hand in the velvet glove – and, sadly, there was all too little evidence of that glove on many occasions. It was a story too of undeniable commercial acquisitiveness and exploitation, frequently tinged with acts that brought little credit to their perpetrators. Yet, as these chapters show, the growth of Empire was also a time of heroism and great self-sacrifice in the service of the Crown. Furthermore, from it all sprang a system of benevolent colonial administration that has had few equals and which was to breed so strong a spirit of loyalty to Britain that it provoked an overwhelming response to our country's need in two world wars.

The years since 1945, when decolonization became the dominating cry in world politics, saw a steady process of the grant of independence throughout the former Empire. This, combined with an upsurge of nationalistic feeling within the resurgent countries, brought change at a gallop, a gallop all too often spurred by malignant ideologies bringing new conflicts in their train. It is all too easy to see the price that has had to be paid when the results of years of honest, disinterested and benevolent work by a network of District Officers and senior Administrators – often typified by practical wisdom, courage and justice – have been thrown to the winds. Where this is not so, the hallmarks of that work live on in new constitutions and administrations, to the lasting benefit of all.

As every chapter in this book reflects, the growth of Empire was based upon an absolute, though misguided, conviction of the God-given superiority of the white man over the black and upon an equally misguided belief in a mission to spread the Gospel of Christ to the detriment of all other religions. Both did far more harm than good and served as a form of self-justification that would be utterly rejected today. Nevertheless, the underlying desire to bring civilization to what our forebears saw as the 'uncivilized and benighted nations' was genuine enough, albeit that their strategies were more influenced by commercial gain than any missionary zeal. That the Commonwealth forum of nations exists today owes much to many people but it sprang from the ashes of the Empire and continues to reflect much that has its roots in our Imperial past.

BRYAN WATKINS

Select Bibliography

Anon: *Told From the Ranks* (1900)

James Edward Alexander: *Incidents of the Maori War* (1863)

C.H. Armitage and A.F. Montanaro: *The Ashanti Campaign of 1900* (1901)

Robert Stephenson Baden-Powell: *The Downfall of Prempeh* (1896)

Robert Stephenson Baden-Powell: *The Matabele Campaign 1896* (1897)

James Bancroft: *Rorke's Drift* (Tunbridge Wells) (1988)

Correlli Barnett: *Britain and her Army 1509–1970* (1970)

Richard Barter: *The Siege of Delhi: Mutiny Memories of an Old Officer* (1869)

Michael Barthop: *The Anglo-Boer Wars* (1987)

Michael Barthop: *To Face the Daring Maoris* (1979)

Nicholas Bentley (editor): *Russell's Dispatches From the Crimea 1854–1856* (1966)

Brian Bond: *Victorian Military Campaigns* (1967)

Demetrius Boulger: *General Gordon's Letters From the Crimea, the Danube and Armenia* (1884)

John Bowie: *The Empire at War* (1989)

Cyprian Bridge: *Journal of Events on an Expedition to New Zealand* (1845)

Colonel George Hamilton Brown ('Maori Brown'): *A Lost Legion in South Africa* (1912)

Bennet Burleigh: *Desert Warfare: Being the Chronicle of the Eastern Soudan Campaign* (1884)

F.R. Burnham: *Scouting on Two Continents* (1927)

The Marchioness of Bute (daughter of the Marquess of Hastings): *The Private Journal of the Marquess of Hastings, KG* (1858)

William Francis Butler: *Life of Sir George Pomeroy Colley* (1899)

C.E. Callwell: *Small Wars: Their Principles and Practice* (1906)

Adelaide Case: *Day by Day at Lucknow* (1858)

William Chambers and Robert Chambers: *The History of the Revolt in India* (1859)

C.B. Cook: *Honours of the British And Indian Armies 1662–1982* (1987)

J.A. De Moor and H.L. Wesserling (editors): *Imperialism and War – Essays on Colonial War in Asia and Africa* (1989)

Arthur Conan Doyle: *The Great Boer War* (1900)

Henry Marion Durand: *The First Afghan War and Its Causes* (1879)

Henry Mortimer Durand: *Sir George White* (1914)

F.B. Doveton: *Reminiscences of the Burmese War in 1824–1826* (1952)

John Alexander Cameron: 'The Fight on Majuba Hill' in *Illustrated London News*, 24 April 1881

Thomas Fortesque Carter: *A Narrative of the Boer War* (1896)

Winston S. Churchill: *The River War* (1898)

Winston S. Churchill: *My Early Life* (1959)

Winston S. Churchill: *The Story of the Malakand Field Force* (1898)

Winston S. Churchill: *Young Winston's Wars*: The Original Dispatches of *Winston Churchill, War Correspondent 1897–1900*, edited by Frederick Woods, (1972)

David Clammer: *The Zulu War* (1973)

W. Walton Claridge: *A History of the Gold Coast and Ashanti* (1915)

Edward Cook: *Letters From the Crimea* (1855)

Edward Cook: *The Life of Florence Nightingale* (1913)

Charles Crosthaite: *The Pacification of Burma* (1912)

Charles Dickens, 'The Great Tasmania's Cargo' in *All the Year Round*, Volume 3, Number 54, May 1860

James Grant Duff: *A History of the Mahrattas* (1826)

John Duncan and John Walton: *Heroes for Victoria* (1991)

Michael Edwardes: *Battles of the Indian Mutiny* (1963)

Frank Emery: *The Red Soldier* (1977)

Byron Farwell: *Queen Victoria's Little Wars* (1973)

Byron Farwell: *For Queen and Country – A Social History of the Victorian and Edwardian Army* (1981)

Byron Farwell: *The Gurkhas* (1984)

Donald Featherstone: *Colonial Small Wars 1837–1901* (1988)

Donald Featherstone: *Victorian Colonial Warfare: Africa – From the Campaigns Against the Kaffirs to the South African War* (1992)

Donald Featherstone: *Victoria's Enemies* (1989)

Peter Fleming: *The Siege at Peking* (1959)

Archibald Forbes: *Glimpses Through Cannon Smoke* (1880)

Archibald Forbes: *Souvenirs of Some Continents* (1885)

Archibald Forbes: *Barracks, Bivouacs and Battles* (1891)

Archibald Forbes: *The Afghan Wars 1839–42 and 1878–80* (1892)

Archibald Forbes: *Memories and Studies of War and Peace* (1895)

John Fortescue: *Military History: Lectures Delivered at Trinity College, Cambridge* (1923)

John Fortescue: *The History of the British Army* (1927)

James Baillie Fraser: *Military Memoir of Lieutenant Colonel James Skinner* (1851)

Brian Gardner: *The African Dream* (1970)

Robert Giddings: *Echoes of War* (1990)

Robert Giddings: *Literature and Imperialism* (1991)

Frederick John Goldsmid: *James Outram: A Biography* (1880)

Charles George Gordon, edited A.E. Hake: *Journals of Major-General Gordon at Khartoum* (1885)

Hugh Gough: *Letters and Dispatches of Field Marshall Sir Hugh Gough* (1865)

James Grant: *British Battles on Land and Sea* (1897)

John Gurwood: *The Dispatches of Field Marshall the Duke of Wellington during his Various Campaigns* (1934–38)

Henry Rider Haggard: *The Last Boer War* (1899)

George Hamilton-Browne: *A Lost Legionary in South Africa* (1912)

T.A. Heathcote: *The Afghan Wars 1839–1919* (1980)

Christopher Hibbert: *The Destruction of Lord Raglan* (1961)

Christopher Hibbert: *The Great Mutiny: India 1857* (1980)

Henry Hook 'Survivor's Tales of Great Events – How They Held Rorke's Drift' in *The Royal Magazine*, February 1905

Peter Hopkirk: *The Great Game* (1990)

Lawrence James: *The Savage Wars – British Campaigns in Africa 1870–1920* (1985)

Alexander Kinglake: *The Invasion of the Crimea* (1887)

John Laffin: *Boys in Battle* (1966)

Henry Atwell Lake: *Narrative of the Defence of Kars* (1857)

Joseph Lehmann: *The First Boer War* (1985)

Daniel Lysons: *The Crimean War From First to Last* (1895)

Alan Lloyd: *The Drums of Kumasi: The Story of the Ashanti Wars* (1964)

Charles Rathbone Low: *The Life and Correspondence of Field Marshal Sir George Pollock, Bart* (1873)

John M. Mackenzie (editor): *Imperialism and Popular Culture* (1986)

John M. Mackenzie (editor): *Propaganda and Empire* (1984)

John M. Mackenzie (editor): *Popular Imperialism and the Military 1850–1950* (1992)

Frederick Manning: *Old New Zealand* (1876)

John Martineau: *Life and Correspondence of Sir Bartle Frere* (1895)

Frederick Maurice and George Arthur: *The Life of Lord Wolseley* (1924)

Herbert Maxwell: *The Life of Wellington* (1899)

John Morley: *The Life of Gladstone* (1903)

Donald R. Morris: *The Washing of the Spears* (1966)

Revd Sydney Godolphin Osborne: *Scutari and Its Hospitals* (1855)

Thomas Pakenham: *The Boer War* (1979)

Thomas Pakenham: *The Scramble for Africa* (1991)

Herbert Plumer: *An Irregular Corps in Matabeleland* (1897)

Melton Prior: *Campaigns of a War Correspondent* (1912)

Robert Rait: *The Life and Campaigns of Hugh, First Viscount Gough, Field Marshall* (1903)

Deneys Reitz: *Commando: A Boer Journal of the Boer War* (1929)

H.I. Ricketts: *A Narrative of the Ashantee War* (1831)

Jasper Ridley: *Lord Palmerston* (1970)

Frederick Sleigh Roberts: *Forty One Years in India* (1897)

J.F.G. Ross-of-Bladensburg: *The Marquess of Hastings KG* (1893)

W.H. Russell: *The British Expedition to the Crimea* (1858)

Tim Ryan and Bill Parham: *The Colonial New Zealand Wars* (Wellington, NZ, 1986)

Florentia Sale: *The Journals of Lady Florentia Sale* (1843)

Frank Scudamore: *A Sheaf of Memories* (1925)

Lawrence Shadwell: *Life of Colin Campbell, Lord Clyde* (1881)

Harry Smith: *The Autobiography of Sir Harry Smith*, edited by G.C. Moore Smith (1901)

A.J. Smithers: *The Kaffir Wars 1779–1877* (1973)

J.J. Snodgrass: *Narrative of the Burmese War* (1827)

Henry Morton Stanley: *Coomassie and Magdala* (1874)

Lord Stanmore: *Memoir of Sydney Herbert, Lord Herbert of Lea* (1906)

Arthur Swinson: *North West Frontier* (1967)

Frank W. Sykes: *With Plumer in Matabeleland* (1897)

George Warrington Steevens: *With Kitchener to Khartum* (1898)

George Warrington Steevens: *From Capetown to Ladysmith* (1900)

Arthur Swinson: *North-West Frontier* (1967)

Sarah A. Tooley: *The Life of Florence Nightingale* (1910)

William Tordoff: *Ashanti Under the Prempehs 1888–1935* (1965)

Lionel J. Trotter: *The Bayard of India: A Life of General Sir James Outram* (1903)

Hedley Vicars: *Memorials of Captain Hedley Vicars* (1856)

The Letters of Queen Victoria 1837–1861, edited by Arthur Christopher Benson and Viscount Esher (1907)

Frederick Villiers: *Pictures of Many Wars* (1902)

William Lee Warner: *The Life of the Marquis of Dalhousie* (1904)

W.A. Wills and L.T. Collingridge: *The Downfall of Lobengula* (1894)

Horace Hyman Wilson: *Narrative of the Burmese War in 1824–26* (1852)

H.W. Wilson: *With the Flag to Pretoria* (1900)

Garnet Wolseley: *The Story of a Soldier's Life* (1903)

Henry Evelyn Wood: *From Midshipman to Field Marshal* (1906)

Cecil Woodham-Smith: *The Reason Why* (1953)

Index